LITTLE GIRL LOST,
LITTLE GIRL FOUND

A Healing Story of Faith, Family & Friends

Year Three
Coming Home

Helen A. Scieszka, Ph.D.

(...and Godzilla the Bear)

Published by
Bezalel Books
Waterford, MI
www.BezalelBooks.com

The choicest first fruits of your soil you shall bring to
the house of the Lord, your God. ~Exodus 23:19

Printed in the United States of America

cover illustration © Helen Scieszka
ISBN 978-1-936453-33-7
Library of Congress Control Number 2016903449

1. Scripture texts in this work are taken from the *New American Bible* with revised New Testament and Psalms © 1991, 1986, 1970 Confraternity of Christian Doctrine, Washington, D.C. and are used by permission of the copyright owner. All Rights Reserved. No part of the New American Bible may be reproduced in any form without permission in writing from the copyright owner.

2. Meaning of Names from: "The Best Baby Name Book in the Whole Wide World" by Bruce & Vicki Lansky, Copyright, 1979. Used with permission.

3. References to Saints, their patronages and the Prayers to St. Germain & the Infant Jesus of Prague retrieved from the SQPN website.

4. Excerpts from the English translation of "The Roman Missal" © 2010, ICEL. All rights reserved. Used with permission.

5. Excerpts from the English translation of "Pastoral Care of the Sick: Rites of Anointing and Viaticum" © 1982, International Commission on English in the Liturgy Corporation (ICEL). Used with permission.

THIS BOOK IS DEDICATED TO ALL OF THE ABUSED, NEGLECTED, AND SEXUALLY MOLESTED CHILDREN OF THE WORLD AND TO THOSE WHO HELP THEM TO HEAL.

ST. GERMAINE COUSIN
PATRONESS OF ABUSED CHILDREN
PRAY FOR US

LITTLE GIRL LOST
LITTLE GIRL FOUND

A Story of Faith, Family, Friends and Healing

YEAR III-COMING HOME

This story is meant to be a work of fiction. As with all human beings my life has been formed by my faith, my education, my work, my family, and other people who have touched my life, the culture I was raised in and my experiences.

I am not alone in this. These items influence all of us and have an effect on whatever we do on a day-to-day basis; whether that be our work, our interaction with others, our thoughts and yes, even what we write.

So, is the story about me? Yes and no. Is this your story? Yes and no. Is it everyone's story? Yes and no. Is it a true story or one based on actual events? Yes and no. All of us will see bits and pieces of ourselves in this work; however, any resemblance to any one person's personal story is not intentional rather please know that it is a conglomeration of all of us.

INTRODUCTION TO BOOK III
by Godzilla

Our journey with Ann continues. She has come a long way on her path of healing and yet a part of her knows that she still has a ways to go. Some of her most challenging days are ahead.

Many have helped her along the journey, but the One that she never really thought was there actually never left her side. Ann's Faith is about to show her how much God really does love her.

*As Jesus said, "...**I am with you always, until the end of the age.**" (Mt 28:20)*

ANN'S STORY
Chapter 1
Getting Closer

Ann felt like she had been on a constant treadmill since before Thanksgiving. Not just the traditional gatherings that went with the holidays of Turkey Day, Christmas and even New Year's, but also the added ones to decorate Tom's tree, then Valentine's Day, Easter and finally little Patricia's birthday. Not that they weren't fun, but it was everything that went with them like gift buying, decorations, and planning. Not that those things weren't fun too, but she just felt like she had been in constant motion for months now. Adding to that were the finishing touches on the research book, not to mention her therapy and the homework associated with it. But, when she woke up this morning, she felt different somehow. She lay there thinking and discerning and suddenly realized what it was. There was nothing she had to do this day, nothing at all. She suddenly felt, as they say, "free as a bird." Whoever "they" are, she chuckled to herself. There were no parties to plan or to prepare to attend, her homework from Dr. Pete was completed for the week, her research book had already been sent to the printer, and she had even worked on her children's book to the point that nothing felt like it was forthcoming. "A day just for me!" she said to all of the stuffed animals in the room. "There is absolutely nothing on the agenda for today," she said as she hugged stuffed bears Godzilla and Sir Lancelot. "I think I will just lie here simply because I can," she said laughing.

But just lying around all day and doing nothing was simply not in Ann's make-up unless she was ill or extremely tired, so, she had to kind of force herself to lie in bed which lasted an entire fifteen minutes. "This would be such a waste of a day," she said as she went by and patted the little lamb Sure To Go, who sat on top of her dresser.

She made herself one of her favorite breakfasts - poached eggs on toast with very crisp bacon, a glass of cranberry juice, and a cup of coffee. Sitting at the kitchen counter she was able to look out the doors to her deck and the backyard beyond. The snow was gone and the sun was shining, and there were hints here and there that spring was definitely in the air. Ann enjoyed the spring, once the rain had stopped being so frequent and the cold dampness left the air. That was the worst part of the season as far as she was concerned. She always preferred snow to rain. Of course, once everything started to bud and poke through the earth there was a special feeling in the air of new life. This day those signs were more hopeful than actually seen.

They always talked about March winds, but Ann's experience was that those days usually occurred during this month, April. "That's when we would go and fly kites," she said to all of her stuffed animals in the kitchen and the family room. "That's it," she suddenly exclaimed, "I think I will go buy a kite and go to the park. It definitely looks like it is windy enough."

As she was getting ready she felt an inner excitement at the thought of doing this. "Just like a little kid," she said to the critters in her room. She then wondered if Tom might like to join her. She was a little nervous about calling him because it did sound kind of childish, but she decided that all he could say was, yes, no or maybe."

"Hello," he answered.

"Tom, it's Ann," she said.

"Well, good morning sunshine, you sound really bright and cheery."

"I guess I am."

"So, what is the good news?"

"Well, the sun is shining and the wind is blowing."

"Yes?"

"And I think that it is a perfect day to go and fly a kite!" she said with a little giggle.

"Oh you do, do you?" he asked teasing.

"And I was wondering if you would like to come and fly kites with me in the park?"

"A play date?"

Ann laughed, "I guess you could call it that."

"I think it sounds like great fun, but I don't have a kite."

"Neither do I. How about I pick you up and we can go buy a couple of them first?"

"Give me a half hour."

"Do you think we should go to that kite store on 10th street or just pick up inexpensive ones?" she asked as Tom got in the car.

Tom smiled, "Personally, I think we should go to the kite store. We may be feeling like little kids today, but our adult selves will really enjoy the fancier kites more."

"I agree," said Ann.

There were so many styles, types, colors and shapes of kites to choose from; it was almost overwhelming, but Ann was having a great time deciding. Tom chose a traditional shaped one, but it had all the colors of the rainbow. It was beautiful. Ann finally decided on one that looked like a Monarch butterfly, feeling that a butterfly really symbolized the freedom she was feeling today.

Once they were at the park, both of them were glad that they had worn mud boots because the grass was still pretty wet and muddy in some spots. Not to mention how good the scarves and gloves felt because the wind still had a bite to it.

It took Tom a couple of tries before his kite caught the wind, but Ann was lucky on her first try of running across the open area. Pretty soon both kites were flying really high and dancing with each other and the wind. Ann found that she simply couldn't stop smiling.

"Oh my gosh," she said, "I can't believe how good this feels."

Tom smiled back at her. They flew the kites for about an hour and then decided that both of them were getting hungry, so they started reeling their kites back in. Tom was able to do his a little faster simply because of it's shape, but suddenly it started to take a nose dive towards the ground and he ran to catch it so that it wouldn't crash and break. In doing so he wasn't paying attention to where he was running and ended up in a muddy area that was very slippery. As he caught his kite down he went face first into the mud. Ann was intent on catching her kite and so had not seen what had happened to him until she turned around. All she could do was to start laughing.

"Oh Tom," she said, still laughing, "What happened?"

"I slipped," he said, "please come and get my kite so I can get up."

Ann laid her kite down and went over to where Tom was. She tried to stay on the edge in the grass so that she wouldn't get all muddy too, however even that was also pretty wet and slippery. So, as she reached forward to take the kite from Tom her one foot slipped out from under her and down she went into the mud too. Now it was Tom's turn to start laughing. Pretty soon both of them were sitting there laughing.

"I wonder if anyone is watching," Ann said.

"If they are, then I bet they are laughing right along with us," Tom answered.

Finally both of them stopped laughing long enough to make some movement toward getting out of the mud.

Ann decided that the best way would be to simply crawl to the edge. Once there she turned and took Tom's kite that he was still holding. Then he crawled over to the side too. Once they stood up both of them started laughing again as they were covered from head to toe in mud.

"Are we having fun yet?" Tom asked.

"I don't know about you, but I sure am! My mother would have been furious if I had come home like this as a kid."

"Isn't it great being a grown-up kid?"

Ann agreed that it definitely was. "Come on," she began, "I've still got blankets in the back of the vehicle from the winter that we can cover the seats and ourselves with."

Once they got everything all set they headed for Tom's house. As she dropped him off he said, "Ann, this was the greatest play date I have ever been on!"

"Yeah, right!" she answered.

"No, seriously. And seeing as how going out for lunch kind of got muddied up, pun intended, how about going out for dinner tonight, my treat?"

"That sounds great."

Tom was still giggling as he got his kite out of the back of the vehicle, "See you later."

Once inside her garage Ann closed the door. She then took the muddy blankets out of the car and also took off all of her clothes. Even her underwear was muddy. "I sure am glad I only have a window on the back door of the garage," she said aloud. She then put everything on the floor by the washer. She was also grateful that she had decided to put in a bathroom with a shower in her basement a few years back. It really came in handy today.

The shower felt good as by then she was feeling a little chilled. Afterwards she put on some clean p.j.'s and decided to take a nap on the couch. Snuggling with her stuffed kitty Sabrina she fell fast asleep. But, it was a very restless sleep as the bad dreams returned. She awoke suddenly, shaking. She was aware that she had been dreaming but couldn't remember what the dream was about other than that she felt really afraid. She grabbed the stuffed bear Father Charlie from the back of the couch and held him in the other arm. "Silly at my age to be comforted by stuffed animals," she said aloud. But, then she remembered the words of Dr. Pete regarding the little girl that was inside of her that needed comfort and healing. Ann just lay there for awhile snuggling with her two stuffed animals and allowing herself to feel okay with doing that.

Tom was right on time and as Ann answered the front door, both of them started laughing again.

"Come my lady," Tom began, "thy chariot awaits thee."

Ann gave him a quizzical frown to which he answered, "Thou wilt understand shortly, my lady."

A short distance out of town they pulled into the parking lot of a restaurant that was built like a castle. The sign simply said, "Camelot."

"Ah," said Ann, "now I understand."

"This is supposed to be quite the dining experience," Tom answered, "lots of fun."

As they approached the entrance a door man dressed as a page welcomed them while he opened the door. Tom turned to Ann and said, "Are thee ready my lady?"

"I am my lord," Ann replied.

After checking their coats another page escorted them towards two very large doors attended by two more pages. Right on cue the two pages opened both doors at the same time into a very large dining hall filled with people at long tables that were surrounding and facing an empty middle section. Plus there were two trumpeters immediately inside who blew an announcement sound.

The page escorting them proclaimed in a loud voice, "The Lady Ann and Sir Thomas!" Everyone inside the room cheered.

They were to find out that this occurred each time new guests arrived. Tom and Ann were escorted to their table. Ann felt as if she had been transported back in time to the Medieval or Renaissance Period. All of their drinks were served in pewter goblets and the food, whose names also reflected that era, were on pewter plates. Of course all of the waiters and waitresses were in period costumes and music of that time was playing in the background.

There really was no opportunity to talk with each other because something was continually happening in the room. Jesters, magicians, and musicians were roaming everywhere. Also throughout the evening knights dressed in armor would periodically come into the middle section and have a sword fight or a small group would do a theatrical performance, poetry, or a scene from a play. It was amazing.

It was also apparent that everyone was having such a good time that no one really wanted to leave, including Ann and Tom. But, eventually, it was time. On the way out they noticed a gift shop.

"Come on Ann, let me buy you something as a memento of this day," said Tom.

"It is I, my lord, who should be gifting thee for this day," Ann answered staying in character.

Tom just shook his head.

They looked around for a while and Ann decided to get four of the pewter goblets that were identical to those used at dinner.

"Two for you and two for me," she said.

Tom said okay. They looked around some more, and then both of them spotted him at the same time.

"Oh look!" they said together.

It was a stuffed doll dressed as a wizard in a wonderful purple robe and a hat to match.

"It's Merlin!" said Ann.

"Do you like him?" asked Tom.

Ann nodded that she did.

"Then, my lady, Merlin the Magician shall be thine. Every lady needs a little magic in her life," Tom answered with a bow.

They laughed and talked all the way home.

"I had never heard of that restaurant," said Ann.

"It's fairly new and I had just read about it recently in an article that gave it great reviews. I was glad that we could get reservations for tonight. Of course being a week night made it a little easier. I've been told that their Friday and Saturday nights are booked at least a month in advance."

"And the food was really delicious," offered Ann.

"That's important," began Tom, "You can have all of the gimmicks in the world, but if your food is not good then the place still won't make it."

"What an incredible day," said Ann, "I can't remember the last time I had so much fun."

Tom answered, "I don't know if you ever came across a stuffed bear that you would put special cassette tapes in that had unique messages." Ann said that she had not. "Well, he was introduced a number of years back and I think he was designed originally to help children who were ill. Today they probably use a CD. Anyway, he offers words of comfort and encouragement to the children."

"Oh Tom he sounds wonderful. How did you learn about him?" Ann asked.

"I found out about him when I was doing volunteer work at Children's Hospital," Tom began. "There was one of his sayings that always stayed with me and this day and you have brought it to mind again."

"What was that?" asked Ann.

Tom smiled as he remembered and then changing his voice to sound like the bear he said, "One shouldn't take life soooooooooooooooo seriously; or something like that.

Ann laughed, "Oh Tom, that is absolutely delightful and soooooooooooooooo true." She said mimicking Tom.

As they pulled into Ann's driveway Tom said, "What is that on your front porch?"

Ann had left both the walkway and porch lights on so they could see that something was sitting there.

"I don't know," answered Ann, "It looks like a large dog. Why would a dog be sitting on my front porch?"

"Maybe it's lost and cold," Tom said. As they stopped the car in front of the garage door Tom exclaimed, "It's a stuffed animal!"

"Oh my gosh," said Ann, "so it is. It looked so real."

As they got closer Ann added, "And it's not a dog at all, it's a lion. A big stuffed lion!"

"He looks just like the lion from the 'Chronicles of Narnia,'" offered Tom.

"Yes he does. And just look at those eyes. They look so real," said Ann. "I wonder who he is from?" she questioned giving Tom a quizzical look.

"Not from me," said Tom. "Remember, I was with you."

"It doesn't mean that you couldn't have had it delivered," Ann answered.

They looked all over for a card or a note, but there was none.

"Would you like to come in for some tea or an after dinner drink?" asked Ann.

"Tea sounds good," said Tom as he picked up the large lion.

"Where do you want him?" asked Tom. Ann pointed to a spot not far from the front door.

Then Tom asked, "Is this the large dog you told us about?" pointing to Cotton Candy.

"Yes, and I still haven't found out who she is from yet either."

"Do you have any ideas?" asked Tom as he sat at the kitchen counter.

"I've asked everyone I can think of, but nobody seems to know anything," she said sitting Merlin the Wizard on the kitchen counter also.

"And now you've got the lion," Tom added.

"At first I thought maybe someone dropped the dog off for me to get cleaned up to take to Officer Brown, but she looks brand new, just like the lion does. So I also checked with him and he said he didn't know anything about it plus he added that she was too large for his purposes.

"Hmm," mused Tom, "a mystery to be solved."

Ann gave Tom a quick hug as she thanked him for a wonderful day.

"And I thank thee too my lady," he answered.
She waved and flicked the lights as Tom beeped his horn as he pulled away.

Ann stood looking at the stuffed lion for a few minutes. "I don't know why," she began, "but there is something very, very comforting that I feel when I look into your eyes and yet..." she paused, "...something a little unsettling too. Anyway, good night my new friend 'Lion.'"

She finished cleaning up the cups in the kitchen and before turning off the light gave Merlin the Wizard a hug.

Ann slept more peacefully than she could ever remember. Not once did she wake up during the night, for anything. She even slept in a little longer the next morning, which was very unusual for her.

She decided that it would be a good day to do some more work on her personal children's book. After getting another cup of coffee she also grabbed Merlin the Wizard and headed for her office. She sat the coffee on one side of the computer and Merlin on the other. "Well, my new friend," she began, "let's see what discoveries we can make today."

THE BOOK
Chapter 1

The next morning everyone had slept in a little later because of staying up late the night before celebrating the new cave mates. Godzilla and his kitchen crew had gotten up just a little earlier so that they could begin fixing a big brunch for everyone.

Ada B. Green and Fuzzy Wuzzy Woof Woof had their children get the table set. "Good to teach them responsibility while they are young," said Fuzzy Wuzzy Woof Woof.

"I couldn't agree more," offered Ada B. Green.

Everyone else was busy making their beds and cleaning up their rooms and any other place they noticed might need a little straightening.

In No Rush was the last one up.

"How are you feeling?" asked the little girl.

"I feel great," he answered.

"You still look a little tired," offered P.J.

"I always look this way," he answered, "that's why my parents gave me this name." Everyone chuckled.

Over brunch the little green rabbit shared how he had been with a family since last Easter, but after a couple of months the children no longer wanted to play with him and he was kind of tossed out.

"Oh how awful," said Sure to Go.

"How did you know to come to Elsie's the Keeper of the Hearts?" asked Little Teresa.

"My parents had told me about her, saying that if I ever became an orphan that I was to make my way to her place in the woods."

"I'm sorry that I wasn't there to greet you," said Elsie.

"But you left a sign and that was a big help," answered In No Rush.

After brunch Peter C. said, "There is another room off of mine if you would like to have that one."

"That would be great," answered the little green bunny.

"Come on," offered little Teresa, "I'll show you where it is."

After they left the room Ada B. Green said, "I think I am going to have to keep an eye on those two." Everyone agreed.

They sat around visiting for a little while before Elsie the Keeper of the Hearts said, "Well, I think it is time that I am on my way. Otherwise Officer Gilbert will start to wonder what has become of me."

There were hugs all around and an extra long one for the little girl as she said, "Take good care of my little friends and of your self." The little girl assured her that she would.

Everyone walked Elsie to the entrance of the cave and suddenly there before all of them stood a wizard in a wonderful purple robe with hat to match. Elsie kind of took a step back saying, "Oh my," as she did.

"I did not mean to startle thee my lady," answered the wizard.

With that a voice was heard from the back of the group, "Merlin, is that you my friend?" yelled Arthur.

"It is indeed my lord," the wizard answered. Within moments both of them were embracing each other.

"And what brings thee to these parts?" asked Arthur.

"I am serving as a traveling companion for another friend of ours," he answered.

With that again suddenly there appeared in the doorway the biggest lion that the little girl had ever seen. She was so startled that she had not noticed that every one of her cave mates had gone down on one knee when the lion appeared.

In a very strong, deep and yet gentle voice the lion said to the little girl, "Do not be afraid. I will not harm you."

It was difficult for her to believe that because his icy stare never changed and his deep voice sent vibrations through her body.

"Honest. He won't hurt you," said Merlin the Wizard.

Barely looking up from his kneeling position Godzilla asked, "And to what do we owe this great honor?"

The lion never took his eyes off of the little girl as he answered, "I'm here to protect her!"

"And I am here to help her," added Merlin.

"But why?" asked Elsie.

Again, the lion did not take his eyes off of the little girl as he answered, "Because I was told that I was needed here."

"We both are," added the wizard.

The little girl was very glad that they were on her side. There was something a little unsettling about both of them, but interestingly enough, she did have a feeling of being safe.

Addressing the wizard the little girl said, "It appears that your name is Merlin," and the wizard gave a little bow, "but may I ask what your name is?" as she looked at the lion.

There was a bit of a gasp from her cave mates and it was at this point that she noticed that all of them were down on one knee and she alone was standing. She looked back to the lion and noticed that there was a flicker of disappointment in his eyes.

"You do not recognize me?" he asked.

Slowly she shook her head no.

The flicker went away. "Just as well," he said, "maybe now I will have some peace and quiet!"

The little girl didn't know what to do so she just stood there.

"Is it all right if I sleep just outside the cave entrance?" the lion asked.

"It might be a little cold," answered the little girl and she invited him to sleep just inside the entrance.

As he settled in, again he looked at the little girl and said, "You no longer have to worry. I will protect you now."

And as Merlin the Wizard headed off to see the room that Arthur and the Prince had offered him near theirs he also turned to the little girl and said, "You will be all right now."

The little girl wasn't sure what either one of them meant, but she was still in a bit of a shock at their arrival. But now it was time to see Elsie the Keeper of Hearts off, so she tried to put it out of her mind.

She then decided that maybe she would walk with Elsie part of the way to start her on her journey. P.J., Lord Percival, and Sure to Go also wanted to go, so of course that meant that Sir Lancelot would go along and now the lion.

It was a beautiful day and everyone was enjoying the walk. After they had walked quite a ways they came to a fork in the road.

"This is as far as I go," said the little girl, "this road to the left will lead you out of the woods."

"Thank you for everything," said Elsie the Keeper of the Hearts.

"No, thank YOU," said the little girl and then added, "Please greet Officer Gilbert for me."

"I will," answered Elsie.

"And all of our friends," said Sure to Go.

"I will," she said again. Then turning to Sir Lancelot she said, "Please take good care of her."

"I will my lady," he answered.

Then to the lion while bending down on one knee she said, "And it was an honor to finally meet you." The lion bowed his head just a little as she continued, "and I am glad that you are here."

She then headed down the path but would stop every few steps and turn to wave. Finally she was out of sight. The little girl stood there and continued to wave even after she could no longer see her because she didn't want her friends to see that she had a tear in her eye. She then kind of cleared her throat as she said, "I am going to miss that good lady."

"Us too," said P.J. as she gave the little girl a hug.

Everyone was quiet as they walked back to the cave just kind of lost in their own thoughts. The little girl kept watching the lion out of the corner of her eye feeling that somehow she should know who he was, especially because everyone else seemed to know. As they got nearer to the cave it suddenly came to her and she exclaimed, "I do know you!"

The lion smiled.

"With all of the reading that I do I should have known who you were right away. You are the lion from "The Chronicles of Narnia" and your name is…but before she had a chance to say his name the lion interrupted her, "Do not say my name aloud; simply call me 'Lion.'"

The little girl agreed and then added, "I am so sorry that I didn't recognize you at first."

Again Lion just smiled.

Over lunch Lion and Merlin both asked everyone to keep their identity and even the fact that they were here a secret.

"OK," said Jacques, "but why?"

Lion smiled, "Because both of us need some rest and relaxation my young friend."

That night the little girl slept more peacefully than she could ever remember. Not once did she wake up during the night; for anything. She even slept in a little longer the next morning, which was very unusual for her. She hadn't even heard all of the critters up and stirring at their usual time. Once up though she decided to take one of her morning walks just to enjoy the fresh air.

THE CRITTERS
Lion and Merlin - The Plan

After Ann left for her walk, they all gathered in the main room. Godzilla began, "Once again, welcome Lion and Merlin to our home."

"We are happy to be here," answered Merlin.

Lion then began, "I need for all of you to keep a secret. Can you do that?"

All of them nodded.

He continued, "As I have already mentioned, Merlin and I need for all of you to keep the fact that we are here a secret. Can all of you do that?"

They again all nodded that they could.

"But, why?" asked Arp.

"Can all of you keep an even bigger secret?" asked Lion.

They nodded again that they could keep the secret.

Lion continued, "We are on a special assignment that we can't talk about and no one is supposed to know that we are here. If certain people found out, it could be dangerous, especially for Ann."

"But Tom knows," said P.J.

"He is okay, as he would never do anything to hurt his friend Ann," said Godzilla.

"But, there are those who have hurt her in the past," Merlin started.

"Like her father?" said R.T. Cold Nose III.

"And her mother?" added Sabrina.

"Then there was this uncle," said Pumpkin-Pumpkin, shaking her head.

"Yes, yes," said Lion, "But, these people are more dangerous than Ann knows. Right now she is feeling somewhat safe because she only remembered a little bit of what her parents did to her. And she has not remembered the uncle at all. But, that's where we come in."

"What do you mean?" asked Beethoven.

Merlin continued, "I'm here to help her to remember and Lion is here to offer extra special protection. That's why we have to keep our presence here a secret, for a while longer anyway."

"I don't understand why it is so dangerous," said Raspberry Sundae.

"And if it is so dangerous," began Joan, "why not just let things stay as they are?"

"Especially because the nightmares seem to have stopped," added P.J.

"If only it was so simple, but it's actually kind of complicated," began Merlin, "basically, because of what these people did to her she does not feel safe. Only, she doesn't know why. There are things about them and more about what they did to her that she has buried deep inside. They were so painful and terrifying at the time because she was so young and felt powerless. It was easier to simply try to forget everything that happened at least on a conscious level. But, down deep, the memories are still there, along with the feelings of terror."

"Is this why she has had so many nightmares?" asked Lord Percival.

Both Lion and Merlin nodded.

"But how can remembering help her?" asked Snowflake the bear, "Won't that just cause her more pain?"

Merlin answered, "Yes, it will be painful as she remembers because she will be feeling the same feelings she had when she was younger, but buried. But, remember, it will also be very freeing for her. This is what Dr. Pete is helping her with."

"I'm not sure I totally understand," said Front Porch the Buffalo Bull. Moose Bear shook his head in agreement.

"As I said, as she remembers," began Merlin, "she will be having the same feelings. But eventually she will also realize that she is older now and an adult and therefore can defend herself against these people."

"But aren't her parents already deceased?" asked Cotton Candy.

"Yes," said Merlin, "but their voices and their actions are still inside of Ann and she needs to face them, but as an adult. And the danger lies in the fact that at first she is going to still feel like that helpless little girl and may feel so afraid that she decides that she does not want to face everything. Also, the uncle is still living and that also causes fear."

"I would be scared too," said Miss Evelyn.

Everyone nodded in agreement.

"However," continued Merlin, "Ann does not have to face all of this alone anymore. She has her good friends, her brother and other relatives, Dr. Pete, Father Jack, and all of us to stand with her."

"Plus her Catholic faith," said Lion, "which is part of why I am here too."

"And that's a lot of power!" said Sir Lancelot.

"Exactly!" answered Merlin. "That will help her get her power back; the power that she came into this world with, which these people took away when they hurt her."

"Wow!" said Jacques.

"How can we help?" asked Jeanette.

"You already are," said Merlin, "just by being here and being her friends."

ANN'S STORY
Chapter 2
Remembering

After that first night of wonderful, undisturbed blissful sleep the tides turned for Ann. The nightmares returned worse than ever. Strange, disturbing and even bizarre were the only way she could describe them. At first she couldn't remember any details, but then slowly people were showing up in them. People that she didn't know, but felt that she should, and they were all screaming and yelling at her. And even stranger is that the stuffed lion that had shown up on her front doorstep also showed up in the dreams, and once he did she somehow knew that she was safe.

Of course Ann talked with Dr. Pete about all of this.

"What are you thinking this means?" he asked her.

Ann took a deep sigh before she answered, "I have a feeling that I am about to remember some more things that happened."

"And isn't that what you wanted to happen as a result of coming to see me?" he ventured.

"Yes, but..." she began, "I'm afraid."

"Of what?"

"Of what it is that I am going to remember. It must be pretty terrible if I have buried it so deep that it has taken this long for it to come out."

"How has it been remembering your father's drinking and some of the abuse from your mother?"

"At first I guess I didn't believe that some of it could actually be true because it was kind of shocking that I hadn't remembered it. I also did not want it to be true. And then there was some hurt as I remembered some of the events."

"And anger?" Dr. Pete interjected.

"Some, I guess," she said, "but actually more sadness that these things had happened, and that it involved my parents who were supposed to love me."

"And now?"

"I think that attending the meetings for those who grew up in alcoholic homes really helped me to understand that my father had a disease and that it had nothing to do with me. Given the disease, he did the best he could. Not that he couldn't have done better, but I think his disease kept him from doing that."

"So, kind of an acceptance?"

"Yes, but also a healing for me. Not that it happened overnight because first I had to process all of that."

"What about some of the abuse from your mother?"

"Not quite as resolved. I can't figure out why she would do some of the things that my brother mentioned or that I began remembering."

"Do you think she had some mental problems of some kind?"

Ann gave a nervous laugh, "I think that anyone who does those kinds of things to kids definitely has a mental problem! I guess that with my father I have kind of figured things out and come to some kind of resolution, but not with my mother."

"Good," said Dr. Pete. "It's sort of like the stages of grief that people go through when they or someone they love is dying."

"Those made famous by Dr. Elisabeth Kubler-Ross many years ago?" Ann asked.

"Yes. There are stages to healing from childhood traumas too. For many, they have to remember them first, then deal with the feelings surrounding all of the things that happened and finally come to some kind of resolution and healing."

"I can see that."

"One more question. Do you feel that you have survived the remembering and the feelings of the incidents so far?"

"Yes, definitely."

"And are healing?"

Ann laughed, "You said one more question!" and then answered, "Yes, why?"

Dr. Pete smiled, "So, what makes you think that whatever you are about to remember will turn out any differently?"

"Checkmate."

Dr. Pete smiled.

"So, why is the lion from the 'Chronicles of Narnia' showing up in my dreams?" she asked.

"Why do you think?"

"I don't know," she said, "that is why I asked you."

"What does he represent to you?" Dr. Pete prompted.

Ann thought for a moment before answering. "I could tell you what various articles say about his character in 'The Chronicles of Narnia.'"

Dr. Pete smiled, "Have you ever read or seen the story?"

"Yes," answered Ann.

"So, what did the lion represent to you personally?" he gently asked.

"When I read the story he seemed to be a very powerful and strong figure, yet gentle and very spiritual. Then when I saw the movie I got more of a sense of him as somewhat of a Christ figure. Even though Lewis seems to have indicated that he did not intend for the lion to totally represent Christ."

Dr. Pete smiled as he said, "You just had to sneak your knowledge in there didn't you?"

Ann hung her head a little.

"Ann, I don't care what Lewis intended or did not intend; I want to know what your view and experience of the lion was. It is your opinion that counts to me right now because it was your dream. Do you understand?"

Ann said that she did and then added, "So, if he is a spiritual, or even a Christ figure for me then his showing up in my dream may be my unconscious telling me that my faith will get me through."

"Good. And how did you say you felt once he shows up in the dream?"

"That I knew that I was safe."

"So, does that give you any other ideas?"

Ann thought for a few minutes and then a huge smile came across her face as she said, "I AM going to be okay, because God IS with me."

Dr. Pete gave her a huge smile back as he said, "Isn't our Catholic Faith a wonderful gift?"

Ann agreed that it was.

Dr. Pete then finished the session by saying, "Ann, I don't want to soft-soap any of this and lead you into thinking that this is not going to be painful, because it is. But, you will get through it and you will be okay. And please remember that I am praying for you."

That very night Ann had another nightmare very similar to the first one. Again, there were people drinking and fighting. She could hear them, but couldn't really see who it was. And this time someone was chasing her as well as yelling at her. Again, the lion showed up in the dream and even though she awoke she knew she was okay and was able to go right back to sleep after grabbing Sir Lancelot and Godzilla.

This continued off and on over the next couple of weeks until finally one night she was able to see who was doing the drinking and fighting, her parents. She had suspected that that was who it was, but now she knew. And in this one her mother was really beating her. She lay there awhile after the dream woke her up and tried to get in touch with the feelings that she had in the dream. She decided that mostly she felt afraid; afraid that her parents would hurt each other or would go after one of her siblings as they had her. Ann still sensed that fear wasn't the only thing she was feeling, but she couldn't quite put her finger on it. She decided that maybe working on her children's book again would help her.

However, the next day she received a telephone call from Father Jack. "How are you Father?" she asked.

"I am doing quite well Ann, and you?" he answered.

"Doing well too," she said.

"I thought that you were because you never called to make another appointment to see me, so I figured you had sorted things out."

Ann laughed, "Not totally."

"Please know Ann, that when you are ready to talk, just give me a call."

"Thanks Father Jack, I will. Now, was there a reason that you called?"

"Yes, of course to see how you were, but also to invite you to attend a program that we have offered before and are going to be offering it again."

"What is that?"

"It's a training program that helps adults to know and recognize the behaviors of child molesters and of children who might be being molested."

"Isn't that part of the program that the U.S. Catholic Bishops recommended after the sexual abuse scandal?"

"Yes, it is. It comes under the Charter for the 'Protection of Children and Young People.' Everyone who has anything to do with our children, whether in the Catholic School, the Religious Education Program, our before and after-school programs, and the lunch program and whether they are a paid employee or a volunteer, have been required to go through the training. And before that we held a special training for all parents."

"I am really not involved in any of those programs, so why do you want me to attend?"

"This year we have decided to offer the training to the rest of our parishioners, starting with a group of those we consider to be leaders in the community. It will of course include our parish council and members of all of the committees, but also people like you. I've also asked Tom and plan on asking Marie and D.J. to attend this first one. After that we will then open it up generally. My goal is to be able to say that 100% of our parishioners have gone through the training."

"I think that is a wonderful idea. What kind of time commitment is involved?"

"Just one evening. And actually, we've scheduled it for next Friday. Hopefully that will work for you."

"Works great. I'll be there."

"Thank you so much Ann. I was hoping that we could count on you."

"I thought about you often during that whole upheaval," Ann began. "How did you handle it?"

"Not well I'm afraid," he answered. "Of course I received taunts when I wore my collar in public, all of us did, but what really got to me is that I could not understand how my brother priests could do something like that to children. I still don't totally understand it, but in taking these classes I've learned a lot more about child abuse, neglect, and the different types and levels of molestation. The fields of psychology and human behavior have a long ways to go in their attempts to understand and treat those affected by abuse, especially those who end up being perpetrators. We've come quite a distance in a very short time as a society, but it is still not quick enough to protect so many children. Through this process I've learned that even up until the late 1960's child abuse was not seen as a problem, and even by the early 1970's many states still did not have laws on their books to deal with these issues. But, you will hear all of this when you come to the workshop."

"That must have been really hard on you," began Ann. "I mean, the vast majority of priests are good and loving and yet all of you had to bear the burden of those few and their actions."

"Actually, the entire Church has had to bear it," he answered, "and the attacks are based upon the knowledge that we have today and not the lack of knowledge and understanding that was in play during those times. Hopefully now we are becoming part of the solution. Just talking about it a little bit has helped me to realize that this is something that is still very upsetting to me."

"I can see how it would be Father. Plus, I've noticed that, like you said, the entire priesthood and the Church are being blamed and attacked because of this. And yet we don't see the same thing occurring in other religious congregations or even occupations. I mean if a doctor, dentist, teacher, or a protestant minister has hurt a child the entire group is not condemned like we have been!"

"I know. The Catholic Church always seems to be a target because we very often stand against the main line culture so they take every opportunity to attack. Anyway, thank you for listening Ann."

"Anytime Father. See you next Friday," answered Ann.

Ann then telephoned Tom to see if he would consider the two of them going together, which he thought a great idea. Ann was grateful that Tom was going too. She was looking forward to it, and yet also felt some nervousness as they would be talking about abuse. After the events that she had already started to remember she was hoping that it wouldn't be too upsetting; at least not so upsetting that she couldn't deal with publicly.

The next few nights were really rough for Ann. The nightmares not only continued, but also increased in their intensity and their clearness. There was so much screaming and yelling in them, and usually it was aimed at her. She dreamt of her father drinking and the fights her parents had which were as her memories had already been. But, now she was also seeing how much her mother not only yelled at her, but also hit her. And then, there was always someone chasing her, but she couldn't see who it was. Then the lion would appear and that woke her up. Often she was still shaking and feeling terrified until she realized that she was awake and that she was okay. Each time this happened she would grab another one of the stuffed animals and put them in bed with her. "Pretty soon there is not going to be enough room for me," she said to all of them one night after another nightmare had awakened her.

As difficult as all of this was, she also knew that these nightmares were also bringing her closer and closer to remembering the events of her childhood that she had forgotten. One night when she was particularly tired, she also brought Raspberry Sundae, Cotton Candy and Moose Bear into her bedroom. "I know it's silly," she said to all of the stuffed animals gathered there, "but somehow I feel safer with all of you here." As she was falling asleep she had a memory from childhood of putting all of her dolls and stuffed animals in bed with her one night. "I'll have to think about that more tomorrow," she thought as she drifted off.

When Friday arrived, as much as Ann was looking forward to the workshop that evening, she was also a little leery about attending. With the nightmares she hadn't been sleeping all that well, and when tired like that she felt particularly vulnerable. It was not a feeling that Ann, the strong one, liked. She tried to take a nap in the afternoon, but was unable to sleep at all.

As the doorbell rang that evening announcing Tom's arrival Ann said a quick prayer asking God to be with her and help her.

"Hey," Tom said as Ann opened the door, "are you ready?"

"As ready as I'll ever be," Ann answered.

"Is everything okay?"

"Just a little nervous," she replied and then explained a little bit about the dreams she had been having.

"Is that why you asked me to attend this with you?"

"Partially, but I also enjoy your company."

"Have you talked with your brother?"

"As a matter of fact, I have and he verified some of the memories and dreams that I have had. At least the ones he was old enough to remember too. Other memories we both figure that he was too young."

"It's too bad that your sister is not still living to help you fill in some of the gaps," Tom commented. Ann agreed.

When they arrived at the church hall before getting out of the car Tom took Ann's hand and said, "I'll be right next to you."

"Thanks Tom," she answered giving him a weak smile.

There was a nice size group already gathering when they got inside, and immediately they found Marie and D.J. who had saved seats in the front.

Great! Ann thought to herself, they had to find seats right up front!

Tom must have sensed her apprehension and gave her hand a quick squeeze.

Father Jack greeted them and thanked them for coming.

Then Ann spotted Dr. Pete. She excused herself and went over to talk with him.

"What are you doing here?" she asked.

"I am part of the presentation," he answered, "and how about you?"

Ann explained Father Jack's invitation. She then said, "I would like you to meet a few of my good friends as I have mentioned them to you in our sessions."

"Do they know that I am your therapist?" he asked.

"I have mentioned you," she answered.

"Okay," he said, "because remember I told you in the first session that even the fact that I am your therapist is something that I keep confidential in addition to all that you share with me. Only you can break that confidentiality."

"I remember," answered Ann, "and it is one of the reasons that I trust you."

Then Ann called her friends over and introduced them to Dr. Pete.

As they were heading back to their seats Tom shook Dr. Pete's hand and said, "Thank you for all that you are doing to help Ann." Dr. Pete just smiled.

Pretty soon it was time to begin the program. Father Jack began with a prayer and then a little explanation on what was going to occur throughout the evening. He then introduced Dr. Pete giving his background and credentials.

Dr. Pete welcomed everyone and began with an overview of child abuse in our country. "When I began my undergraduate studies in Psychology in the late 1960's I took one of the very first courses ever offered on child abuse in this country. One of the things that really struck me was that physical child abuse was not even viewed as a problem in our country at the time. There were very few laws, if any, on the books to protect children, other than labor laws, basically because it was not viewed as a problem. And even this undergraduate course dealt only with extreme physical abuse and neglect and didn't even touch on emotional abuse or sexual abuse. I remember my professor telling us that part of our responsibility as future therapists would be to bring these issues to light and to make sure that they would finally be viewed as a problem in our country. I can still see in my mind's eye some of the photos that were included in the text book. Of course, these were some of the most serious cases of abuses that we covered because the authors, as well as my professor, were trying to make a very strong point. Plus, much of this information was also going to be included in the training of medical personnel so that they could also begin to be more aware of the patterns of child abuse that would be showing up in their offices and ER rooms."

"The second part of this problem," he continued, "is that legislation needed to be introduced that would protect physicians, other health care workers, teachers, and what we today call 'mandated reporters' from being sued for their reporting, and also assuring that it could be done anonymously. This would eventually include anyone, whether it be a neighbor, friend, or family member who had witnessed something or was simply suspicious. Once these were in place it made it much easier for these incidents to be reported; prior to that most were afraid of repercussions."

"Wow," Tom whispered to Ann.

Ann nodded and whispered back, "This is some of what Officer Gil Brown shared with me too."

"Another problem," he continued, "was that at the time there was no one definition of what child abuse was, and there were definitely very inaccurate methods of keeping track of the number of cases. One of the better surveys at the time was an attempt in 1965 from Brandeis University to get some kind of handle on the number of abuse cases in the United States by reviewing newspaper stories for the six-month period from July to December of that year. Obviously, we have come much further in our reporting methods, but I wanted to give you an idea of where we were at the time. What they found were 504 incidents reported in newspapers nationwide. Of these, 164 resulted in the death of the child and 340 were non-fatal. If we look at the age groups the highest percentage of abuse was 15.3% in the three to five year old range. The second highest, and most disturbing, was 14.3% for those under the age of 6 months."

Ann along with the rest of the audience made audible gasps.

Dr. Pete continued, "In 2010, there were 3.3 million reports of child abuse that involved more than 5 million children and every day in our country 5 children die as the result of abuse." Again, the audience gasped as Dr. Pete said, "However, remember, it's not necessarily that we have more abuse in this country than we did in the 1960's, it's just that we have much, much better awareness and reporting. And finally, there was the treatment of the abusers, as well as the children abused. Psychology is not an exact science, and in the early years of treatment we were trying different treatment methods with various levels of success. It also depended on what the problematic issue was. For some parents it might have been stress on the job, in the marital relationship or even in their parenting skills, and thus they would lash out at the child. These cases were treated differently than those that stemmed from their own abuse. Sometimes alcohol or drug abuse was at the root, so these had to be dealt with first."

Tom reached over and grabbed Ann's hand giving it a squeeze.

"Now remember," Dr. Pete continued, "So far we have only been referring to physical abuse and neglect. But, this evening, what we are going to focus on is sexual abuse or molestation. Of all of the abuse cases reported in the United States currently, 9.2% of them are considered to be sexual abuse or about 1.3 million children per year.

Let's first define what child sex abuse or molestation is. Of course there are cases which involve actual body contact which includes erotic kissing as well as oral, anal, or vaginal sexual activity; but it can also involve touching children on their private parts or showing children one's private parts as in 'flashing,' forcing children to watch pornography, or to show their body to someone as well as having sexual intercourse in front of children. Child pornography and prostitution also fall under this definition. Thus, we can see that there are different levels and types of sexual molestation and abusers.

So, who are the abusers? About 95% are known by their victim, with 30% of them being the victim's, father, mother, brother, uncle, cousin, or some other relative; the other 65% would include family friends, babysitters, neighbors, teachers, coaches, school counselors, or other people who would have direct contact with the child. Yes, mothers or other females; they account for about 6% of abusers in the cases reported by girls and 14% reported by boys. The estimates today say that there are somewhere between 250,000 and 500,000 sexual abusers living in the United States. Most molesters were also sexually abused in their own childhood, but not every child molested becomes a sexual abuser. This is something that those of us in the fields of psychology and psychiatry are studying in the hope of understanding more.

There was a time in the earlier days of the 1970's when we thought that by simply separating the particular child victim from the abuser that everything would be okay. Unfortunately this is also what the field of psychology advised the Catholic bishops at the time who turned to us for help and advice. It was dealt with almost as in the early days of treating alcoholics when it was thought that if whiskey was what was causing you problems then you removed that, but that wine or the beer would be all right. Today we know better; that alcohol is alcohol, and children are children, and that it is most often what is convenient rather than what might be preferred."

Dr. Pete then took a quick drink of water, and Ann realized that she had kind of been holding her breath, which she slowly let out.

"Finally," Dr. Pete began, "let us take a quick look at the victims. We now know that those who have been sexually abused, depending on the level and type, may not show any effects, but that is pretty rare. Most often they will show various psychological problems that may include, but not be limited to: depression, anti-social behavior, suicide attempts or self-destructive behavior, neurosis of various types, eating disorders, cruelty to animals, anxiety or panic attacks, and even what we now call post-traumatic stress disorder. Or they may have chronic 'aches and pains' that cannot really be attributed to any physical disorder, plus they may also have angry outbursts, fear of being alone, sleeping problems that may or may not include nightmares as well as learning problems. For example in one study it was found on the SAT exam for college entrance women who were not sexually abused scored much higher than those who were abused. And finally, very often their own behavior and relationships with others tends to be highly sexualized. All of these can of course continue into adulthood."

Ann was beginning to feel highly uncomfortable and hid it the best she could.

Dr. Pete continued, "Today in the United States alone it is estimated that there are 60 million survivors of sexual abuse with 20 million of these being victims of their own parents. It breaks out to about 1 in every 4 girls and 1 in every 6 boys have been sexually abused. So, that means that out of this group of about 30 people, 5 of the men have ostensibly been molested and 8 of the women. Let's see what that looks like."

Ann felt herself going numb as she suddenly remembered what she had forced herself to forget.

First, Dr. Pete chose 5 of the men from throughout the audience including Tom, and then asked them to stand. He then chose 8 women, gratefully not including Ann and asked them to stand. There were a few audible "wows" throughout the audience.

"Now," began Dr. Pete, "I want to make it even more dramatic. Would everyone on this side of the audience please sit down and those on this right side all stand with the exception of these two," he said pointing to Tom and Ann. "Again," Dr. Pete began, "out of this group of about 30 these are the number who statistically would have been sexually molested."

"Absolutely incredible," Marie said.

Dr. Pete then thanked everyone and had them all sit down. "Now, you are going to watch a video where they will talk about the signs that a child may have been sexually abused. We will then take a short break and the second part of the video will include interviews with actual molesters."

Ann really wanted to just run out of the room and to keep running until she could run no longer, but instead, she forced herself to stay seated.

Tom reached over and whispered, "Are you doing okay?"

Ann nodded a lying yes, but her mind was now a thousand miles away and years ago to when she was a child. It was the uncle that she had seen in those photos!

Marie sitting on the other side of her then also whispered, "This is kind of scary hearing all of this. If anyone would try anything with our little Patricia I know I wouldn't care about the consequences of my behavior."

"Neither would I," D.J. chimed in, "and I'm an attorney."

It took everything Ann had to stay in her seat, but she really couldn't tell you what was being said in the movie. She was glad that they would have materials to take home with them. During the break Ann got up to get some water and Tom went with her.

"Are you doing okay?" he asked.

Again she nodded that she was, but avoided eye contact with him. Just then Dr. Pete came over and asked what they thought. Tom jumped right in answering that he was learning so much, and even though it was all so sad and tragic he was glad that he had come.

As they were walking back to their seats Dr. Pete gently steered Ann to the side and said, "I have an appointment available at 9 tomorrow morning."

Without looking at him she answered, "Thank you. I will be there."

Ann was grateful that Marie and D.J. had to get home because they had a sitter and Tom said that he had an early morning meeting too, as the last thing Ann wanted to do that night was to go out and talk about all of this.

Driving home Tom said that his head was just swirling with all of the information they had been given and then asked, "How about you?"

"I am so exhausted from all of it," answered Ann.

"Was some of it hard for you?"

All Ann said was, "Yes."

"Would you like to talk about it?"

Ann managed to say, "Thank you, but not tonight."

When they arrived at Ann's house Tom started to get out of the car to walk Ann to her front door when Ann said, "It's okay Tom. I can make it from here."

Tom knew that tone. It was the strong, tough Ann, but he also sensed that this was not the time to challenge her.

"Okay," he said gently, "I'm here if you need me."

"Thanks," she said getting out of the car. She flicked the porch light once she was inside and he flicked his car lights back.

"Be with her this night Lord," Tom said aloud as he pulled out of her driveway.

Ann felt like she had been hit and run over by a fleet of semi-trucks! She took an ibuprofen hoping that would help her head and body aches. And for some reason she felt the need for a warm shower even though she had showered earlier in the day. Once in the shower she shed a few tears as she allowed the memory that had shown up earlier in the evening to return. That uncle had tried to force her to stay in a room in his house and was touching her where he shouldn't be.

She remembered him saying, "It will just be our little secret."

Somehow, she was able to get past him and to rejoin the cousins in the living room.

"I can't believe it," Ann said aloud, "that scumbag!"

She put on her favorite, most comfortable p.j.'s and made herself some hot cocoa with milk to help her to sleep. She thought that she would fall right to sleep because she was so tired, which she did, but within ten minutes was wide awake again and feeling very fearful. "That's it," she said aloud, "silly or not I am going to do it."

With that she got out of bed and gathered every single one of the stuffed animals and dolls in her house and brought them into the bedroom. She placed those that would fit into the bed with her between Godzilla on one side and Sir Lancelot on the other. The rest of them were surrounding her bed and everywhere else there was a spot. She then decided that she had better set her alarm so as not to miss the appointment with Dr. Pete. With that Ann crawled under the covers and snuggled as close as she could to all of her stuffed animals and fell fast asleep. The only dreams she had that night were of her and her stuffed animals all having fun together.

The next morning Ann felt a little more rested, but still like she had been hit by a truck.

Dr. Pete was waiting when she arrived at his office.

"I didn't know you had Saturday appointments," she said.

"Sometimes I do," he answered.

Once they were seated in his office he gently asked, "You remembered something, didn't you?"

"Yes, how did you know?"

"Because the color in your face began to slowly drain, and then there was this moment when you looked like you had seen a ghost."

"Nothing like being right in the front row."

"Ann?" he gently prodded.

She then told him what she had remembered and how she had been feeling through the entire talk.

"Do you remember any other times with him?"

"No, but he must have been around because I have come across some photographs of him, and I remembered that he didn't live that far from us."

"Do you know if he is still living?"

"I think so, why?" Ann answered with a certain level of fear.

Dr. Pete smiled, "Don't worry, you don't have to contact him, but we need to find out where he is and if he might have access to children."

"Do you think he would do something to a child today? I mean, he must be fairly old at this point."

"It doesn't matter what age they are, but we won't worry about that for now. How are you feeling today?"

"Pretty drained and yet kind of okay. Last evening was pretty intense for me."

"I bet it was."

"Unfortunately I don't remember much of the video."

"That's all right. Sometime down the road you can borrow it from me if you wish, but for now I think you have enough going on. How are you feeling about the memory?"

"There's a part of me that wonders if it really happened or if it is just my creative imagination, but it seemed so real."

"Why don't you do some writing on your children's book and see what comes out?"

"Do you think it really happened?"

"Ann, I have suspected for some time now that something like this had happened to you."

"Why?"

"Because you were exhibiting some of the things that would point to that."

"Like what?"

"Now, I can't give away all of my trade secrets," he said smiling. "Just trust me."

"Okay."

Ann decided to spend the rest of the weekend resting; so on the way home she stopped at the store and picked up food for the weekend and a bouquet of flowers. Monday would be soon enough to work on the children's book. She watched cartoons and old movies. She laughed and clapped at the shows. She even made a few healthy meals, instead of the quick things like pizza and sandwiches. It was the best two days Ann had ever had in her entire life. She also moved the icon of St. Germaine Cousin to one of the nightstands next to her bed.

Both nights she slept like a peaceful child with all of her stuffed animals around her and St. Germaine at her side.

THE BOOK
Chapter 2

What a glorious walk the little girl had that morning. She did enjoy the middle to late spring time before they got into the heat of the summer. It was wonderful seeing all of the new life that was coming forth throughout the woods. By the time she returned to the cave she was actually whistling. It did all of her little friends good to see their friend happy. But, all of that was about to change, again.

That night the bad dreams began to return and they were kind of strange and very disturbing. There were people in them that she didn't know and yet she felt that she did. They were screaming and yelling at her and she felt very afraid until there appeared a critter that she knew. It was Lion and she knew she was safe. The next morning she didn't tell anyone about the dream.

Over the next couple of weeks the little girl had many dreams very similar to the first one. Usually, the people were fighting and drinking. Sometimes they would chase after the little girl yelling and screaming at her. Sometimes they also slapped her or were beating her with sticks and belts. Just when she would become so terrified that she thought she would be killed, Lion would appear and protect her.

And often he would say the same thing, "I would have been here sooner, if you had called for me." The little girl could never figure that part out neither during the dream nor even after she was awake. How could she call for someone if she didn't know they were there? Besides, sometimes she was just so terrified that she couldn't call out.

Then one night it happened. The dream came as always, only this time it was somewhat different. First, the people in the dream weren't just people she didn't know, they were her parents who were fighting and yelling and it was her mother that was beating her. And as if that weren't bad enough she also dreamt that a man was touching her in places that were hers alone and she couldn't get away from him. The man was an uncle of hers! She was so startled and afraid that this time, she screamed! Immediately Lion appeared in the dream and protected her.

What the little girl didn't realize is that when she screamed in her dream she had also screamed out loud. So when she opened her eyes as she came out of the nightmare, there were all of her cave mates surrounding her and all of their eyes were as big as saucers.

"Here we go again," said R.T. Cold Nose III.

"Shhh," said Godzilla and gave the little seal a bit of a scolding look.

Sir Lancelot snuggled close to the little girl as did P.J., and urged her to talk about the dream.

"It was more like a memory," began the little girl.

Merlin and the Prince nodded.

"The fights and the drinking weren't just at Christmas as I remembered before, but happened off and on throughout the year. And that was the scary part because I never knew when it was going to happen and how bad it was going to be; these fights seem to come out of nowhere so you couldn't prepare for them."

"I can see how that would be really scary," said Lord Percival. The rest of the critters nodded in agreement with him.

The little girl then became quiet and one tear rolled down her cheek. Everyone sat quietly waiting for her to continue.

Then Godzilla gently asked, "Did you remember something else?"

The little girl nodded that she had. "I have shared with you that sometimes my mother would hit me," she began.

Everyone nodded again.

"I also dreamt that not only would she hit me, but sometimes she would beat me too with belts or sticks. I would beg for her to stop, but she wouldn't. I would also ask them not to fight and yell at each other and me, but again they never listened to me. They were so much bigger than me and I was so scared. I finally gave up trying and just tried to stay out of their way."

By now, her critter friends all had tears in their eyes and the little girl whispered, "No one ever listened to me."

After a few moments Lion stepped forward and gently asked, "You remembered something else too didn't you?"

The little girl looked up at him and with tears in her eyes nodded yes. She took a deep breath so as to stop the tears that were starting to well-up as she began, "I also dreamt of a man who was my uncle who would hold me against my will and touch me in places that he shouldn't have."

"Oh my," said Ada B. Green softly as she hugged both Jacques and Jeanette. Fuzzy, Wuzzy Woof Woof also hugged Arp and Godzilla put an arm around R.T. Cold Nose III.

The rest of the night the little girl shared with her friends all that she could remember from the dreams. She was also able to tell them her feelings of fear and of anger, but they all noticed that she never really cried. It was a pretty strong wall she had built to try to protect herself.

Finally, in the wee hours of the morning the little girl stopped talking and was able to fall asleep with all of her friends around her. They all snuggled so close to her and each other that there really was no room to move. But, she slept peacefully for the first time in a long time. In fact, all of them slept most of the next morning; a long, restful sleep that was long overdue.

When everyone finally awoke the little girl felt almost like a new person. She said that she wanted to take a long, warm, bubble bath. Godzilla got his kitchen crew together to fix a huge and healthy brunch for everyone. Meanwhile the rest of the critters set about cleaning and straightening up the cave.

After cleaning up from the brunch everyone sat around and told stories, sang songs or did skits all afternoon. The little girl sang, laughed and clapped her hands with delight at all of the talent her friends had. Of course, the critters were all having a good time too.

All in all it was a really good day. One of the best the little girl had ever had in her life. She slept like a peaceful child again that night with all her friends surrounding her.

ANN'S STORY
Chapter 3
Can One Ever Have Enough Stuffed Animals?

Ann did go back to working on her children's book and found it helpful to express some of her feelings through her main character. Somehow it enabled her to sort out exactly what she was feeling.

Later in the day Marie called. "Boy, wasn't that material intense on Friday evening?" Marie began.

"It sure was," answered Ann.

"D.J. and I didn't talk all of the way home. Finally on Saturday we decided to sit down and share how we felt about all of it," Marie added.

"Yeah, Tom and I didn't talk either," answered Ann.

"Anyway," Marie continued, "D.J. and I would like to invite you and Tom to dinner on Thursday. You are Patricia's godparents and we have never had you over and we would like to do that so we can spend time together and you can also spend time with Patricia."

"That would be wonderful," began Ann, "I know that I have neglected my duties as a godparent recently. I just don't know where the hours and days go."

"You have been great! Don't think for a moment that you haven't," answered Marie.

"Can I bring anything?"

"Just your beautiful self. D.J. is going to call Tom today too, so don't be surprised if you hear from him."

"Thanks for the warning," giggled Ann.

Sure enough a couple of hours later Tom telephoned Ann.

"Hey lovely lady," he began.

Ann laughed, "Always the charmer. Now, I suppose that you are calling to ask me if I would like for you to pick me up on Thursday to go to Marie's and D.J.'s."

"Actually," began Tom, "I was calling to see if you would pick me up?"

"Is something wrong with your vehicle?" asked Ann seriously as picking Tom up would be going in the wrong direction.

"No," he said, "you just seemed so sure of yourself that I decided to give you a hard time."

"Funny guy."

After they arranged the time that Tom would come by he asked, "How are you doing?"

"You know Tom, I am okay. Actually, I am better than okay."

"That is great to hear. I knew that the talk Friday evening was difficult for you."

"Yes, yes it was, very difficult and I would like to share it with you, but not over the telephone."

"Fair enough. Just let me know when you are ready."

Ann promised that she would, and they finished making the arrangements for Thursday prior to hanging up.

Ann decided that she wanted to bring a little something, not just for Marie and D.J., but also for Patricia, so she took a run out to the Catholic Religious Gift Store in the mall. As Ann entered the store she was happy to see that the same lady was working who had snuck the icon of St. Germaine Cousin in her bag last fall.

"Hello," Ann said in greeting.

"Hi, how are you?" answered the lady obviously recognizing Ann.

"I am very well, thank you," Ann answered and then continued, "I am glad that you are working today because I wanted to thank you in person for the icon of St. Germaine Cousin."

"There is no need to thank me," answered the lady. "I only try to follow what the Holy Spirit guides me to do."

"Well," began Ann, "as difficult as this is for me to share with you I want you to know that you were correct. I was supposed to have that icon. Just last week I had a memory of being molested, and there have been other memories of abuse." Ann then swallowed hard because she realized that she had said the words out loud and to a stranger.

"Oh, I am so sorry that happened to you," said the lady, "I was really hoping that giving you the icon maybe had something to do with your work or maybe with someone you knew. May I give you a hug?"

Ann said that it would be okay. The lady came around from behind the counter and gave Ann such a long, gentle hug that it almost brought tears to her eyes.

"I will keep you in special prayer," the lady offered.

Ann thanked her and then began looking for something for Patricia. She finally decided on a book about Mary.

As Ann got ready to leave the store she thanked the lady again for the icon to which the lady replied, "Again, no need to thank me. Just do the same thing for someone else someday." Ann liked that idea.

Ann then found a nice box of different flavored coffees for Marie and D.J. On the way to the car she decided that she just had to go by the stuffed animal store.

Of course the owners remembered her saying, "And how is one of our very favorite customers?"

"Just fine," answered Ann, "and how are all of you?" as she swept her arm to include all of the stuffed animals in the store.

The owners laughed, "All of us are just fine. So, how can we help you?"

"Oh, you know me; I can't come to the mall without stopping by and seeing what is new in your store. I just love looking around," Ann answered.

"Well, look to your heart's content," said the husband.

Ann looked around a long time and thoroughly enjoyed all the different kinds of stuffed animals that were in the store. And then she spotted him- a little pink piglet.

I don't have a pig in my collection, she said to herself, and he is just so cute. His tag said that his name was "Fast Eddy." What a strange name for a pig, she thought to herself. As she headed to the counter to pay for him she spotted a little dog that was almost identical to one she had at home, except that this one was just a little bit smaller. You look like you are related to Amelia, she said to herself, and to the little grey and white stuffed puppy, and we can't have sisters separated.

"So, you found two more," said the wife.

"One can never have enough stuffed animals can one?" Ann asked smiling.

"Not as far as I'm concerned," the woman answered.

Ann then asked about the pig and his name. The husband explained that there had, at one time, been a set of stuffed barn yard animals and they had all been given names at the factory. The pig was the only one left.

"Just such a funny name for a pig," remarked Ann, "as one doesn't think of pigs as being fast."

"Unless it's an angry mother pig," the man answered, "then look out!"

Once home Ann placed Fast Eddy on a shelf in the kitchen and the new puppy next to her twin sister by the stereo. "No longer separated," she said, "but Amelia, what is your sister's name?" For some reason the name of a friend from childhood came to mind, "Tali." "Well, I guess that's your name then," said Ann.

Tom was right on time. Ann answered the door.

"Hey lady," was Tom's greeting. "Whoa, love the top!" he added.

"Thanks," said Ann.

"I think this is the first time I've ever seen you wear something with a little color and pattern other than your plaid flannel shirts," he added. "It just really looks nice on you. Fun!"

Again, Ann just said, "Thanks."

They talked a little bit on the way to Marie and D.J.'s, but mostly just catching up since they had last talked. Little Patricia went right to Ann and then the rest of the evening would switch back and forth between her and Tom.

"I think she's glad to have others around besides mom and dad," said D.J.

"I just can't believe how much she has grown and how strong those little legs are getting," said Ann.

"Yes," said Marie. "She is right on the brink of walking on her own but is still hesitant to try. Of course that wagon that the two of you got her has helped as she walks a lot using it."

It was fun to watch how D.J. and Marie both shared in the care of Patricia before, during, and after the meal and how much they cared for and respected each other. They also showed respect for Patricia. Marie had given her some carrots, and after she tasted them she made a face, and when Marie tried again Patricia shook her head no. Marie then tried some peas, which Patricia liked and ate some each time they were offered.

"Sometimes getting her to eat vegetables is a challenge," said D.J., "but, we don't want to force things on her at this age. We can only hope that with patience and time her taste buds will mature."

Tom and D.J. offered to do the dishes while Ann and Marie visited for a bit in the living room. Patricia had been pulling herself up and walking around using the couch, tables, and chairs, to hang onto. After the dishes were done Tom came out into the living room followed by D.J. Patricia turned and gave her dad a huge smile.

"Hey little princess," he said stooping down to her level, "can you come to Daddy?"

She looked back at Marie who said, "Go ahead, go to Daddy," and with that Patricia took three steps on her own before falling into D.J.'s arms. Everyone cheered and Patricia clapped her little hands.

"That's my girl," D.J. said as he scooped her up and gave her a hug and a kiss on the cheek. She then put out her arms to Marie who did the same thing.

After a while everyone could tell that she was getting sleepy, especially when she curled up on D.J.'s lap and started to suck her thumb.

"I think I'll put this little one to bed," he said.

Marie said to Ann and Tom, "Blow her kisses. We have been trying to teach her that."

So, they both did and Patricia managed to blow one back. While D.J. put Patricia to bed Marie warmed up everyone's coffee and then excused herself saying, "D.J. and I try to put her to bed together every night that we can." In a few minutes they were back and both were smiling.

"I know that I am her dad, but have you ever seen a cuter, brighter, or more precious little girl?" D.J. said. Both Ann and Tom agreed that they had not.

"She is such a joy," said Marie.

D.J. continued, "Marie and I talked after the presentation last Friday and both of us are really struggling thinking about how anyone could do those things to a child!"

"I think it brought it home to us because of Patricia's age and how many children are abused at that age. It just made me sick to my stomach," added Marie.

"They are just really sick individuals," said Tom, "and somehow, we have to remember that. Like Dr. Pete said, the majority of them were also abused."

"That's what really got to me," began D.J. "You would then think they would remember what it was like and would choose not to do that to another child!"

"I agree," said Marie. "How can they not look into the face of a child and see what they are doing is so very, very hurtful?"

"Somehow, they aren't able to control it," said Tom, "I really don't understand either, but I have to keep reminding myself that they are children of God too."

Marie turned to Ann and asked, "Ann, you went through some hard times in your family, what is your perspective?"

Ann took a deep breath before answering, "This is very difficult for me." Tom reached over and took her hand. "Tom knows some of this," she began, "and Marie you know about my father's drinking and the fights that he and my mother had. In addition to that, my brother shared with me and I have now had some memories of my own of how abusive my mother was with all of us."

"I don't mean to appear dumb, but abusive how?" asked Marie.

Ann continued, "Well, both of them yelled a lot, but my mother was also very physically and emotionally abusive."

"I remember your sister telling me how she was always putting all of you down, but I did not know about the physical stuff," said Marie. "I am so sorry."

"Me too," said D.J. "No child should have to go through that."

Ann squeezed Tom's hand and took another deep breath, "There's more. The other evening during the talk I had a memory of some minor sexual abuse from an uncle."

"Oh Ann," said Marie as she reached over and gave her a hug.

"What do you mean?" asked D.J.

"Well, the memory is of him touching and grabbing me in places that he shouldn't have," she answered. "It's not like it was intercourse."

It was Tom's turn, "But I am sure that you were still terrified." Ann indicated that she was. "Do you remember how old you were?" he asked.

"I think about eight years old," she answered.

"Was that the only time?" he asked.

"At least that I remember at this point. But, Dr. Pete indicated when I met with him on Saturday that I shouldn't be surprised if more memories surface."

"How are you doing with all of this? I mean, you seem fine, but we all know you Ann, you are very good at hiding things and being the strong one," Marie offered.

Ann laughed a little and Tom gave her a wink. "I guess everyone knew that except me," Ann began. "I'd be lying if I said that I was okay. It's just that this is all new. When I first realized it, it was a shock and Friday night was rough. But after meeting with Dr. Pete on Saturday I did feel a little better. I think it's because part of me now feels free. It's very hard to talk about, especially with all of you."

"But we are your friends," said Tom.

"That's what makes it hard because I don't want you to think badly of me," she answered.

"Ann!" exclaimed Tom, "I'm sure that Dr. Pete told you that in no way was this your fault or your doing."

"He did," answered Ann.

"But it's hard for you to truly believe that, isn't it Ann?" asked Marie.

Ann nodded.

D.J. added, "That was something that Dr. Pete said is very hard for victims to understand."

Ann nodded as she continued, "Yes, as I keep thinking that there is something that I must have done to cause this, that it was my fault."

"Oh Ann," Marie said.

Ann continued, "And beyond that that I should have been able to stop them."

"But Ann," began D.J., "you were just a kid. And from what you have shared, you did try."

"I know that it doesn't make any sense," said Ann, "but that's what the feelings are. I mean, otherwise why would they choose to do this?"

"Boy," said Marie, "it makes me just want to go and punch that uncle and your Mom. Aren't you angry?"

"A little bit," said Ann, "but actually, a little more afraid."

"Of what?" Marie asked.

"I'm not really sure," Ann answered.

Tom offered, "But your mother is already deceased so she can no longer hurt you. And what about the uncle?"

"I know, I know," began Ann, "and again, this is going to sound crazy, but even though my mother is deceased I still somehow feel afraid of her. As far as the uncle is concerned, I think he is still alive and you can bet that I will not be going anywhere near him."

"I know that Dr. Pete is going to be a huge help in your healing and recovery from all of this, but what can we do as your friends?" asked Tom.

Ann smiled, "Just keep being my friends. Without any of you knowing it you have been helping me so much more than you will ever know."

"How is that?" asked D.J.

"For one thing you have all accepted me just the way that I am, and I am hoping that you will be able to continue to feel that way about me."

"Oh Ann," said Marie, "of course we will."

Ann continued, "I also heard Dr. Pete share the stats that many who are abused or molested also become what they were victim of."

Tom jumped in, "He also said that most do not."

"That is correct," said Ann. "I think at some level it becomes a choice and my choice has always been to protect children."

"That has been obvious to all of us," said D.J.

Ann continued, "I am also going to ask all of you not to share this with anyone else. I am not even going to tell my brother for awhile. I'm just not comfortable enough to share it with a lot of people at this point."

"Understood," said D.J.

"Why not?" asked Tom.

Ann pondered a moment, "I think it's because I feel safe with the three of you. Not that I don't trust the others or feel safe around them, but this is something different. I'm not quite sure how to explain it."

"I think I understand," said Tom.

"Thanks," said Ann, "which brings me to another way that you three, and actually the rest of the group too, have helped. Part of why I was finally able to remember these events is because, what Dr. Pete calls, the damaged and injured little girl inside of this adult body has finally felt safe enough to do so."

"Gosh, how did we help with that?" asked D.J.

Ann smiled, "Well, in addition to totally accepting me, I also learned that I could trust all of you, and finally by all of your gifts of the stuffed animals and the dolls."

"Really?" asked Marie.

"I know, I know, stranger than fiction. But, somehow having all of those stuffed critters around has helped."

Tom gently said, "The little girl is healing and is finally getting to be a little girl."

Ann didn't answer but knew that she would think about that later.

"Oh my gosh," Marie said suddenly, "I almost forgot!"

"Me too," added D.J. as Marie jumped up.

When Marie returned she was carrying a plastic bag that had something in it. After sitting down Marie pulled out a stuffed mouse saying, "We found this in the park when we took Patricia there the other day. We tried to clean him up a little, but as you can see weren't able to do a very good job. Both of us immediately thought of you Ann because you have such a way with these stuffed animals. Do you think you can help him?"

The little mouse looked like he had been through every war there ever was, but when Ann held him something stirred inside, "I'll sure try," she answered.

She then held him up and looked at his eyes which seemed to sparkle in the light.

"Did you give him a name yet?" she asked. Both Marie and D.J. indicated that they had not. "Then I shall call him 'Bright Eyes,'" said Ann.

They talked a little more before leaving. Both D.J. and Marie gave Ann long hugs and told her that they were there for her, whatever she needed. For the first part of the drive home both Ann and Tom were quietly lost in their own thoughts.

Finally Tom said, "Ann, I cannot begin to tell you how proud I am of you. It takes great courage to face all of this. And as hard as it has been and will be, you are going to be stronger for it."

"Thanks Tom," Ann answered, "you are the best friend anyone could ask for."

"And just so you know," he added, "anytime little Ann wants to go and fly kites, little Tom is more than ready."

Ann laughed. "You've got a deal."

Once in the house Ann decided to see what she could do to start getting the little mouse cleaned up. She ran some warm water in the bathroom sink and used some gentle soap and gently rubbed his fur. Every time Ann looked into the little mouse's eyes something stirred inside of her. For some reason she felt a special kind of tenderness towards him, which of course made no sense because he was a stuffed animal. "You are going to be okay little one," she said.

After she had gotten all of the dirt and other marks off of him she took a big towel and gently dried him, trying to fluff up his fur as she did. She then set him near one of the heat vents so that he could dry thoroughly. Interestingly she found herself giving him a kiss on the forehead before going off to bed herself. Again, Ann was surrounded with all of her stuffed animals which made it a little difficult to get into her room and bed, but she didn't care.

It was a good night's sleep and Ann actually woke up quite early. She immediately went and checked on the little mouse and found that he was dried through and through.

In deciding what to do with her day she thought she might make a huge pot of homemade vegetable beef soup and maybe see if Tom wanted to join her. After a while she telephoned him.

"I was just getting ready to call you," he said. "How are you doing?"

"I'm okay," Ann answered, "just trying to process all of this."

"I bet."

"Anyway, I know that we were just together at Marie's and D.J.'s for dinner last night, but I decided to make a pot of homemade soup and wondered if you would like to join me."

Tom laughed a little, "That's why I was calling you, to see if you wanted to go out for supper. Great minds and all of that! But, as long as you have got everything started, I would love to come over."

"It's nothing fancy."

"I bet it will be delicious. How about I bring a bottle of wine?"

"That would be really nice." They then decided on a time.

After Ann got the soup started in the crock pot she then spent a good part of the day gently combing and untangling the fur on the stuffed mouse. It was tedious, but somehow Ann felt good about doing it. Once finished she couldn't believe the transformation in him. "Now, all you need is a ribbon or bow or something," she said to the little mouse. After going through all of her craft stuff she finally found a light blue one that was perfect. Even Ann couldn't believe how good he looked when she set him on the couch. "Let's see how long it takes Tom to notice that it is you," she said.

Even though the weather was warmer it still wasn't warm enough to eat outdoors so Ann decided that sitting at the kitchen counter would be good for the two of them. Now, what to wear. It was interesting that she had chosen a top with colors and patterns the night prior. Tom was correct, she thought to herself, she usually didn't wear those styles; she was always much more subdued in both color and pattern as those tended to hide a 'multitude of sins.' Interesting! What had she been trying to hide? I'll think about that on another day. Of course she would wear her jeans and finally decided on a white, long sleeved casual 'big shirt' as they were called. They were much more comfortable than tight fitting ones.

Of course Tom was right on time. When Ann opened the door there he stood arms filled with a dozen red roses, a stuffed bear, and of course the wine.

"What is all of this?" Ann asked.

"For you my friend," Tom said as he handed her the wine, "the rest is for me." Ann laughed. "Where do you want the roses?" he asked.

She steered him to the coffee table and then handed her the bear, saying, "There's a story that goes with him."

"Do tell," said Ann as she led him to the kitchen to pour them each a glass of wine.

"Well," Tom began, "He was supposed to be one of your Christmas gifts. I had actually found him back in September. I had put him on a shelf in the spare room closet and totally forgot about him until I had to get something from that closet this morning and he fell off the shelf into my arms."

"Just a gentle reminder," giggled Ann.

"Wait, there's more. When I first came across him in the store the same thing happened. He just suddenly fell off of the shelf as I was standing there."

"Whoa," said Ann.

"I know. So, I knew that I had to get him for you. When I went to pay for him the clerk said that he had just come in that day so he was brand new."

"Meant to be."

"It gets better."

"What?"

"When I got home I had to look at my calendar for something, and do you know what day it was?"

"Well, you did say that it was September, but I can't think of any day that would be related to a stuffed bear."

Tom started to laugh as he said, "It was the Fall Equinox!"

As Tom kept laughing Ann was scowling, "I'm sorry Tom, I don't get it."

Tom was still laughing as he tried to answer, "The Fall Equinox and he FELL off of the shelf."

Then Ann started to laugh, "I guess then that his name must be 'The Fall Guy.'"

With that both of them busted out in laughter. "Oh that's good, that's really good," said Tom in between laughing.

It was a nice evening just sitting and talking with each other and neither of them bringing up anything that Ann was going through. After supper they decided to go into the living room to drink their coffee and that was when Tom noticed Bright Eyes.

"And what do we have here, another new stuffed animal?" he asked.

"Don't you recognize him?"

Tom looked closer and even picked him up before finally saying, "This is NOT the mouse that Marie and D.J. gave you last evening?"

"It is."

"You are a miracle worker," he said. Then Tom kind of glanced around the room and added, "I noticed that there was something different when I came in, but I couldn't figure it out until just now."

"What's that?"

"Where are all of your stuffed animals?"

Ann took a deep breath and said, "I will tell you only if you promise to tell no one." Tom of course promised. With that Ann motioned for him to follow her and when she got to her room she turned on the light.

"Oh my! Is there room for you?" Ann assured him that there was. "It's helping isn't it?" he again asked. Ann just nodded. With that Tom leaned over and kissed Ann on the forehead saying, "I'm glad. Every little girl needs to feel safe."

Ann felt some tears welling up but fought them as she said, "Thank you so much for understanding Tom. There's not many who would."

Tom smiled, "That's why I brought The Fall Guy for little Ann and the roses are for the grown-up Ann."

"You are the best," she said.

After Tom left, Ann finished cleaning everything up and got it loaded in the dishwasher. She then sat at the kitchen counter and just kind of stared out into the back yard. "This had been a most interesting week," she said to herself. "If anyone had told me that I would have the memory that I did and would be sharing it with my three best friends I would have told them that they were nuts. I just hope they don't think that I am nuts. I think I will work more on my children's book tomorrow."

She took The Fall Guy and Bright Eyes with her and as she crawled into bed she glanced over at P.J. on the nightstand. Grabbing her she prayed, "Please Lord, don't ever let anything like what happened to me ever happen to Patricia. Keep her safe."

THE BOOK
Chapter 3

Ever since her bad dreams and memories started the little girl began most every morning with a walk. Of course, Sir Lancelot was with her, but these days he usually stayed at a distance as the little girl did not seem to want to talk. And Lion followed at an even more discreet distance. Her cave mates knew that she was thinking and processing all of the information that had come to light in her dreams and memories, so they didn't push her to talk about it, they simply stayed close.

One morning as she left for her walk P.J., Lord Percival and Sure to Go asked if they could go along too. The little girl said that would be fine. And Sir Lancelot followed. As they walked through the woods all of them were quiet as then they could hear the sounds of all of the birds and other creatures that were living there. Once in awhile they would stop and point to a woodpecker digging for bugs in a tree, a robin singing, or a beautiful eagle flying overhead. Of course, there were lots of flowers in bloom now too. The forest was coming alive with new life once again.

One of the things that Sir Lancelot had noticed on these morning walks is that more often than not the little girl would take paths that lead them closer to the edge rather than the ones that took them deeper into the woods. He found that interesting and also reassuring. This morning was one of those mornings. Recently the little girl would go as far as the point where she told Elsie the Keeper of the Hearts farewell and this morning was no exception. However as they reached that point and were starting to turn around to head back to the cave the little girl suddenly stopped and listened intently.

"What is it my little lady?" asked Sir Lancelot.

"I thought I heard something," she said.

All of her friends perked up their ears to listen.

"It's someone moaning," said Sure to Go and immediately headed off into the direction that she heard the sound which was towards the edge of the woods.

The little girl said, "Wait," but Sure to Go was too fast.

Lord Percival had also started sniffing the air, but couldn't detect any smell. By then the little lamb had run off of the path and into the overgrowth with the little girl following and Sir Lancelot following the little girl.

P.J. said to Lord Percival, "We had better try to catch up."

So off both of them ran trying to follow the other three. The only way that the little girl could follow the lamb is that now and again she could see her little head bouncing just above the ground cover and then she couldn't see her at all because she had stopped.

"Sure to Go, where are you?" the little girl said in a loud whisper.

"I'm over here," the little lamb answered, "Please hurry."

The little girl and Sir Lancelot ran as fast as they could to where the sound of Sure To Go's voice had come from and P.J. and Lord Percival did their best to catch up.

When the little girl arrived she saw a very ill little white mouse. At least she thought it was a mouse and thought it was white, but she couldn't be sure. The little mouse looked like he had been through every war there ever was. Gently as the little girl picked up the mouse and held him in her arms something stirred inside of her. She could tell that he had been through some really rough times and was very, very sick.

"I wonder what his name is," said the little girl.

"I couldn't find a tag or anything," offered Sure to Go.

By then P.J. and Lord Percival had arrived, "Oh, do you think you can help him?" P.J. asked anxiously.

"I'm sure we can," answered the little girl, "but what I need for the three of you to do is to please hurry as fast as you can back to the cave and tell everyone what has happened. Have them get a warm bubble bath ready and have the Prince add some of his minerals and herbs. Also, tell them to make sure that the main room of the cave is nice and warm and tell Ada B. Green that we need one of her wonderful fluffy towels and ask Godzilla to get something warm ready for him to drink. Sir Lancelot and I will be along as quickly as we can."

With that the three of them ran off back to the path. Of course Sure to Go was faster than P.J. and Lord Percival, but they knew it was really important that everything be ready so they ran as hard as they could.

The little girl was glad that she had worn a sweater that morning because a wind had just picked up and she was able to hold the little mouse close to her inside the sweater to protect him. As she held him closer he slowly opened his eyes and looked up at her. As their eyes met again something stirred deep inside of her. She smiled and assured him that everything was going to be OK now. His eyes danced ever so slightly with life in answer.

"Well, hello bright eyes," she said. The little mouse gave a slight smile back and then closed his eyes again as the little girl snuggled him closer to her under the sweater.

When they arrived at the cave everything was ready just as the little girl had asked. She gently placed the little mouse into the warm water with the mineral and herbs and very gently bathed away all of the dirt on him. She could tell by the way that he would move that his body hurt no matter how gentle she was. Once in awhile he would open his eyes slightly and just look at the little girl and give her a little smile. Each time he did, it would stir something in her and she felt this tremendous tenderness towards him.

When she finished Ada B. Green handed her one of the large fluffy, soft towels that she had been warming by the fire to dry him with. This took a little doing as it turned out he had a lot of fur, but pretty soon he was all dry.

Then little Jacques stepped up and said, "These are a pair of my jammies. I think they will fit him and I also warmed them by the fire."

The little girl smiled at Jacques as she said, "What a very kind thing to do." Jacques just kind of shrugged his shoulders and looked a little embarrassed.

P.J. said, "Here, put him in my bed as my quilt will keep him nice and warm."

"And I brought him a couple of my soft, fluffy pillows," said Jeanette.

"What wonderful young cave mates I have," the little girl said to both of them.

Amelia had brought out a cup of warm broth which the little mouse sipped with the little girl's assistance. Arthur then handed the little girl a book with lots of stories in it. The little girl picked one about a little mouse and a lion. But she had hardly begun when she noticed that the little mouse was already fast asleep.

While he slept Godzilla and his kitchen crew got busy making some wonderful vegetable soup. It had a nice thick broth with noodles and lots of good things like potatoes, carrots, and cabbage. The cave smelled so wonderful, warm, nurturing, welcoming and safe. While the soup was simmering everyone, including the little girl took naps. It was just that kind of day.

Everyone slept for quite awhile but immediately upon awakening the little girl checked on the little mouse; he was still sound asleep. He looked very peaceful and comfortable so she let him sleep. He even slept through supper. After all the dishes were cleared and done she checked on him again and this time the little mouse opened his eyes and smiled. He was quite hungry and ate two bowls of the soup!

After he ate the little girl kind of moved his little bed and pillows closer to the fire around which everyone had gathered. That way he could share in the conversations if he wanted to. However, he just listened and before long he had fallen asleep again. He just seemed so worn out. So, the little girl gently moved everything back next to her sleeping area. All through that night she would awake and check on him.

Over the next few days she did everything she could to comfort and care for him. Slowly he started to get better. In a week's time he was up and around and was able to eat his meals with everyone else. He even sat outside the cave entrance in the sun one day with P.J. and Lord Percival. He was getting stronger and stronger, but he still didn't talk. He only smiled and when he did his eyes would just sparkle.

One day after his bath the little girl decided that it was time to try and untangle some of his fur. She took him to a little room off of the library and as gently as she could she worked at it off and on for much of the day. Her cave mates were struck with not only how caring she was, but also how loving, gentle and patient. What she didn't share with them is that actually it felt really good to be able to care for something as tiny and helpless as this little mouse and the bonus was that he seemed to thrive on it! When the little girl finished even she couldn't believe the change in the little mouse! He looked, well, beautiful! He was so white and fluffy that he almost sparkled like new fallen snow.

She then stood him in front of a mirror, the little mouse smiled and his eyes lit up like the stars.

"Well, what do you think, 'Bright Eyes?'" she asked.

He put his arms around her and hugged her and hugged her and hugged her! Both of them had tears in their eyes. What a gift they had given each other! Then she put a beautiful blue ribbon around his neck and tied a little bow in it. He looked so good!

When they came back into the gathering room the rest of the critters cheered and "oohed" and "aahed." They couldn't believe how different the little mouse looked! It was like an entirely different critter the change was that amazing.

From then on the little mouse always stayed close to the little girl wherever she went. He never did talk, but he sure smiled a lot and of course his eyes always sparkled.

As the days warmed into summer inside the cave, although filled with lots of activity things were also a lot more peaceful. Or maybe it would be more accurate to say that it was the nights that were more that way! The little girl could feel the changes too. It was nice not to feel so afraid all of the time.

One day little Amelia came running into the cave so filled with excitement that she could hardly contain herself. Everyone went running to the main room to see what all of the commotion was about. They all started giggling when they saw the little puppy; she was so filled with joy that she was jumping straight up and down.

"Oh, it's so wonderful!" she kept saying over and over.

Finally, the little girl was able to get a word in. "What is? What is?" she asked.

"I just got word that my little sister Tali that I had been looking for when we got lost does live in these woods and is coming to visit and I haven't seen her in so long!" exclaimed the little puppy now out of breath.

"Hooray! We can have a party!" said R.T. Cold Nose III.

Pumpkin-Pumpkin just shook her head at him, "That's all you ever want to do is party," she scolded.

"And what's wrong with that?" he retorted, pretending to be a little hurt.

"There's more to life than just to party. Besides, it's a lot of work preparing for a party," she answered.

"But, life is a party! Besides, if everyone helps out, it won't be so much work." He smiled because he knew that he had her now.

Of course, all agreed to help.

Finally the day arrived and the cave never looked nicer. Some of the critters had even picked fresh flowers to place in the main room and of course, also in Amelia's room which she hoped her sister would share with her.

Amelia couldn't wait any longer so she went and stood outside of the cave entrance to see if she could see her. Pretty soon, off in the distance she saw her approaching. "There she is!" she hollered, "Tali!!!" They both ran towards each other.

"Amelia!!!" The excitement built the closer they got! Both of them calling, "Tali!" "Amelia!" Finally they embraced! The rest of the critters had gathered outside of the cave by now along with the little girl and there wasn't a dry eye in the group.

It was very clear that they were sisters. Both were grey and white with big round eyes and they even wore the same style pink bows!

As they reached the top of the hill Amelia said to her friends, "This is my sister, Tali."

"We know!" they all exclaimed and everyone laughed.

It was a wonderful day. They danced and sang and played games. And then they had a wonderful picnic. It was like a family, at least what the little girl often thought that a family should be like. But, she wasn't really sure because her family had always fought on occasions like this, not to mention every other occasion; especially the holidays.

As the little girl took a break from playing the games she sat on a log and was just watching everyone. Pretty soon Godzilla brought her a slice of watermelon and sat down next to her.

"Thank you," she said.

"What are you thinking about?" asked Godzilla.

"I was just wondering if this is what families are supposed to be like," she said.

"In what way?" he asked.

"Well, everyone seems to be having such a good time. And even though some of the games we are playing are a bit competitive, there's no arguing, or yelling, or fighting. I mean, we are all cheering and laughing," she answered.

"And it wasn't this way in your family?" he asked.

The little girl shook her head no.

Godzilla then said, "You are correct. This is the way that families are supposed to act towards each other. Not that there is not any arguments, but you are to have fun together and treat each other with respect and love."

"I am really glad to hear that," she answered, "I always suspected that it was supposed to be like this, but I wasn't sure. And the best part of today is that not only am I learning how families are supposed to be, but this is also a lot of fun!"

Godzilla laughed, "I am glad my young friend. I am glad."

As they were cleaning up everything from their day outdoors Moose Bear and Front Porch the Buffalo Bull suddenly went on full alert.

"I smell a bear," said Front Porch.

Moose Bear gave him a funny look as if to say "Really?" while he said, "No, it's a pig."

By now all of the protector critters had their noses in the air trying to catch the scent and their ears peaked for any sound.

Suddenly they all saw something racing full speed up the hill towards them, but because it was small it was hidden in all of the brush. Before they knew it there stood a little pink pig in front of them all out of breath but smiling and weakly saying, "I won, I won."

"And who, may I ask, are you?" said Godzilla.

"My name is Fast Eddie."

"What a funny name for a pig," Arp whispered to his father who gave him a scolding look back.

"And what did you mean that you won?" asked Joan.

"I beat my friend up the hill," he replied.

Just then a honey colored bear poked his head up over the lower ridge and said, "I'm coming."

When he reached the top of the hill he too was a little out of breath and he looked like he had been rolling in dirt.

"You got a lucky break," he said to the pig.

"How do you figure that? I won fair and square," the pig answered.

"Well," began the bear, "I tripped over a rock and then I rolled part of the way back down the hill."

"It's not my fault that you are such a klutz," said the little pig with a smile.

Everyone tried not to chuckle. The little pig then said, "I would like to introduce you to my friend. His name is 'The Fall Guy' because he was born on the Fall Equinox, but I think his parents already knew how clumsy he was going to be and that's really how he got his name."

"Very funny," said the bear, "but then added, "it is nice to finally meet all of you."

"Finally?" asked the Prince.

"Yes," answered The Fall Guy, "We were supposed to be here last fall, but my buddy here doesn't always stop to ask directions; he just races around and so we got a little lost."

"You two sure are a pair," said Godzilla and then suggested that everyone go inside as the night chill was beginning to descend.

After dinner they all sat around the fire and told stories of all of their travels. Fast Eddie and The Fall Guy had every one in stitches as they shared all of their adventures or maybe mis-adventures would be a better term. The little girl laughed so hard that her sides ached.

Of course everyone wanted them to stay and so they moved into rooms on the second floor of the cave right next to each other. Even after everyone had settled down to go to sleep laughter could be heard from the rooms upstairs as the two were still sharing stories with those who had rooms up there. Plus, they could hear Amelia and Tali giggling from their room near the kitchen. Finally, everyone was quiet as all had finally fallen asleep.

The days following the arrival of these new critters were filled with great fun. It was summer so they spent a lot of time out of doors playing all kinds of games; games that the little girl had forgotten about that she had once played like Hide and Seek, Tag, Jump Rope, and just exploring for birds, bugs and butterflies. Her friends had never seen her so happy and the little girl had to admit that she was having a great time.

In the evening The Prince or Arthur or even the little girl would read stories to everyone. Sometimes they played card games or board games. The little girl was really learning how to enjoy herself, and to laugh, and to play. There were a lot of smiles around the cave that summer.

ANN'S STORY
Chapter 4
Summer Outings

Summer was definitely here as the days were longer with light and the air warmer. Ann loved that she could open her windows wide to let in all of the fresh air that was out there. As much as she loved fall and winter she also really enjoyed the late spring and early summer. There wasn't as much rain and it had not turned beastly hot yet. "Thank goodness for air conditioning," she said to no one in particular. But those days weren't here yet and the warm fresh air felt good.

Ann's sessions with Dr. Pete were moving along pretty well. She had had a couple more memories regarding the abuse and molest and as difficult as it was she also knew that it was part of the healing process.

One Friday morning as she was straightening up around the house her phone rang.

"Ann?" the female voice asked.

"Yes," answered Ann trying to place the voice.

"This is your cousin Lucy."

"Oh my goodness," said Ann, "How long has it been? How are you? And where are you?"

Lucy started laughing, "It has been too long, I am fine and I am living on the West Coast."

"That's where my brother is," Ann answered.

"I know that's how I got your telephone number."

They chatted for a few moments catching up on this and that. Ann had always liked Lucy. She was much quieter than Ann as a child and not as in to sports, but she always enjoyed playing with her. Ann wondered if Lucy had any idea of what her step-father had done to

Ann, but Ann didn't have to wait too long to find out the answer to that question.

"Ann," Lucy began, "I have something that I would like to share with you."

"Okay."

"When I talked with your brother we talked about your parents and what you all had to go through with your father's drinking and your mother's temper. It was good to get some of that family background."

Ann heard Lucy take a deep breath before she continued, "Ann, I have been in therapy because I began having memories of being abused and...." She halted a moment, "and molested when I was younger."

"It was your step-father wasn't it?"

"Yes, how did you know?"

"Because he got me too."

"Oh Ann, I am so sorry."

"And I am sorry about you."

"Does your brother know, because he didn't say anything?"

"No, I haven't told him yet. It's hard to talk about."

"I know what you mean."

They then talked more about the events that they remembered. As hard as it was to listen to what had happened to Lucy at the hands of her step-father it also validated what Ann had remembered. Up until that moment she had had her doubts about if this could really be true or not.

"I remember you being at our house," said Lucy. "You are just a bit older than me so we were sometimes able to play together."

"I remember that too."

"You know, I remember him sharing one time that before he and my mother were married that he used to babysit you when you were quite little."

Ann's mind suddenly went blank and she almost felt like she was going to faint.

"Ann? Ann, are you okay?" asked Lucy.

"Yes, yes, I'm okay. I just spilled my coffee," Ann lied.

They talked for a few more minutes and then Ann said, "If I remember anything else that might help you in your healing I will let you know."

Lucy responded, "And I will do the same for you."

"By the way," asked Ann, "are you in touch with your step-father?"

"No way, but I do know that he is living in South Carolina," answered Lucy.

"I totally understand," said Ann.

Lucy then added, "I think that he also got to one of my half-sisters, which is his own biological daughter, but she is still in denial so she doesn't want to talk to me either. Maybe if I tell her about you that would help her."

"Okay," Ann said weakly.

"And Ann," said Lucy, "I think you should tell your brother. He loves you so very much and has been concerned about you."

"Okay I will. Thanks Lucy."

After they hung up Ann went and got Godzilla from her bedroom and just sat on the couch hugging him and going over the conversation with her cousin in her head, just feeling kind of stunned. She didn't feel upset, except maybe for Lucy, but definitely not for herself. She was more curious about her reaction to Lucy sharing that her step-father had been Ann's babysitter when she was little. The only feeling other than stunned that she could come up with was that she also felt numb.

As she was trying to process this her phone rang again and startled her.

It was Marie, "Did I catch you at a bad time?" she asked.

"No, no," Ann lied again.

Marie began, "I was wondering if you weren't doing anything tomorrow if you would like to go to some garage sales with Patricia and me. D.J. has to bring some work home from the office so I want to give him some alone time plus I want to find some outfits for Patricia for the summer."

"Oh Marie, I would love to. It sounds like great fun," said Ann, "and maybe we could stop for lunch, my treat." They arranged a time for Marie to pick her up in the morning.

Ann spent the rest of the day doing some laundry and general cleaning in her house. She had heard somewhere that when a woman was upset she cleaned. Ann had to admit that there were therapeutic values to it.

As Marie was pulling into the driveway the next morning Ann could see little Patricia in her seat in the back trying to jump up and down and was waving both hands. Ann first opened the back door of the car as little Patricia was desperately trying to get out of her seat to get to Ann, so Ann leaned over and gave her a big hug and then got into the front seat.

Marie was laughing and shaking her head, "She has been like that since I told her we were coming to see you."

As they pulled out of the driveway Patricia was still making all kinds of sounds trying to get Ann's attention. Ann finally reached back and held her little hand.

"She is making more and more sounds that are getting closer to actual words," Marie said, "it is so fun."

"I bet," said Ann.

When they got to the first garage sale Marie quickly got out and looked around.

As she got back in the car she said, "Mostly baby clothes; nothing that would fit Patricia."

So they went onto the next one which was huge. "This looks like a multiple family one," said Ann. Even from the car Marie could spot clothes that would fit Patricia, so at this one they got the stroller from the back to make it easier to get around.

Marie couldn't believe the outfits that she was finding.

"Gosh, these are almost brand new," she said.

Ann replied, "I guess that kids grow so fast at this age that really don't wear them that long."

Marie also found some things that Patricia would probably grow into for the fall. "And the prices are so cheap," she said, "I almost feel guilty."

As they were going down one aisle of tables Patricia suddenly reached up and tried to grab a yellow shirt.

Marie laughed, "It's her favorite color and luckily it will fit her."

Ann moved on ahead at one point just looking mostly to get ideas for her house, not that she needed anything. Sometimes it was just nice to do a little redecorating, but she did not see anything that she absolutely couldn't live without. However, she did find a darling sun dress that was yellow and white checkered with matching panties that was in Patricia's size. Then she came down the aisle where all of the stuffed animals were.

"Oh boy," she said to herself, "I'm in trouble now."

There were lots of wonderful ones, but nothing that particularly caught her eye. Then, she spotted him! A good size sheep dog! What a face! She thought to herself, you can't even see his eyes for all of the fur. But, I don't really need another stuffed animal. As she was checking him over she discovered that one of his ears was missing and that was all that Ann needed to convince her to buy him.

She got finished before Marie and so was already paying for her purchases when Marie and Patricia came up. As Marie was paying Ann showed Patricia the outfit she had bought for her. Immediately the little one grabbed it to feel the material with her little hands and got very excited. Ann just started laughing, "You are definitely a little girl. All about the dresses aren't you?"

"Oh Ann," said Marie, "what a darling outfit! Thank you. And I see that you also found a little something for yourself."

Ann nodded, "He's missing an ear, but that's okay."

"A missing ear, huh, then you should name him Van Gogh."

"Perfect! Van Gogh it is!"

They stopped at one more sale but didn't really find anything, so they decided to go and have lunch.

After they had gotten settled and ordered Marie asked, "How are you doing?"

"You know," began Ann, "I have my moments that are difficult, but by and large I am doing pretty well."

"You seem so much more relaxed."

"Thanks, because I am pretty much feeling that way. I know that this is an ongoing process but I am hoping that most of the rough stuff is over. Of course the minute I think that then something else pops up."

"Like what?"

Ann then told Marie a bit about the telephone call from her cousin.

"Oh my, that poor girl," said Marie.

"I know," said Ann, "I feel worse for her than I do for myself."

"But at least now you can help each other."

Ann agreed. Ann had also decided not to say anything about learning that this uncle had babysat her when she was little. It did no good to do so until she could learn or remember more.

The rest of the lunch Marie and Ann took turns helping little Patricia with her food and just talking about various events in their lives.

As Marie dropped Ann off she said, "Ann, I agree with your cousin. I think you should tell your brother."

"Yes, I think you are right. I thought that maybe I would call him tomorrow," Ann answered.

Ann gave Patricia a hug and a kiss on the cheek. She stayed in the driveway waving goodbye until she could no longer see the car with little Patricia's hand waving back.

When Ann checked her messages there was one from Tom.

"Hey lovely lady. And where might you be on this beautiful day? Give me a call when you get back."

Ann put Van Gogh in the family room where she could work on cleaning him up a little bit and then returned Tom's call.

"So, were you out bumming?" asked Tom.

"Actually, I was," answered Ann, "It was a girl's day out at the garage sales." Ann then filled Tom in.

"Oh, then you may not be interested in the reason that I was calling," he said.

"One never knows unless one asks," said Ann.

"Well, the weather is so beautiful I thought that tomorrow would be a great day to go to the swap meet," he said.

"That's a wonderful idea."

"Are you going to Mass today or tomorrow?"

"Well, if we want to get an early start tomorrow I think that I will go to 4 p.m. today."

"That's what I was thinking too."

Mass was kind of crowded. When Ann saw Tom afterwards he said, "It looks like everyone had the same idea." They then discussed what time he would pick her up before parting ways.

Ann decided that as long as she was now going to be gone on Sunday that she would give her brother a call this evening after dinner. She poured herself a tall glass of raspberry iced tea and settled on the couch before calling.

"I had a feeling that I would be hearing from you," he said.

"What a surprise to hear from Lucy after all of these years," she added.

"How did your talk go?" he asked.

Ann then filled him in on everything except her own molestation. Finally she said, "I have something to tell you." She then shared with him what she had remembered.

He was quiet for a moment and then said, "I was angry when Lucy told me what had happened to her and now I am really angry. That son of a....well you know! Boy, if he was in the room right now with me I don't know if I would be able to control myself. It's a good thing I didn't know about it when we were growing up, I just know I would have slugged him. It's a good thing Dad didn't know about it, he didn't seem to like him too much anyway. Oh Ann, I am just so furious!" He ranted a bit more and then said, "Aren't you angry?"

"I feel bad, especially for Lucy, but I don't know that I feel any anger."

"Well you should," her brother replied.

"I don't know, you seem to be feeling enough anger for both of us."

"I guess I am but, gosh, sis, I mean...how dare he?! It just infuriates me. Do you think Mom and Dad suspected anything?"

Ann thought a moment, "If they did, they never said or did anything that I can remember. But like you said, Dad didn't seem to be too fond of him, so maybe he sensed something about him."

Ann's brother finally calmed down a bit and then they talked about how her therapy was going and how helpful it was. Her brother shared that he had started going to the meetings for those who had grown up in alcoholic homes and was just amazed to find so many others who had experienced what they had.

"Well, if you ever want to go a little deeper I will send you the link for the Catholic therapists' organization," she offered. He said that would be good. Then Ann asked, "How are things going with your girlfriend?"

"Really well," he began, "she is just wonderful. I just know you are going to like her once you get to meet. Are you planning any trips this way?"

"I hadn't thought about it," Ann answered, "but who knows."

They talked a while longer before hanging up. As Ann crawled into bed that night amid all of her stuffed animals, including the new Van Gogh she thought about her conversation with her brother. She found it interesting that he was so angry, and that she couldn't honestly say she felt that way at all.

Ann's sleep was a little restless that night, and she knew she had dreamt but couldn't remember anything upon waking. All she knew was that she was really glad to have all of her stuffed animals there with her, and that she was going to be spending the next day with Tom.

As she got ready she thought about Tom and what a good friend he was. Not just because he was kind and caring; or even that he was so giving; but mainly because she felt very safe with him and lately they had been having a lot of fun and laughs together.

When Tom rang the doorbell Ann had just grabbed her first cup of coffee.

"Hey girl, are you ready to go?" Tom greeted.

"Just let me take one more swallow of coffee," she said.

"No need! Your favorite caramel iced coffee and doughnuts are already in the car."

"How did you know that I hadn't had breakfast?"

"I didn't, but isn't there always room for coffee and doughnuts?"

Ann laughed, "You are not very good for my waist line."

"Oh you are going to walk all of this off today."

The fresh air and warmth of the sun felt good as they walked up and down all of the rows of the vendors. There seemed to be more this year and they were selling everything imaginable. Of course Tom and Ann both liked looking at the old books and spent a fair amount of time at that booth. Ann found herself looking at the books for young people like the "Little House" series by Laura Ingalls Wilder.

"Didn't you ever read those?" asked Tom.

"I remember reading one of them about the house in the big woods, but not the rest."

"How about the 'Anne of Green Gables' series?"

"I saw a couple of them that were made into movies for television, but I don't think I ever read the set as a young girl."

"And you an author," he teased.

"Does reading most of Shakespeare count?"

He laughed, "Ann, Ann, Ann, always with the serious stuff."

"He did write comedies too," she protested.

"Comedies by Shakespeare are like a hockey player trying to do figure skating," he teased.

"What?" said Ann. "That makes no sense!"

"I know," he said and then started laughing.

Then Ann started laughing and both of them stood there laughing. Pretty soon the vendor was laughing and he didn't even know why, which made Ann and Tom laugh all the more. Finally they all calmed down enough to make their purchases. Ann decided that Tom was correct that she needed to read both series, secretly wondering what Dr. Pete would think. Tom found a book for himself and something else that he didn't let Ann see.

They stopped at another booth that had some prints of famous paintings.

Ann and Tom were both looking through separate bins when Ann said, "Oh my gosh!"

"What?" asked Tom.

"My sister and I used to have this picture hanging in our bedroom. It's a Guardian Angel guiding a little girl and boy over a rickety bridge high above a deep cavern filled with water. I wonder what ever happened to that." Ann looked at the picture a long time remembering her sister and the fun they sometimes had. "I'm going to get this for my spare bedroom."

After that purchase they decided to stop for a bit of lunch. As they sat eating Tom suddenly said, *"For God commands the angels/to guard you in all your ways."*

"What?" said Ann.

"I was trying to remember the quote from the Bible that had to do with the Guardian Angels."

"I think it's from Psalm 91," Ann said.

"Boy, my Guardian Angel has sure been kept busy with me," Tom said.

Ann didn't say anything.

"So, what do you think about when you look at that print?" he finally asked.

"I just kind of remember some of the things my sister and I did together."

"Did you have fun together?"

"Sometimes. But, she was younger and so for a long time it was like she was just tagging along. But, as adults we had a few good times together before she died."

"Were you close?"

"Sort of."

"What about you and your brother?"

"Hey, what's with all of the questions?"

"I guess I'm just curious. You don't talk about your family too much."

"Would you if you came from a whacked group like mine?" she said a little sternly.

"Whoa Ann. What's going on?"

Ann sat there a minute before answering, "I'm sorry," she began, "it's been a rough couple of days and I thought I was handling it okay, but obviously I'm not."

"Do you feel like talking about it?" he gently asked. Ann then briefly told him about the phone call from her cousin.

"Oh Ann," he said, "how awful."

"And my brother is so angry," she added.

"Aren't you?"

"I didn't think I was, but how I responded to your questions lets me know that maybe there is a little anger there."

"Ya think?" he teased, sensing that she didn't want to get into too serious of a conversation at this point.

"I'm sorry Tom. I really did not mean to snap at you."

He took her hand as he said, "I know. How about we get back to our shopping?" Ann was really glad to have that diversion.

Of course they eventually came to the area where all of the stuffed animals were and found the vendor where Ann had found the little seal, R.T. Cold Nose III.

"Boy, there have been a few additions since him," Ann said.

"I'll say," offered Tom.

"Hey," began Ann, "you are the one who not only started all of it, but have also been a big part of adding to the collection."

"I know," he said, "and you love it!" That brought a tiny smile to Ann's face.

Then Tom said, "Now here is a fine looking critter who reminds me of my dear friend Ann."

Ann rolled her eyes and then exclaimed, "What?!" as Tom held up a little French Bull Dog.

Tom laughed, "Yes. He's cute and gentle, but don't mess with him because the bull dog part will come out strong."

"Very funny," said Ann. "I thought I was getting better at that."

"You are because, as with the little bull dog, all of your friends know that it's all show. You wouldn't really bite anyone."

"Of course not," Ann said with her voice softening a bit.

"I think you need to have him," Tom said as he pulled out his money to pay the vendor. Ann just shook her head.

The last area of the swap meet they went to was filled with antiques. Something else that Tom and Ann both liked looking at. Ann found an old coffee grinder for her kitchen, and Tom found a coal bucket that would look good next to his fireplace. "This has really been a successful day," he said on the way to the car. Ann agreed.

When they got to Ann's house she invited him in, but he said that he had some work to do prior to a meeting the next morning. However, he did help carry the purchases into the house for her. As he was getting ready to leave he handed her a bag.

"What's this?" she asked.

"Open it and see," he said.

"Inside were two children's books about a little girl named "Investigator Anne" by Mark and Sarah Treu. They seemed to be mystery books for a child.

"Everyone should have books that have their name in the title," he said. "Just a personal belief of mine."

Ann thanked him and then started to apologize again, but Tom stopped her. "Ann I know this is all very painful and difficult for you; you have had a lot thrown at you at once. I also know how hard you are working at healing and getting better. So for now, there is no need to apologize." He then gave her a kiss on the cheek.

After putting the books in the library and setting the print in the spare bedroom she sat on the couch holding the little French bull dog. "You need a name my new little friend," she said. "Who do I know that is French?" she said. As she couldn't think of a name, she set him on the coffee table and decided to watch some TV before fixing supper. As fate would have it she found a channel playing an episode of one of her favorite Star Trek series and there he was - the Captain whose character Ann really enjoyed. "Well, what do you know?" Ann said to the little bull dog. "Welcome to your new home Jean Luc."

Ann had quite a session with Dr. Pete the following week. What with the phone call from her cousin and the conversations with her brother, Tom, and Marie, she had a lot to sort out.

He explained that if her uncle had done something to her when she was quite little she might have been too young to have had a conscious memory of it and so her body may have been what reacted by simply going numb.

"So, you don't think that I was just reacting to what had happened to my cousin?" she asked.

"I don't think so from how you described the sequence of the conversation. You were upset and consoling when she told you about her molest, but it seems to have been later in the conversation that she mentioned her father babysitting for you when you were younger. Is that correct?"

Ann thought a moment and then said, "Yes. But, why am I not feeling anger like my brother?"

"Why don't you think you are?"

Ann thought for a few minutes. "I think I felt some anger that he would do that to his own step-daughter."

"Okay, but how about anger at what he did to you?"

Ann thought and thought, "I'm just not coming up with anything."

"That's okay. You will when it's time."

"You know Dr. Pete I don't want to say that I was glad to hear about what happened to my cousin, but it did help me."

"Because you found out you were not alone?"

"More than that because it validated my memories."

"Had you doubted them?"

"I think I just kept questioning how this could have happened and maybe I was having a false memory of some kind."

"But you no longer feel that way?"

She shook her head no as a tear slowly ran down her cheek, "Now I know that it really did happen."

"And how does that feel?"

"Sad, really sad, but also a kind of relief that I wasn't imagining it."

Dr. Pete nodded, "Ann, remember that this is a process that is not going to happen overnight. As I explained to you before it's like peeling back the layers of an onion one layer at a time, and we never know what the next layer is going to bring. But, I think that you are doing remarkably well in processing and coming to grips with all of this."

Ann then added that her cousin thought that her step-dad now lived in South Carolina.

Dr. Pete answered, "That is good to know." He continued, "Ann, by law I am required to make a report to the authorities on what happened to you."

"Even though it was so long ago?" she asked.

"Yes," he replied, "some states do have a statute of limitations and ours is one of them. However, I still make the report because as we discussed before he could still have access to children and if anything comes up in the future, by reporting what happened to you there is at least a basis for a pattern. I will also be making the report to South Carolina because that is where he currently lives."

She let him know that she understood.

Ann really felt tired when she got home from her session. In the past when she felt this way she would have simply ordered a pizza, but she was learning to take a little better care of herself so decided instead to have some raw vegetables and dip plus to finish off a bowl of cut up fruit that she had put together. She did treat herself to a little ice cream for dessert. "After all a girl just can't survive on fruit and vegetables," she said to Jean Luc.

After dinner as she was just settling in to watch some TV her phone rang.

It was Maggie. They hadn't talked in a while so Ann was happy to hear from her.

"So bride to be, how is it going?" asked Ann.

"There seems to be a thousand details to take care of," Maggie answered, "but J.R. and I are having fun. That was something that Father Jack mentioned to us when we first met with him. He said that our wedding day is going to go so fast, so to be sure to have fun while we were planning."

"Good advice," said Ann.

Maggie continued, "I was wondering if you are available next week Wednesday evening for a dress fitting. Lynn can make it and my sister is coming to town for something else during the day."

Ann quickly checked her schedule and said that she was free, "I can't wait to see the dresses."

"I can't wait for you to see them, now something else. Do you remember the craft show that you and I went to over at the Catholic Parish in Johnsville last summer?"

"I sure do, that was a great show."

"Well, this year's show is this weekend. If you are available would you like to go with me?"

"Definitely."

"With our wedding being during the pre-Christmas season I thought I could find some things or at least get some good ideas. And Ann you are so great at decorating I would really welcome your input."

"Well, I don't know about that, but I will be happy to help where I can. And I would be happy to drive this year."

"Sounds good." They arranged the time that Ann would pick her up and then hung up.

"You can sure tell it's summer between all of the garage sales, swap meets, and craft shows," Ann said to Jean Luc.

ANN'S STORY
Chapter 5
Planning a Wedding

Ann woke up early on Saturday anxious to go to the craft show and to be with Maggie. Maggie was waiting at the door when Ann arrived. Of course they did a drive through to get their caramel iced coffee and giggled about their tradition. Maggie was filled with wedding plans, well actually, it was more like wedding ideas. Ann could now see why Maggie had asked for her help, she needed a little of Ann's organization skills.

They arrived a bit before the sale opened so they were one of the first ones in line. Ann was glad that she and Maggie both liked to get to places early to beat the crowds that were sure to be there later in the morning.

Maggie said that she and J.R. had decided on a smaller wedding and reception with just family and their best friends as neither one of them really enjoyed large crowds.

"And with it being an evening wedding we wanted to also have a dinner after and a short time to dance. It is definitely not going to be one of those all night deals," Maggie shared. "So, I need to find some decorations for the tables and maybe for the church too. As that weekend is the first Sunday of Advent I told Father Jack that we would purchase a couple of white poinsettias for near the altar and the ambo and then simply donate them to the parish. He also suggested that I meet with Sally, who is responsible for the environment that we could work together. So, I also wanted to have some ideas before I meet with her next week."

"Sounds like a really good plan," answered Ann.

They decided to do a quick run through of the show to see what ideas they could gather and then go back, if necessary, to purchase items they had decided on.

About half way through Maggie turned to Ann and said, "Gosh, this is going to be harder than I thought. I've already seen so many things that have sparked a hundred ideas that are now running through my head."

"Ask God to guide you," suggested Ann.

"Even with wedding decorations?" questioned Maggie.

"Of course. After all He designed the universe, so who better?" answered Ann.

"I guess I just never thought of bothering Him with little things," said Maggie.

"I think if the truth be known," began Ann, "He likes us to bother Him about everything."

"It's worth a try," said Maggie who then stood silently for a moment with her eyes closed. At the very next booth Maggie exclaimed "Oh my gosh! Look Ann!" Maggie was pointing to a large crystal glass one horse drawn sleigh. There were also some smaller sized ones. "These are perfect," exclaimed Maggie.

Maggie could see that there was room for a small votive or tea light candle in each one but asked the lady if the glass could handle the flame. The lady suggested instead that they use the battery operated candles, not only to keep the crystal from cracking, but also for safety reasons.

"What do you think Ann?"

"Tell me what you are thinking."

"Well, seeing as how a winter sleigh ride was part of J.R.'s proposal I love tying that in with our wedding. We could put the large one on the main table which I would then keep for our home, a beautiful memento, and maybe the smaller ones on each of the tables. What do you think?"

"I think that it is a beautiful idea. Do you think J.R. will like it?"

"Both of us decided on the color scheme for the wedding and, actually, one of the invitations that we are leaning towards has an embossed one horse sleigh with a couple in it and a church in the background. I think he will like this."

"Then go for it."

"Of course I want the large one, but how many of the smaller ones will we need?" She was kind of talking out loud to herself.

Ann asked how many tables at the reception and after counting Maggie knew there would be eight. They then decided to add two more of the small ones for the ends of the main table and two for the cake table; so twelve total. Maggie paid the lady and then said that they would be back after completing their shopping. The lady told them to take their time as she had a lot of special wrapping to do.

"Boy God sure does work fast," Maggie said as they walked to the next booth. Ann giggled.

After they had walked the entire show they got a glass of iced tea and a snack and went and sat at the tables that were set up for that.

"Okay," began Ann, "what ideas did you see that you liked?"

"Oh gosh," began Maggie, "there were a lot of different ones; of course finding those crystal sleighs and horses really helped to narrow down the search as they became the centerpieces."

Ann pulled out a small tablet and pen.

"I can sure tell you are a writer," laughed Maggie.

"Yes, have pen and paper will travel but let's get a little organized here."

At the top of the first sheet of paper she wrote "Reception" with sub categories of dining tables, cake table, gift table, and decorations. On the second sheet she wrote "Church" at the top with sub categories of altar, ambo, and pews. On the third sheet she wrote "Wedding Colors" with sub categories of bride, maid of honor, bridesmaids, best man and groomsmen.

"Okay, let's start with this last one first," began Ann. "Are you willing to share with me the colors of your wedding yet?"

With that Maggie pulled out two swatches of material from her purse. The first one was a white velvet and the second one a red velvet.

"The white is for my dress and the red for the bridesmaids," she said.

"Oh Maggie, how beautiful!" exclaimed Ann.

"Also all of the dresses will be trimmed in white fur around the bottom and we will also be wearing short capes trimmed in the white fur."

"Oh Maggie, they sound absolutely elegant."

"Plus, all of you will be carrying white fur muffs and I was thinking how pretty it would look for you to have one red rose pinned on the front."

"Will you also have a muff?"

"Yes, but I won't carry it in church. Instead I will have a bouquet of white roses."

"That makes sense because you want to have your hands free."

"My thoughts were that the jackets and the muffs would almost be easier than coats and gloves for everyone."

"I think you are correct," began Ann, "after all, that is pretty much all they had around the turn of the last century."

"True."

"How about the suits for the guys?"

"J.R. decided that he wanted the classic black tuxedos with a short tail and white shirts for the guys. At first he wasn't sure if he wanted cummerbunds and bowties or vests and regular ties for the guys. But after talking with the guy at the tux shop, because it is an evening wedding and J.R. is more traditional they decided to go with bow ties and cummerbunds. J.R's tie and cummerbund will be white and the groomsmen's will be red."

"I can't wait to see those guys all dressed up," Ann offered.

"He also wanted top hats for the guys, but thankfully the guy at the store said that wasn't really appropriate for an evening wedding any longer."

"How about the parents?"

"Our dads will also have the tuxedos, only theirs will be a dark grey pinstripe and their bow ties and cummerbunds will be silver. Our mothers decided to go shopping together. I don't know how many stores they ended up going to, but my father decided that all they were really doing was using it as an excuse to go shopping."

"Why would he think that?"

Maggie laughed, "Because the dresses they ended up getting were from the very first store they went to."

Ann laughed, "I see what you mean."

Maggie continued, "Their dresses are similar in that they are long with short jackets and nothing fancy; very classic lines. J.R.'s mother decided on a black one. At first she wasn't sure she wanted black, but the jacket is beaded with black crystal beads. It really is beautiful and with her color of hair it looks absolutely gorgeous on her. My mother's, like I said, is very similar in style with a jacket and same classic lines only it is a medium silver gray color and it has clear crystal beads just on the top half of the dress. Again, with my mother's hair coloring she looks absolutely stunning in it."

"Oh Maggie, it is going to be such an elegant wedding."

Maggie kind of giggled.

"So, your basic colors in addition to the white of your gown are red, black, and a silver gray."

Maggie nodded.

"So what were you thinking of for decorations near the altar and the ambo?"

"From what Father Jack shared you are correct in that those are basically the only two places we can have anything, and of course I will be meeting with Sally, but I was thinking of something kind of wintry. You know, evergreens that maybe have been flocked to look like they have snow on them. And in the middle of them J.R. and I were thinking of a huge white poinsettia for in front of the ambo and a couple of smaller red ones in front of the altar. Nothing fancy or overwhelming but simple and elegant."

"Yes, as you mentioned Father Jack pointed out that it will be the beginning of Advent so one does not want things over decorated."

"Exactly. The other thing I was thinking of today after we talked about the battery operated candles for the glass sleighs was that we could also have them in different places throughout the church."

"What do you mean?"

"Well, I know that every year they also place evergreen boughs on each of the window sills with red ribbons so what do you think of placing the flameless candles in the middle of each of those?"

"I think that would be lovely."

"With it being an evening wedding J.R. and I decided that we wanted as few church lights and as much candlelight as possible and this would be one way to add to it. Father Jack said that he can get by with limited lighting in the sanctuary as even the secondary lights are bright enough for everyone to see and yet add a softer tone than adding all of the big lights." Maggie could tell that Ann had also thought of something so asked, "Yes?"

"Well, I don't know if you saw them or not, but one of the booths had tall, wooden candle holders with a glass chimney on top. I was thinking that we could wrap some of the evergreen boughs around them and also use the flameless candles in those to line the main aisle with."

"I know that we really can't hook anything on the pews."

"No, these were free standing and they had different kinds of woods, some light but also some darker like our pews."

"Did you see how much they were? Because we have a very long aisle in our church and that could get really expensive."

"True. We will have to check on that. Okay, then the last thing will be the reception and dinner hall. What do you think?"

"I seem to remember that the hall manager said that they had red tablecloths which will be perfect. And we have the glass sleighs and flameless candles. How about getting some of the fluffy cotton batting from a craft store, sprinkling it with silver glitter and have the sleighs sitting on that in the middle of the tables?"

"I like that. It's simple yet elegant as you said. And maybe we could also find some white netting kind of material and intertwine it with the small white Christmas lights to hang from the ceiling and maybe across the front of the main table and the cake and gifts tables. Of course that will depend on the outlet availability as we don't want cords all over the place."

"I think I have seen some of those that are battery operated. In fact, I think I saw a table with them today. Afterwards we can use them as part of our decorations at home for the holidays."

"Nothing wasted."

"Exactly. Also, maybe we could put them under the cotton batting on each of the tables as long as we don't have to worry about cords."

"Good idea and I just thought of something else. How about an evergreen bough too?"

"Or those little artificial trees?"

"I like that even better. I know that you have the glass sleighs for the cake table, but do you want anything on the gift table?"

"Other than the string of lights in the front I don't think so. But what about something near the bandstand?"

"That's right, how about some red poinsettia plants?"

"Perfect. I think we have some shopping to do!"

They decided that they could get the cotton batting, the flocked evergreen boughs, the little artificial Christmas trees and the flameless candles at the craft store as they would probably be less expensive than here at the craft show. However they did find some beautiful red and white velvet ribbon so picked up a couple rolls of each, just in case they thought of something they might need them for. And also the battery operated string of little white lights. They decided to get a couple of extra ones in case they thought of another location to place them. When they got to the booth where the tall candle holders were that Ann had seen, Maggie fell in love with them.

"Oh Ann, these would be so perfect, but...," she said looking at the cost, "there is no way I could afford to purchase the number we would need."

With that the booth owner came over. "I couldn't help over hearing your conversation," he began, "what event are you looking to use these for?"

"My wedding," Maggie said, "we thought they would be perfect to line the main aisle with next to each pew, but we have a pretty long aisle in our church."

"May I make a couple of suggestions?" asked the man.

Maggie said "Of course."

"First," he started, "I would suggest that you place them at every other pew. You can even stagger them but making sure that the front pews have one on both sides."

"That sounds good," said Maggie and Ann agreed.

"Second," he said, "I do rent these out for just such occasions as yours!"

"Really!" Maggie exclaimed almost loud enough for the entire craft show to hear her.

The man started to laugh, "And, I even have the supplies to decorate them however you wish."

"You mean like with evergreen boughs and red ribbons?" asked Maggie.

"Yes," said the man, "and we also supply the flameless candles."

"Oh my gosh," said Maggie and then stopped her excitement long enough to ask his price. After he told her Maggie got excited all over again.

"That is very doable," she said.

Maggie took the man's contact information and gave him the date of her wedding and how she wanted them decorated. The only thing she would have to get back to him on would be the number.

"Oh Ann," Maggie said as they headed back to the booth to pick up the crystal, "can you believe how all of this is coming together?"

"See," Ann began, "I told you, and all you have to do is ask God to be involved."

Maggie gave Ann an impromptu hug.

When they arrived at the glass booth the lady had everything all bubble wrapped, packed and ready to go in about four huge shopping bags. She also gave Maggie her card just in case something were to happen between now and her wedding.

"And I have a wedding gift for you," the lady said.

"Really?" said Maggie.

With that the lady pulled out another small box also all wrapped up in bubble wrap. As she handed it to Maggie she said, "It is very fragile like a marriage can be sometimes, so take very good care of it. Also, this is for you and your fiancé so do not open it until you are with him."

Maggie gave her a hug and thanked her.

"Let's go put everything into the car and then come back in as I spotted something earlier that I think I would like to get," said Maggie.

"Me too," said Ann.

Ann had some blankets in the back of the car just in case she ever wanted to stop for a picnic or to sit under a tree or on the beach. She took these and wrapped them carefully around the bags with the crystal sleighs in them.

"I don't think these will go anywhere," she said.

When they got back inside Maggie made a beeline toward one of the side booths.

"They are both still here," she said as Ann was just catching up to her.

"They," as Ann could see were two identical, fluffy white rabbits. She had the young girl put them into two separate bags and after paying for them handed one to Ann.

"What?" said Ann.

"Just a little memento of our day together and to thank you for all of your help," said Maggie.

"Oh Maggie, that wasn't necessary. I have really enjoyed this day."

"Me too and having you along not only made it easier, but a lot more fun."

"So, why did you choose the white rabbits?"

Maggie smiled, "'Alice in Wonderland' was always one of my favorite stories and I especially liked the rabbit in that story. I think it was because my mother used to sing his song to me almost every morning."

Both of them started singing it at the same time.

And then burst out laughing. Of course everyone was looking at them and smiling but neither Maggie nor Ann cared.

"Ann," Maggie began once she stopped laughing, "this is a symbol of my childhood which I am about to trade in as I become a woman. I just never want to forget."

Ann hugged her friend as she said, "I won't let you."

"I know, that's why I wanted you to have the same rabbit."

"Maggie, just because you are getting married doesn't mean that you aren't still going to have fun."

"I know but it's just going to be different. I now have to consider another person when I make decisions and eventually even more when we start having children. It means that I am no longer just responsible for myself."

Ann nodded, "Well, whenever you feel you need a play date just give your single friend Ann a call."

Maggie flashed her a big smile, "I think that we should both name our bunnies 'White Rabbit.'"

"I agree."

They looked at each and every booth both getting great ideas for crafts and decorating.

"By the way, I think J.R. and I have found a house," Maggie said.

"That's great," said Ann, "where is it?"

"Just down the block from the parish and the Catholic school."

"We have made an offer on it and hopefully J.R. will hear today. Then all we have to do is sell our own homes."

"Oh Maggie that's wonderful."

Maggie continued, "We have already put our homes on the market about two weeks ago and there have been a couple of nibbles, but that's it. We decided that whosever home sells first then that person will move into the new home until the wedding. If the second home sells before the wedding then whosever home that is will stay with their parents until the wedding."

"Sounds like a great plan. Tell me about the house."

"Oh Ann, not only is the location perfect, but so is the house. It is similar to yours in that it has a living room and formal dining room, but also has a great room connected with the kitchen and another room that can be used as a play room or a home office, but the master bedroom and three other bedrooms are all upstairs. There is a small room off of the master bedroom that could be used as a nursery or eventually a home office."

"It sounds perfect."

"I know it's kind of large, but we are hoping for at least four children. Oh and there's a huge back yard that is all fenced in."

"Well, we will pray first that your offer is accepted and second ask for St. Joseph's help in selling both yours and J.R.'s house. I know they sell kits of some kind with a statue of St. Joseph and you are to bury him in the ground upside down."

"I've heard that you are supposed to do that but never knew why."

"I'm not really sure either. I would guess that it has something to do with him being the patron of families, fathers and husbands. Guess I will have to check that out online."

"I wonder where we can get a couple of those kits."

"I've seen them in the religious goods store in the mall."

They continued walking around looking at all of the booths until they came to the booth that Ann had wanted to check out a little more closely. The lady made stuffed teddy bears of all sizes and colors and then different kinds of outfits for them.

"You sure do put a lot of work into these," Ann said to the lady behind the table.

"My daughter and I, and now my granddaughter as well, work on them together. It's become our traditional time together. I was never much of a cook but I loved to do a little sewing and so was able to teach my daughter and we are both teaching my granddaughter."

"That is so wonderful," said Ann, "and it's obvious that there is a lot of creative talent among you."

Maggie agreed, "I have never seen so many cleverly dressed teddy bears in my life. It looks like you have one for just about every occupation there is."

"That is part of what we tried to do," answered the lady, "and we will do special requests if you don't see one that you like."

Ann looked them all over saying, "I wish I could take them all home."

Maggie laughed and shook her head, "Aren't you running out of room yet?"

Then Ann spotted her; a little bear in a safari type outfit. "Oh, she looks like she is ready to head into the jungles of Africa. I just love her."

"Well, now that you have found Jane maybe we can find Tarzan," said Maggie.

"Sorry," the lady said, "I sold him earlier this morning, but how about this chap?" She held up a bear of about the same color as the Safari bear only he was wearing a little blue jacket and a big red hat.

"He reminds me of that famous English bear only his hat is red instead of blue," said Ann.

"I know which one you mean," said Maggie. "I think he was named after one of their rail stations in London."

"The children's books?" asked the lady.

"Yes," both Ann and Maggie said together.

"So are you going to get both Jungle Jane and the other one?" asked Maggie.

"Of course," answered Ann laughing, "I think they belong together."

After they left that booth they realized that they had missed an entire smaller room that was off of the main hall. There were maybe four or five tables.

Maggie said, "Are you game?"

"I am if you are," said Ann, "after all Heaven forbid that we miss anything."

Maggie laughed, "Then after we can go to lunch."

When they walked in Ann couldn't believe her eyes. There was the clerk from the religious goods store in the mall that had given her the icon of St. Germaine Cousin.

"What a wonderful surprise," said Ann as she gave the lady a hug. She then introduced her to Maggie saying, "We were just talking about your store today."

"Must be a God incidence," the lady said.

"Definitely," said Ann. "My friend and her fiancé are looking to sell their homes and I was telling her that you had the St. Joseph home selling kit in your store."

"Do you mean this one?" she said pulling out a box from behind the counter.

"That's it," said Ann. "Do you have two of them?"

"I sure do," she replied.

"Sold," answered Ann.

Maggie protested, "You don't have to purchase them for us."

"But I want to," said Ann. Then she asked the clerk, "Do you know anything about how this tradition started of burying St. Joseph's statue upside down in the ground to help sell your house?"

The lady then explained, "The only thing that I have ever heard is that it began with an order of religious nuns hundreds of years back who would bury their St. Joseph medals in the ground and pray for his intervention. And somehow it has evolved into what it is today. It's not that it is a superstitious practice, but more of a religious tradition that involves prayer. All of that is included in the kit."

"That is wonderful," said Maggie, "Once more our Catholic Faith is intertwined with our daily lives."

"As it should be," said the lady.

As the lady was wrapping up the two packages she asked Ann, "How are you doing?"

"I am doing okay, thank you for asking," Ann replied.

"I am still praying for you," the lady answered.

"You are?" Ann responded.

It always surprised Ann to learn that people were praying for her or even that they thought of her at all. The lady just smiled at her. After exchanging a few pleasantries Maggie and Ann were ready to go.

As they headed towards the main door Maggie asked, "Why is she praying for you? Are you okay?"

"It's a long story that I will share with you someday soon, but in the meantime just know that I am just fine, my friend," answered Ann giving Maggie a hug around the waist.

When they got outside standing next to Ann's car was J.R. and Tom!

Tom greeted them with, "I was right. They did go back to buy out the other half of the craft sale."

"Ha, ha," said Ann.

"And I'm starving," said J.R.

"You're always starving," giggled Maggie as she gave him a kiss in greeting, "What are you guys doing here?"

Tom said, "I thought that I would take all of you to lunch."

"Well, that is very nice of you Thomas," Ann replied, "but how did you know that we would still be here?"

Tom laughed, "You, Maggie, shopping...really?!"

"So, what's the occasion?" asked Maggie.

With that J.R. took Maggie's hands in his and gently said, "They accepted our offer on the house."

"What?!" exclaimed Maggie, "Really?" Of course Maggie and J.R. ignored the congratulations from Ann because they were too busy hugging and kissing.

"Come on, let's go to lunch," said Tom. They decided on a restaurant that was in Johnsville, but on their way home.

When they got in the car Maggie said, "Oh Ann, I can't believe that all of this is happening. God is being so good to us."

Ann agreed and then said, "Now, all we have to do is get yours and J.R.'s houses sold."

Maggie giggled, "Well, St. Joseph is ready to go."

When they got to the restaurant Maggie decided to take in one of the St. Joseph house kits so that J.R. could take his home right away and get the statue buried and the prayers going. She also decided that it would be a good time for them to open the gift that the lady at the glass booth had given them.

After they had received their drinks and ordered their lunch Maggie gave J.R. the St. Joseph house kit and had Ann explain the tradition.

"Ann gave me one too," said Maggie.

"Ann, that was very generous of you," said J.R.

"I just want to do my part to help you get your dream home," Ann replied, "and of course, that means getting St. Joseph involved."

"I wonder why he is to be buried upside down?" pondered Tom.

J.R. laughed, "Maybe that way he will work harder at getting the house sold. After all, who wants to be buried upside down?"

During lunch Maggie shared with J.R. and Tom the ideas that she and Ann had come up with for the decorations and the items they had purchased. J.R. was very happy with all of the ideas and choices.

"In fact," he said, "I think that I would like to go with you to the craft store to get the remaining items."

Maggie gave him a huge smile, "How did I get so lucky to get such a wonderful guy like you?"

They all decided to get a little something for dessert convincing themselves that a little treat now and again was good for the soul. Maggie thought that this would be the right time to share the wedding gift she had received that morning.

"J.R.," she began, "we have received our first wedding gift."

"Are you kidding?" he responded, "and we are what, four months or so away?"

Maggie explained that it was from the lady who had the glass booth. The gift was really wrapped well in bubble wrap both in and outside of the box it was in. Finally they got the last piece of bubble wrap off. No one could believe their eyes!

In fact Maggie started to cry, "Oh this is absolutely gorgeous."

"It sure is," J.R. said in almost a whisper.

It was a single horse drawn sleigh very similar to the ones that Maggie had purchased, only much smaller and inside the sleigh were a couple; the lady was wearing white and the man black and they were covered with glass that was made to look like a red blanket. Behind them were also a miniature glass church and an evergreen tree.

J.R. said, "Look, he's wearing a top hat!"

Maggie through tears said, "What a gorgeous topper for our wedding cake."

"Is that what it is?" asked J.R.

"I think so," answered Maggie, "If not, I think we should use it for that anyway."

"I agree," said J.R. "but how are we going to thank her?"

"She gave me her card," answered Maggie, "So I will definitely be writing her a note."

"And sweetheart," began J.R., "I don't know what you think, but now I think that we should definitely order the announcements that have the sleigh and church on the front."

She nodded in agreement.

On the way home Maggie said, "What an incredible day!"

"You can say that again," answered Ann. "I don't know about you, but I think I am going to wait and go to Sunday morning Mass rather than this evening. I'm pooped. It's a good tired, but I am still tired."

"Me too," said Maggie, "but first I am going to get St. Joseph buried in my yard before I do anything else."

Ann helped Maggie carry all of the packages into the house before heading home herself. As she drove she thought, yes, an incredible day to say the least!

After carrying her packages inside she decided that eventually she would place White Rabbit in the spare bedroom, but for now she placed him among all of the critters in her bedroom. "And now for you two," she said to the two little bears, "but first I have to come up with a name for your buddy here, Jungle Jane. I don't want to name him after the more famous bear, but he sure does look like he is from London. That's it! Your name is 'London.' Eventually you two will go in my office, but for now I want everyone in my bedroom. Weird, I know." All of her stuffed animals just smiled back at her.

Ann spent the rest of the day sitting on the back deck reading, writing, praying, and doing a lot of thinking. Her sessions with Dr. Pete had really been full and intense lately as they talked about what she had remembered. She was really glad to have some down time to process part of it.

There was a gorgeous sunset that evening and Ann stayed outside watching it until the stars began to come out. She felt more peaceful than she had in a long time, but she also felt very much alone. Slowly a tear started, but instead of trying to stop it, Ann just let it run down her cheek.

Eventually she crawled into bed amid all of her stuffed animals and fell asleep.

THE BOOK
Chapter 4

One very warm summer day when everyone was resting after lunch outside under the shade of the trees all of a sudden all of the critters' ears and noses perked up.

"I hear something," said Sabrina.

"And I smell a rabbit," said Pumpkin-Pumpkin. Ada B. Green who was standing next to her nudged the puppy. "Not you," said Pumpkin-Pumpkin, "from out there."

Pretty soon everyone could hear this voice coming from down the path, but approaching quite rapidly and singing as fast as he seemed to be running.

Of course all of the protector critters went on full alert especially Godzilla, Raspberry Sundae, Cotton Candy, Lion, Sir Lancelot, P.J., Lord Percival and of course Bright Eyes who all moved closer to the little girl.

"Wait, I know who that is," said R. Rabbit and Topo G. together.

"Me too," added Dale E. Woof.

"Oh my gosh," said Ada B. Green, "It's the rabbit from the story about Alice."

Sure enough before anyone knew it a white rabbit went running by all of them and straight for the cave. All of them that is with the exception of Lion who was suddenly blocking the entrance, "And where do you think you are going my friend?" he asked in his deep voice. Of course the rabbit stopped dead in his tracks still mumbling something about being late and then bowed down to Lion.

"Yes," answered Lion, "I know that you are late, but you have arrived."

With that the rabbit kind of plopped down on the ground. Everyone could see that he was totally worn out. Immediately Amelia and Tali went and got him a tall glass of cool water. Finally, the rabbit caught his breath.

"I am sorry that I am late," he said.

"Late for what?" asked Ada B. Green.

"I was supposed to be here in the spring for Easter," he answered.

"So what happened?" asked Jeanette.

"Well, there was this mean woman who was chasing me and of course, I didn't want her to know that I was coming here so I led her on a very merry goose chase so deep into the woods that she will never find her way out," he answered.

"Are you sure you lost her?" asked the little girl trying not to let her fear show.

"Yes," said the rabbit, "plus I talked with her husband who is a decent fellow who promised to always keep her away and said he would take her on a long trip to another world." The little girl breathed a sigh of relief.

They spent the rest of the afternoon listening to all of the tales of the rabbit some of which seemed to be pretty tall ones. At one point the little girl asked him why he came to the cave.

"Why," he answered, "to be with you my fair young lady."

The little girl smiled. Of course everyone wanted him to stay. Ada B. Green said that there was a room near hers and the children's that he could have and that she would make sure that he was never late again. Everyone laughed.

The happy little group in the cave in the woods was having a wonderful summer. Not only did they play a lot of games, but they also went swimming. Which of course R.T. Cold Nose III really, really liked to do. And they went on a couple of trips to their favorite camping spot they had been to the previous summer when they met Kris, Front Porch the Buffalo Bull, and Moose Bear.

When they arrived at the site for their final camping trip for the year they were surprised to find two critters already camping there. One looked like a French Bull Dog and the other a big English Sheep dog who seemed to be missing one of his ears, although it was kind of hard to tell for sure because his hair was so long.

"Greetings," Godzilla said.

The bull dog responded, "Bon jour."

"Uh, he said 'Good Day,'" added the sheep dog, "He's French but is learning English with my help. My name is Van Gogh and this is Jean Luc."

"Enchantee," Godzilla said to Jean Luc.

"Parlez-vous français?" asked Jean Luc.

Godzilla smiled as he responded, "Un peu. Parlez-vous anglais?"

Jean Luc smiled back at Godzilla as he answered, "A little more than a little."

"Bonne," said Godzilla, "Tres bien."

And then both of them laughed. Godzilla turned to rest of his friends and said, "I told him that it was nice to meet him and then he asked me if I spoke French. I told him a 'little' and then I asked him if he spoke English and he said, well, you all heard what he said. So I said that was good, very good." Everyone laughed.

Then Lion stepped forward and the minute that the two puppies saw him they bowed down.

"Arise, my friends," said Lion.

"It is you," said Van Gogh.

Lion reached out and touched where the dogs ear had once been, "Yes my friend, it is I. How are thee?"

"I am well," answered Van Gogh, "Thanks to you."

In the meantime Jean Luc was trying to contain himself but was so excited that he reverted back to his French and just kept saying, "Oh mon, oh mon. C'est le Lion."

Godzilla placed a paw on the little dog's shoulder and said, "Yes, it is the Lion."

The little girl then asked if it would be OK if she and her friends also set up camp?

"Of course it is," answered Van Gogh, "It will be good to have more company."

In the meantime Jean Luc took a walk down to the lake all the while muttering to himself, "Oh mon. C'est le Lion."

Van Gogh shook his head as he said, "He'll get over it."

At the campfire that evening the little girl found herself sitting next to Van Gogh. For some reason she felt drawn to him, but she didn't know why.

Eventually she got up her courage and said, "Van Gogh, may I ask you a personal question?"

The dog smiled at her as he answered, "You may ask, but I may not answer."

"Fair enough," she responded and then continued, "How did you lose your ear and how do you know Lion?"

"That's two questions," he chided her. The dog got very quiet for a moment, staring off as if seeing something that only he could. "When I was a little puppy there was a bigger dog that would attack me. Most of the time I could run away, but one time he grabbed my ear and almost pulled it off with his teeth." The dog took a deep breath before continuing, "But somehow I was still able to get away and ran and ran until I knew he couldn't catch me. Then I went and hid in the woods and was hoping that the ear would heal, but it didn't. Instead it got infected. That was when I met Lion. He couldn't save the ear, but he did clear up the infection and helped me to heal in other ways too. I consider him a very special friend."

The little girl had a tear in her eye as she reached out and gave him a hug, "Thank you for telling me."

He gave her a hug back and whispered, "You, too, will heal."

After a couple more days they decided that it was time to get back to the cave. Of course by now Jean Luc and Van Gogh had become friends and were invited to come and live in the cave too. Jean Luc thought it would be a good opportunity to learn English from the

Prince and of course Arthur. The Prince said that there was a room next to his that Jean Luc could have.

Arthur said, "There is?"

The little girl giggled and said, "He has his sources."

Arthur kind of scowled and Sir Lancelot said, "I will explain it my lord to thee later."

Of course all of the way back to the cave the group was singing and laughing and even doing a little dance here and there. As they neared the cave a few of the critters suddenly stopped with their noses and ears perked, but Lion kept moving forward. After he got a little ways ahead of the rest of them he also stopped and turning around said, "It is OK my friends for I know who our guests are as I have been expecting them."

When they got closer to the cave entrance Lion gave a greeting and the two little bears that were sitting by the entrance waved back. One was dressed in a safari outfit and the other in a blue jacket and large red hat. As Lion approached them, they both bowed down on one knee.

"Greetings my friends," said Lion, "I am happy that you have made it back from all of your travels." He then turned to the rest of the group and said, "I would like to introduce my friends Jungle Jane and London."

London gave a little bow and then said with a very clear English accent, "I say old chaps is that you Arthur, Lance and Merlin?"

"Tis I, old friend," answered Arthur. Sir Lancelot and Merlin bowed in agreement.

The little girl then introduced herself and invited the two travelers into the cave. Everyone excused themselves as they went to put away all of their camping gear, but Godzilla did first bring each of them a cool glass of water.

"We have just returned from the last of our summer camping trips," said the little girl, "so we are happy, but also a little tired from the walk."

"We are a little tired too," said Jungle Jane "as actually we arrived just a short time before you came back."

"I suggest that we all take a nap before dinner then," said Godzilla, "and then we can hear all about your adventures."

"Adventures," said Jacques and Arp at the same time.

Fuzzy Wuzzy Woof Woof said to his son, "There will be plenty of opportunities to hear all of their stories."

Ada B. Green gave her son a look that said, "Listen to what Arp's father just said."

Everyone had a wonderful summer's afternoon nap all waking to the sound of activity in the kitchen. Godzilla and his crew were busy putting together a wonderful meal with lots of fresh fruit and of course some honey.

After cleaning things off the table and getting the kitchen straightened around it was decided to build a small fire outside the cave and enjoy the beautiful summer sky. Of course Jacques and Arp were all ready to hear about all of the adventures that Jungle Jane and London had been on but Lion began the evening's storytelling by saying, "I think that your new friends would enjoy hearing about how the two of you first met."

Everyone applauded, even Arp and Jacques as they were learning how to be polite young gentlemen.

"Well, actually," Jane began, "We're both originally from England; at least we were born there. Our parents were friends and they lived very near to each other. In fact, both London and I were born about the same time and knew each other as infants."

She turned and smiled at London who started to say something but Jane went on. "Only we don't quite remember the events of those days." Again, she turned to London and smiled and again he started to speak, but Jane went on. "When we were still quite young, my parents decided to move to Africa. It was a wonderful place, with so many animals everywhere."

The little girl loved animals and had always wanted to travel to Africa to see them so she made a mental note to ask Jungle Jane about them sometime.

"I especially liked being in the jungle, any jungle," she giggled, "And that's how I got my nickname! London also has a nickname," she said as she turned towards him. Once more he started to speak but instead just smiled and nodded. It was apparent that he was the quiet sort, especially when Jungle Jane was around.

"Only a few people know it anymore, she continued, "As it was from when he was quite young. It seems that after we moved away, London really missed me and used to go to the railroad stations looking for me and waiting for me to return. There was one in particular that he went to the most often and because he didn't talk much and wouldn't give anyone his name, they started calling him by the name of the station. It stuck for awhile; even his family and friends still call him by that name sometimes."

London just nodded and smiled leaning back and waiting for Jungle Jane to continue with her story, which he knew she would.

"Anyway, when he got old enough he took off on his own to look for me by traveling to Africa, to the rain forests and to any other jungles that he had heard of. He even went to Peru. But he kept missing me as I too kept traveling to every jungle I could find. The last information that he received was that I was on my way back to England. So, he decided to return there too." She looked toward her friend, who had his head tilted back and his eyes closed, but he was smiling.

So, she continued. "In the meantime, I had been off on all of my adventures and along the way I had met a lion who informed me that he was on his way to America. 'Whatever for?' I inquired. To which he responded with this amazing story about this little girl he had heard about who was lost. Actually, she had kind of lost herself and was on this difficult journey trying to find herself. He said that she needed help and protection. Can you imagine anyone losing themselves? Well, I couldn't, so I wanted to see for myself. Plus, if a lion was going I knew that the journey had to take place in the jungles of America and I definitely wanted to see those. Of course I have since found out that the jungles of America are actually very large cities. Weird. Anyway, I decided to stop in England on the way as it had been so long since I had been there and I did wonder from time to time what had become of my childhood friend. As chance would have it, as my plane was arriving from Africa London's plane was arriving from Peru! We ran into each other as we were gathering our luggage. I would have known him anywhere!"

She turned to her friend once more who opened his eyes, smiled broadly and said, "I would have known her too!"

And getting the last word in, because that is what she usually did, Jungle Jane added, "And we have been together ever since!"

Everyone cheered.

"Wow! What a story!" said the little girl, "It's a wonderful example of how love always triumphs! But, did you ever find the lion or the little girl you were looking for?"

"Well, after first arriving in America," Jungle Jane began, "we started asking around and we did hear some stories about this place. That it was a place where there was a little girl who loved critters, but it was in the woods and not a jungle and no one had ever heard about a lion living here. But after some exploring that didn't bring any results we decided to try here anyway."

"You are correct, this is not a jungle," said the little girl, "and Lion just recently arrived."

With that Jungle Jane and London looked at Lion who nodded and cleared his throat which caused the little girl to exclaim, "You're the lion!"

With that Jungle Jane said, "I thought you knew. I guess I really put my foot into it this time."

"It's all right," said the little girl, "I had already suspected that I might be the little girl you had been looking for."

"Well, how are you, my dear?" London had the presence of mind to ask, "Have you found yourself yet?"

"Well, I have found out a lot about myself, and I would guess that that is at least on the right track," she answered.

"And what have you learned?" asked Godzilla.

"I remembered things that had happened to me when I was younger, which helped to explain why I had so many nightmares and why I felt so afraid much of the time and alone. Yet, I was also afraid to get close to people and to make friends."

"Why was that?" asked Pumpkin-Pumpkin.

"Because, I thought that no one liked me or wanted me around. No one really seemed to care; even the ones that I felt close to all left. I really felt terribly alone but also afraid to get too close to anyone because I didn't want to be hurt again."

"Does it still feel that way?" asked R.T. Cold Nose III.

"Sometimes," the little girl answered.

P.J. started to squirm a little, "Even with us?" she asked.

"No, I've learned to trust all of you and that it is OK to be close. I feel safe and cared for with all of you; even our new cave mates that are just joining us."

"We feel the same way," said Sabrina, "You really do take good care of us too."

"That's what I like about our relationship," said the little girl, "It's a mutual sharing and caring. Being respectful of each other, accepting and supportive; never one-sided."

The Prince smiled as he answered, "I believe that's what they call unconditional love."

"Yes. I do love all of you," said the little girl.

"And we love you too," cheered all of her little friends. The little girl squirmed a little.

"What's wrong?" asked Godzilla, "Don't you believe us?"

"Oh yes," she answered, "It just feels strange and uncomfortable."

"Why?" asked P.J. and Lord Percival together.

"I guess it's because the people who said they loved me before either hurt me or left me. So, it still feels a little scary to hear someone say they love me." Seeing the distressed look on her friends' faces she didn't want to hurt their feelings so quickly added, "But I am sure that those feelings will pass."

The sun soon went down and everyone sat there quietly watching the stars come out; all lost in their own thoughts.

THE CRITTERS
Facing the Unknown

It was time for another meeting of all of the critters and gratefully Ann had left for one of her walks. When all had gathered Godzilla began, "We are heading into the next stretch of challenges for our friend Ann."

"But she has been through so much already," said Sure to Go.

"I know," said Godzilla, "but this next part is going to be very, very important."

"How so?" asked P.J.

"Because she is going to have to face the feelings that go with the memories of her past," he answered.

"Like what?" asked R.T. Cold Nose III.

"Like fear and anger," Godzilla answered.

"Gosh, why do the feelings always have to be such difficult ones?" asked Joan.

"That's a very good question," Godzilla said, "but this time she will also have to face feelings of being loved and cared for."

"Well, that should be a cinch," said Pumpkin-Pumpkin.

"Not necessarily," Godzilla began, "remember what she said around the campfire the other night?"

"I do," said P.J., "that it is still scary for her to hear someone say that they love her."

"That surprised even me," said the Prince, "I thought that by now she would feel more comfortable accepting being loved."

"She has to deal with the other feelings first before she can allow that love in," answered Godzilla.

"So, what do we do?" asked Amelia.

"Just keep loving her," answered the Lion.

ANN'S STORY
Chapter 6
Facing More of the Past

Ann had never remembered a summer that seemed to fly by as fast as this one was. Here it was already at the end of July. She was also very grateful that even though it had been quite warm so far they had not had the super hot days like the previous summer. As much as Ann was very grateful for air conditioning it was always nicer to have the windows opened and the fresh air flowing through the house.

She had worked a fair amount on her children's book and at the request of her publisher had also started working on her other research book. Both of these and the sessions with Dr. Pete sure kept her head full and busy.

As much as she was getting out of the sessions with Dr. Pete they were also difficult at times especially when he had her talking about how she felt regarding the things that had happened to her. As she had faced the memories of the things that had happened to her, at least the ones she could remember, she did notice that the nightmares had pretty much disappeared, and she didn't wake up feeling afraid as she had been for a long time. In fact, she had even moved all of her stuffed animals out of her bedroom and back to their places throughout her house except of course those who belonged there. She still did sleep with Godzilla and Sir Lancelot. It just felt comfortable.

In her last session Dr. Pete had asked her if she was upset about what had happened to her.

"Of course," had been her reply, "anyone would be."

Then he asked, "Are you upset with your parents and uncle?"

"I don't know if upset is the correct word," she began. "Of course I now understand that my father had the illness of alcoholism, which in his day we didn't know a lot about, so it wasn't entirely his fault."

"You are pretty forgiving," said Dr. Pete.

"Hmm, I don't know about that. Maybe just towards my father at this point."

"How about your mother and uncle?"

Ann took a deep sigh, "I guess I still simply do not understand why they did what they did."

"How do you feel about their actions?"

"Sad."

"Is that all?"

"And hurt. I mean, why would they do something like that to a kid?"

"Are you still blaming yourself?"

"I guess I am a little bit even though you and a couple of my friends have told me that it wasn't my fault."

"Why don't you believe us?"

"It's not that I don't believe you, it's just so hard to accept that they would do the things they did without some kind of provocation."

"Ann," Dr. Pete began, "maybe this will help. In a child's mind, especially a very young child, they think that the world revolves around them, that they are somehow controlling it and thus are responsible for everything. Of course, as they mature they learn differently. I think that because we think that some of the molestation happened to you at a very young age your mind is still sort of stuck in that mindset. Does that make sense?"

"I think so. It also explains why I have tended to want to control everything."

"Tended?" he asked gently.

Ann laughed, "For a long time I had a sign in my office that read, 'If it is to be, I am the one to make it be.'"

Dr. Pete laughed, "Is it still there?"

"No, after about a year of attending the meetings for adults from alcoholic homes I realized that I was not in charge."

"But there is still a part of you that tries to control everything, isn't there?"

"Yes."

"That is very understandable. As a child your entire world was pretty much out of your control and you have been trying ever since to get that feeling of security and of things being right in your world back. Well, maybe not back, because I am not sure it was ever there for you in the first place."

"So, what do I do to feel more secure?"

"As you began to learn in the meetings, you must rely more on your higher power which of course we call God. He will take care of you."

"I'm still not 100% sure about that."

"This may be the time to meet with your pastor to discuss this as he can perhaps help you with the last bit of that. Also, I would like to make another suggestion. I have a group of people that meet once a week and I would like for you to join us. All of them were also sexually molested as children. I think listening to their stories and sharing yours will be very helpful for all of you."

"Do you mean I have to share what happened to me with strangers?" Ann asked a little alarmed. "Only a couple of my closest friends and my brother know about this. I haven't told anyone else."

Dr. Pete smiled gently, "You do not have to share anything that you don't want to with anyone. Just come and sit in as I believe hearing others' stories will help you to see that you are not alone."

"Okay, I can do that."

"Great, we meet tomorrow evening at 6:30 p.m. Also, Ann, before our next session I would like you to think about why you do not want to tell anyone that you were abused and molested, okay?"

Ann nodded "Yes."

On the way home she decided to stop into the craft store just to walk around and get ideas. She liked to do that, especially when things were heavy on her mind.

She had walked down a couple of aisles when she heard, "Ann!" It was Maggie and J.R.

"We finally got here to get the rest of the items for our wedding decorations," said Maggie.

"I can see that you found a couple of extras from the look of your cart," Ann said kidding.

"And would you believe that those are items that J.R. wanted after how much he and Tom kidded you and me at the craft show," Maggie said laughing.

"By the way Ann," began J.R. changing the subject, "we were actually going to call you this afternoon. My house has sold and Maggie was told this morning that there is someone who might be interested in hers."

"Oh that is great," answered Ann.

"Plus, the people buying my place are currently living in an apartment so they have asked for a two month escrow, which means that I will be moving into our new home the beginning of October, he continued."

"And," began Maggie, "the person that might be interested in my house is being transferred here from out of state and won't be arriving until the end of December."

"Oh my gosh," said Ann, "so you can stay there until after the wedding."

"I know," said Maggie, "I love my parents, but the thought of moving back home as an adult was really going to be stressful for all of us."

"Especially with the wedding," added J.R.

"Well, when you get ready to move just give me a call. I will be happy to help," offered Ann.

"Thanks," they both said together.

"So, did you find everything you needed for the decorations?" asked Ann.

"Yup," began Maggie, "cotton batting, the flocked evergreen boughs, the Christmas trees and the flameless candles, which were on sale! Plus, I met with Sally at the church and she loved all of our ideas. She suggested that because the Christmas lights were battery operated that we could also put a string amidst each of the displays in front of the altar and the ambo with the poinsettias and the evergreen boughs. She also has some red twig dogwood branches that she will have in vases, just to add a little more of the winter flavor. Plus she said that she would be available to help decorate Thursday evening after rehearsal."

"I can help too," offered Ann.

"That's what Maggie and I are hoping," began J.R. "That our parents and all of our attendants can help so that it won't take that long."

"Oh and the guy with the candle holders said that he will also put all of the holders up that afternoon for us," added Maggie. "I was concerned about decorating on a Thursday evening because of morning Mass on Fridays, but Father Jack said that it is a smaller crowd of retired people so nothing will be in the way."

"Sounds like everything is coming together perfectly," said Ann.

"Now, all we have to worry about is the weather," said J.R.

"Shhh," said Maggie, "It's going to be just fine."

"Well, it may not be on your 'to do' list, but it's on mine," J.R. said kidding her.

"You know," said Maggie, "there is a part of me that is concerned because everything is coming together so perfectly and items are getting checked off that 'to do' list right and left..."

"Waiting for the shoe to drop?" asked Ann.

"She sure is," chided J.R. "And Father Jack even told both of us that something is going to go wrong; it is something that we can pretty much be sure of, either the day of or the day before the wedding. He said to pray that it is nothing serious, but assured us that it will all be okay and it is what will make our wedding, our wedding."

"I wish he hadn't told us that because now I keep thinking about all of the things that can go wrong," said Maggie.

Ann laughed, "We humans! By the way, any word from Fred and Barb?"

"Nothing yet," said J.R., "but her doctor told her about a week or so ago that it could be any time."

"Be sure to let me know," said Ann.

"Yes," said Maggie, "we have the phone thing all set up to notify everyone like we did for Marie and D.J." They chatted for a few more minutes and then Ann continued her shopping.

Ann thought a lot about Fred and Barb and how excited they must be at the impending birth of their first child, just like Marie and D.J. were. She couldn't help but wonder if her parents were excited about the births of herself and her siblings and, if so, what went wrong?

The next evening Ann went to the support group for the first time, and to say that she was nervous would be putting it mildly. In fact, she was so nervous that she almost took her big bears Godzilla and Sir Lancelot with her in the car, but then decided it would be better to take something smaller, so she took the little mouse Bright Eyes which could be more easily hidden in the car. As she got ready to leave she looked around at all of her stuffed animals and said, "Wish me luck," and for a moment she could almost hear them say, "We'll be with you in spirit."

Gratefully Ann wasn't the first one there, as two other women had already arrived. And pretty soon they were joined by five other women, all of them different ages. Ann momentarily wondered why there were no men in the group but put that thought in the back of her head to ask Dr. Pete later on.

Dr. Pete introduced Ann and asked that each woman give her first name and just a short summary of why she was in the group. He also said that Ann had the option of not sharing if she so chose. Ann was amazed at how open each woman seemed to be about what had happened to them, and she also felt overwhelmed with feelings. One woman had been molested by her godfather who was a close family friend, another by a neighbor, the third one by a female coach, and the fourth one was the one that bothered Ann the most as she had been abused and molested by both her parents and a few of her older siblings. The fifth woman had been molested by a boyfriend of her mothers. The next woman was molested by her stepfather, and the last one by an uncle like Ann had been. And all of occurrences were at different ages ranging from early childhood to mid to early teens. When it got back to Ann she swallowed hard and found herself saying, "It was one of my uncles."

Immediately a couple of the women said, "Ann, we are so sorry that happened to you."

Ann's head was spinning as she thought, they are sorry about what happened to me, what about what happened to them?! But all she did was nod her head in reply. Ann just sat and listened during the rest of the group trying to process everything she was hearing.

At the end of the session each of the ladies came over and told Ann how glad they were that she had come to the group.

Ann just said, "Thank you for having me."

As there was only one other lady who hadn't left yet Ann felt comfortable asking Dr. Pete why there were no men in the group.

"Let's see if I can give you an abbreviated version," he began, "as we've discussed before there are different levels and types of molest. If it's a man and a female child, that brings up one set of issues, but if it's an adult of the same sex as the child, that brings up another set of issues. Also boys have the 'being a man' thing and being able to defend themselves that also comes into play."

"So, what you are saying is that it is probably easier for men to relate with other men who have been molested than it would be for them to relate to women."

"Basically, yes," Dr. Pete replied. "So, otherwise how are you feeling?"

"Blown away," Ann said.

Dr. Pete laughed.

The other woman who was still there said, "I felt the same way the first time I came to the group too. Often we feel so alone and isolated and suddenly here we are in a group of women who have been through the same or similar things that we have. It's okay."

"Thank you," said Ann.

"See you next week?" the lady asked. Ann nodded in the affirmative.

When she got into the car Ann picked up Bright Eyes and giving him a hug said, "Oh my little friend this has been a difficult evening." She then sat him on the seat and drove home. When she got into the house she found herself saying aloud, "I'm home," patting Cotton Candy and Raspberry Sundae as she passed by them and giving Godzilla a huge hug when she got to her room. This was one night she was glad they were all there.

She had noticed that she had a message on her phone. It was from Tom, but she was so tired that she decided to call him back tomorrow. Instead, she ran herself a wonderful, full bubble bath and poured herself a glass of wine. For some reason her body ached like she had just run a marathon so the water and the wine and felt wonderful.

She fell right to sleep but in the morning was aware that her sleep had been a little restless, like maybe she had been dreaming but couldn't remember what about.

After having breakfast on the deck she returned Tom's call.

"Well, good morning," he said.

"Sorry I missed you last evening," she replied, "what's up?"

"Well, I hadn't talked to you in a few days so was just kind of checking in. How are you doing?"

"Okay, how's by you?"

"All good. Hey have you talked to Maggie in the last day or so?"

"I ran into her and J.R. at the craft store the day before yesterday, why?"

"So you know about his house selling."

"Yes, but any word on Maggie's?"

"She accepted an offer today."

"Was it from the person that is being transferred here?"

"Yes. Isn't that great? Good old St. Joseph did it again!"

"I never doubted him for a moment," giggled Ann.

"Onto another topic, I was wondering if you would like to get Maggie and J.R. the pontifical blessing for their wedding gift like we did for Barb and Fred?"

"That's a great idea. I had totally forgotten that we had done that."

"Should I get the book to look at again or do you want to do the same design?"

"Why don't we take a look at the book again just to make sure."

"As we are already into August if you're not doing anything today I could pick it up and pop over."

"Just working on a new book so an interruption would be welcomed."

"How about I pick up a couple of our favorite burgers, some fries, and drinks?"

"How about a burger and a chocolate milk shake?"

"You've got it! No fries?"

"Trying to be a little good and it is so nice out we can eat on the deck."

"Sounds wonderful. I'll see you about 11:30."

Ann went to work on getting thoughts, notes and cards organized for her research book and before she knew it was 11:30 and her doorbell was ringing. Tom greeted Ann and then said, "Hi guys," to all of her stuffed animals.

Ann laughed a little as she said, "Reminds me of kids with their invisible playmates."

"Only yours are not invisible my friend," answered Tom.

Ann was glad that she had opened up the huge umbrella over her round picnic table as it had become a little warmer since she had been out there earlier. They ate and looked at the booklet with the pontifical blessings, finally deciding on one that was a bit different from the one they had got for Marie and D.J.

"I'm glad you suggested I pick up the book as this one looks more like Maggie's and J.R.'s taste," he said.

As Ann was clearing the table off her phone rang.

It was Maggie. "J.R. just called and Fred just took Barb to the hospital. It's time! See you there?"

"Of course," Ann replied and added, "Tom is here so that will save you a phone call."

"Great," said Maggie and hung up.

Ann went and told Tom and all he said was, "My car, yours, or separate?"

"Yours," said Ann and off they went.

On the way to the hospital Ann said, "Darn, it's only August 3rd and I was hoping that their little one would be born on August 4th the feast of St. John Vianney."

"Well, whose feast day is today?"

"I forgot to look this morning so I don't know."

"Any day is a good day when a child is born healthy."

"Yes. Santo Bambino, please pray for Barb and her child."

By the time they had gotten to the hospital Maggie and J.R. were there.

"I'm sure glad I have a great boss," said J.R.

"Me too," said Maggie, "Marie will be here as soon as Patricia Jane wakes up from her nap and D.J. will be here after work."

"The same with Randy and Don," said J.R. "Did you get a hold of Lynn?"

"Darn it," said Maggie grabbing her cell phone, "I'll go call her right now."

J.R. shook his head, "I'm afraid as to what she is going to be like the closer we get to the wedding."

A moment later Maggie returned, "She will be here after work too."

Just then Ann noticed a little older couple sitting down the hall. "Isn't that Barb's parents?"

"I think so," said Maggie.

"I'll go check and see if they want to come and sit with us," said J.R.

Just as he got to them Fred's parents also arrived, so J.R. brought them back to the larger areas where the group was sitting.

Barb's mother said, "What wonderful friends that you would be here."

"We're not all here yet," said J.R., "There's at least five more coming."

"Fred's brother is on his way," offered his mother.

"And so is Barb's sister," said her Dad who was already pacing.

Barb's mother whispered, "I think this is harder on him than when Barb was born because then he had to help take care of me."

About an hour later Fred came out to give an update. Barb was doing fine and resting in between contractions which still seemed to be far enough apart that her doctor was not even here yet. He thanked everyone for coming and gave his and Barb's parents hugs. Barb's dad went back to pacing.

Marie arrived with Patricia Jane who was dressed in one of the outfits that she and Ann had found when they went to the garage sales. Marie put her down and she walked to Ann with her arms outstretched. A little wobbly still, but she was getting this walking thing down.

"Well look at you," said Tom. Patricia flashed him a huge smile as she grabbed Ann who picked her up and gave her a hug.

A little while later Randy arrived saying, "I'm glad I was on for the lunch crowd today and not for dinner. Don't want to miss this."

About 5:30 p.m. the rest of the group arrived from work. So when Fred came out at 6:00 p.m. to give an update he was surprised by the crowd that had gathered. Again, he shared that Barb was doing fine and that the labor pains were still a ways apart, but her spirits were good.

At various points during the evening members of the group took turns going to the hospital cafeteria to get a bite to eat. The parents went first as it seemed they had a better chance of eating and getting back before their new grandchild would be born.

Eventually, as the hour got later, Patricia curled up on her mom's lap and went to sleep. She was followed by many of the adults dozing in their chairs too. Interspersed were the updates from Fred who eventually started saying, "I'm sorry this is taking so long."

J.R. laughed, "Hey dude, we just feel bad for your wife."

"I know," said Fred, "she's getting tired and just when she dozes off another contraction comes."

"We are all praying," said Ann, "to Santo Bambino." Fred smiled.

At about 11:45p.m. Tom whispered to Ann, "You may get your wish after all."

Ann said, "It really doesn't matter anymore I just hope that Barb and the baby are okay."

At 12:30a.m. Fred came out and was smiling from ear to ear, "First, Barb is just fine, a little tired but just fine. And we are pleased to announce the arrival of John Paul at 12:15a.m., 20 inches long, and weighs 9 pounds and 1 ounce."

Everyone stifled a cheer because of being in the hospital, but there were a lot of hugs all the way around.

"By the way," Fred added, "my friends may not know this, but John is my father's middle name and Paul is Barb's dad's middle name not to mention that St. John Paul II is a favorite of ours, so it only made natural sense to us."

"And it is the feast of St. John Vianney," said Tom.

"That's right," said Fred, "wait until I tell Barb. We forgot about that. Thank you again for all of the support, love, and for being here. It means a lot to both Barb and I and now John Paul."

"Would it be okay if we came to visit tomorrow evening?" asked J.R.

"That would be good as I think Barb is going to need to rest tomorrow morning, and I am hoping that the grandparents and the godparents of John Paul will come tomorrow afternoon." Again, he gave everyone a hug and headed back to his wife's room.

Ann was glad that Tom had driven as she was feeling really tired. After they got going she asked him if he knew who Fred and Barb had asked to be the godparents.

"J.R. told me that they had asked Fred's older brother and Barb's younger sister," answered Tom.

"Weren't the two of them their witnesses for their wedding?" she asked. Tom said they were.

Tom waited until Ann flicked the front porch light before pulling out of the driveway. Ann felt simply exhausted. "What was that that a friend of mine said to me years ago? Ah yes..." she said to all of her stuffed animals as she passed by them. "I am so tired that if I could drive to bed I would.'" She let out a little chuckle as she dropped all of her clothes on the floor, put on her p.j.'s, and slipped into bed between Godzilla and Sir Lancelot. As she was falling asleep she said, "Thank you Santo Bambino for the gift of little John Paul."

She was really grateful that she was able to sleep in the next morning as when she awoke she had a bit of a headache and the start of a sore throat. "Gosh, I wonder how everyone is doing who had to go into work today." Later Tom called to see if she wanted to go to the hospital with him that evening to see Barb and John Paul. She explained that she wasn't feeling that well and so didn't think it a good idea.

"Do you need anything?" he asked.

"No. Thanks. I'm just fine," she answered, noticing that there was an edge to her voice.

Hopefully Tom didn't notice, but his answer indicated that maybe he did, "Uh, just checking. I'm sure you will let me know if you do."

Ann softened her voice, "Yes, thank you Tom for asking and please greet Barbara, Fred, and John Paul for me."

"I will be happy too."

When she got off of the phone Ann wondered why she was feeling a little crabby, "Maybe it's just because I'm not feeling my best."

Over the next couple of days Ann worked on her research book, happy to be lost in that work. By the weekend she felt that she had a pretty good handle on the project and so decided to work on the gifts for John Paul. She wasn't sure when the baptism would be, but she wanted them ready. She had decided to do the same paintings like she had done for little Patricia; first the water color painting with the quote from the prophet Isaiah (43:1), *"I have called you by name: you are mine,"* then underneath his names in calligraphy and their meanings.

John
"God is Gracious"

Paul
"Small"

Ann chuckled at the meaning of the name "Paul" as John Paul was anything but small, weighing in at over 9 pounds.

For the second water color painting Ann decided to do more of a summer outdoor scene whereas the one she did for Patricia was a spring one, depicting the time of year that each of them were born. She again planned on putting the Apostles' Creed in calligraphy in the middle of it, and then below that John Paul's name and his patron saints.

John Paul

St. John Vianney
Priest

St. Paul
Apostle

St. John Paul II
Pope

Please Pray for Us

After Mass on Saturday Ann decided that it was probably time to schedule a meeting with Father Jack and luckily she was able to talk to him alone for a couple of minutes, long enough to ask if he was going to be around this coming week. He thought that he was available Wednesday but asked her to call the rectory Tuesday afternoon when he had his calendar in front of him.

"Gosh, this is going to be one really busy week," she said to her stuffed animal friends when she got home, "Father Jack, Dr. Pete and the group! It's either going to be really good or really rough, especially because I now have this little cold."

Ann was kind of glad that her phone had not rung on Saturday nor again on Sunday. She really wanted to simply be alone and not be bothered which was kind of strange as she hadn't felt that way since, well, since she couldn't remember when. She just chalked it up to not feeling well and yet something inside told her that that was not the entire reason. But, she still spent all day Sunday just resting on the couch. She watched TV, she read, and she slept and by Monday was feeling much better. In fact she was feeling well enough to give Barbara a call just to see how they were settling in with their new little one.

She was aware that she had not heard from Tom. "Maybe he's just away on business," she tried to tell herself but she actually believed that he was really giving her a little space. "As crabby as I have been lately," she said to her stuffed animal friends in the living room, "I wouldn't want to talk to me either."

Ann was able to make the appointment with Father Jack for after morning Mass on Wednesday. She decided to attend Mass knowing that being there would help her with her meeting.

Ann felt immediately at ease in Father Jack's presence and his gentle ways reassured her of the trust she was about to place in him. She told him that she had been going to therapy and that it had been a huge help in facing and uncovering things from her childhood.

"Are you feeling better?" he asked.

"Yes and no," she answered. She then took a deep breath and told him about the memories of being more abused by her mother and of the molest by her uncle.

"I had wondered about the molest," he said gently.

"Does it show?" Ann asked a little alarmed.

"No, not exactly, but remember I have now sat through quite a few of those training sessions that you attended and I recognized a couple of possible signs. I was hoping that I was wrong. Ann, I am so sorry this happened to you."

She nodded her head in acknowledgement before continuing, "What I am struggling with now is that I am not sure that I trust God because of all of this. I mean, why would He allow this kind of stuff to happen to children?"

"It also sounds like you might be a little angry with Him," he said.

Ann then shared the story about yelling at God for not helping her family when she was a kid, and that Dr. Pete had suggested that she think about ways that maybe He did help them.

"So, did you come up with any ideas on how He did help your family?"

"The only real thing that came to mind was that He gave us the gift of our Faith."

"That's a pretty big one. Anything else?"

"Well, despite the problems, my parents did stay together until the death of my mother, so we did have both parents, and from what I have read recently that is a positive."

"Yes. Studies have shown that kids from broken homes do worse in school, tend to get in trouble with the law, and generally have difficulties in their lives."

"And none of those things happened to me or my siblings. We all did pretty well in school and my sister's marriage was not the best, but it was not the worst either."

"How about your brother?"

"He's had some relationship problems but seems to be working those out and he has started going to church again."

"Is that it?"

"The other ways I think that God helped my family do not sound very nice."

"Try me."

"Well, my father is no longer suffering from his alcoholism because he is deceased."

"That sounds okay to me."

"And my mother who is also deceased can no longer hurt anyone."

"Have you forgiven her?"

"What's to forgive, it is what it is."

"How about your uncle?"

"Same thing, not much can be done about it now."

"Hmm," was all that Father Jack said, then asked, "Did God help you?"

"I guess when I was older and able to leave the house."

"But, not as a kid?"

"I can't think of anything other than church and school."

"Were there any people that you could turn to when you were a kid?"

Ann thought a moment and remembered her neighbors, a couple of teachers, a priest, and a couple of relatives, "But none of them knew any of this was going on," she added, "so I guess it would have been difficult for them to do anything about it. In those days it was kind of like what happened in the house, stayed in the house."

"But you still felt safe and comfortable with them?"

"Yes."

"Did you ever think that maybe God put them in your life for a reason?" he ventured.

"Hmm, I guess I never thought about it that way."

"And is He helping you now?"

"I would say that He is. As hard as this all is at least now I am able to deal with the truth of all that happened."

"Ann, sometimes it is really hard to see God's hand in things, especially things like this. Do you remember the conversation that we had on the gift of free will?"

"Yes."

"And remember that I said that when we are the victims of the actions of someone else's free will that God will give us everything we need to get through it if we are open to it?"

Ann nodded.

"Well, think about it," he began, "it was too much for you to face as a child with no one around that you felt you could turn to, so all of the events were buried until you were old enough to face them. Do you think God had a hand in that?"

"I can see that He would."

"And, when it was time for the memories of those events to surface you used your own free will by saying yes to finding out what the bad dreams were about and God sent you people to help you to do that."

"It hasn't been easy."

"I'm sure it hasn't, but can you imagine what your life would be like if you hadn't had the courage to face the truth and to accept help?"

"I've thought of that. Plus, I've also become aware of how independent and strong I am because of what I have gone through. Not always in healthy ways, but I'm getting there."

"Exactly. Now you are understanding."

"I guess God did help me. I just wish He had chosen a different way of helping."

"Like how?"

"Like never allowing it to happen in the first place."

"I know," said Father Jack, "I know."

In her session with Dr. Pete that week Ann shared about her meeting with Father Jack.

"Still a little angry with God?" he asked.

Ann had to admit that she probably was.

"I'm glad that you can see that. And now that you have faced God, so to speak, do you think you are ready to face some of the people from your childhood?"

Ann felt some panic, "Why would you want me to do that? I mean, what purpose could that serve?"

"Maybe that's what you need to find out." Dr. Pete saw the need to be gentle with her so added, "And I am not necessarily talking about those who hurt you at least not right now. Instead, let's start with those whom you felt close to."

"But so many of them are deceased."

"That's okay, you can still write letters to them and you can either bring them to one of your sessions to share with me or if you know where they are buried you can visit the cemetery.”

“What about those that are living, should I mail those?”

“If you wish, but if you are not sure about mailing them let’s talk about why in one of your sessions.”

“What should I write?”

“Just start and see what happens. You may end up telling them what they meant to you in your life as you never really have had the opportunity to do that.”

“But what if they don’t want to hear what I have to say or maybe they don’t even remember me?”

Dr. Pete smiled, “It’s a risk that we all take when we put our feelings out there. And remember, you aren’t doing this simply to get a response; you are doing it because you have things that need to be said. If you do it with any expectations, positive or negative, it won’t work. These letters must come from your heart.”

“Okay. I’ll give it a shot.”

Dr. Pete smiled, “And will we see you at group tomorrow evening?”

She said that she would be there.

After she arrived home she decided to give Tom a call.

“Hey,” she said when he answered, “I thought I had better check and see if all was well with you.”

“Doing good,” he answered, “how about you?”

“Well, I think my cold or whatever it was is gone, so feeling better.”

“Glad to hear it.”

"Tom, I think I have been a little crabby lately and I just wanted to apologize."

"Yes you have. Apology accepted, but what has been going on as I'm not the only one who has noticed it?"

"Really?"

"Our friends have been calling me and asking what is going on with you as you seemed withdrawn and kind of short with people; which is not like you at all," he began. "Of course Marie, D.J., and I are wondering if it has to do with your recent memories of being molested, but we are not saying that to the rest of the group because you asked us not to say anything about that to them."

"I really appreciate that as I am just not ready for the rest of the world to know. I think that you, Marie, and D.J. may be correct that my mood is related to the memory and I'm not quite sure what to do about it."

"What does Dr. Pete say?"

"Well, he did suggest that I talk to Father Jack, which I did this week."

Ann then shared with Tom some of the conversation that she had had with their pastor, especially about being angry with God and not trusting Him.

"Did it help?" Tom asked.

"I'm still processing everything, but I feel a little more at peace than I did. Also, Dr. Pete gave me an assignment to begin working on this week, and even though I think it is going to be difficult I can also see how it is going to help. Plus, when you were last here I was going to share something else with you when the call came in that Barb was in labor, so I didn't get to tell you."

"What was that?"

"Dr. Pete had me join a group of women that he meets with once a week and all of them have been molested by various people in their lives. I went for the first time last week."

"How was it?"

"Oh Tom, it was so hard hearing what had happened to these women. My head was just spinning by the time I left and I felt so bad for all of them."

"Did you get an opportunity to share?"

"I did, but I was a little uncomfortable so only said that it was an uncle."

"How often do they meet?"

"Once a week. I go again tomorrow evening."

"A lot happening," Tom said gently, "and then on top of it you also caught a cold."

"Oh Tom, thank you so much for understanding. I don't know what I would do without your friendship right now."

"I'll always be your friend, but just know that sometimes I simply do not know what to do to help so at those moments I pray for you."

"Probably the best thing to do, as I don't always know what to do with all of this either, and I definitely don't want to push my friends away with my crabbiness."

"As you seem to be in a pretty good place today, maybe it would be a good idea to reach out to your friends."

"I'm not ready yet to share with all of them what is going on with me, except Marie and D.J."

"Well, then just tell them you have been ill, which is not a lie, because you have had this cold."

"Good idea. Thanks."

"And if you need any help with the assignment that Dr. Pete gave you, I'm here."

"Thanks Tom, but I think it's something that I have to do on my own; at least this part of it."

"Then I will at least be praying for you and know that I am nearby."

"How can I ever thank you?"

"No need to as that is what friends are for."

Ann spent the rest of the day calling her friends and in-between worked on the research book. She decided that the assignment from Dr. Pete was going to have to simply wait a day or two. She called Barb and Fred first and apologized for not getting over to see the new little one, but with her cold she really had not wanted to infect any of them.

"Plus, I think I get a little cranky when I am not feeling good."

Barb answered, "I think we all do. Also, we will be bringing John Paul to church for the first time on Sunday at the 10 a.m. Mass so maybe you can see him then."

"I will be there," answered Ann.

"And, we have set the baptism for the following weekend, also during the 10 a.m. Mass," Barb added.

"I just marked it on my calendar," Ann said. Before hanging up she told Barb to give Fred and John Paul a hug from her.

"Whew, one down," she said after she hung up. She then telephoned Maggie to see how the house sales and the wedding plans were going. Maggie caught her up on the latest and also added that she was glad that Ann was over her cold saying, "You just didn't seem like yourself."

Ann hung up from that call thinking, "And just who is it that I am?"

Lynn was next on her list and she had just had lunch with her brother Don at the restaurant that Randy works at, so she was able to catch Ann up on what was happening with all of them.

"We sure are glad that you are feeling better," Lynn said, "As we were all worried about you."

Ann hung up and said to her stuffed animals in her office, "Why would they worry about me?"

She saved her last call for Marie as she knew that one would take a little longer.

Marie was thrilled to hear from Ann, "I was going to call you today," she said, "just to check in and see what was going on with you."

Ann then told her about her conversation with Tom that morning and that probably the three of them were correct about it being related to her newest memories.

"Plus having a bad cold didn't help," she added, "I'm not a happy camper when I am not feeling well."

"I'm sure that added to it," began Marie, "but, you also just seemed a little angry rather than just crabby. Are you angry?"

"I didn't think I was."

"Why not? Tom, D.J. and I are all angry about what happened to you."

"I kind of gathered that but, I don't know, to me it is what it is. I can't change what happened to me, but I am the one left to deal with it and to make the most of my life."

"True, but I think that your therapist would probably tell you that it is okay to be angry about what happened."

"I'll have to think about that and I will ask him, I promise."

They then talked about all of the new things that little Patricia was accomplishing and some of the funny things she had done.

Ann felt a little tired after all of her telephone conversations but decided to at least make a list of the people that she wanted to write letters to; that way she could begin working on them first thing in the morning.

In the morning she awoke feeling refreshed, which was a good thing considering the task that lay ahead. While making her morning coffee she said to her stuffed animal friends in the kitchen, "I think this is going to be a p.j. day while I work on all of this. I know that you guys don't mind." For a moment Ann thought that her stuffed animal friends had actually smiled back at her.

When she was ready to she headed for her office with Godzilla, Sir Lancelot, P.J., Lord Percival and Bright Eyes in toe. "I need all the support I can get," she said aloud. Then sitting at the computer she asked God to help her and began the task at hand.

THE BOOK
Chapter 5

The next morning the little girl awoke early and snuck out of the cave to go on one of her walks. Of course the protectors of the cave's entrance knew that she had left, but never let on; simply indicating which direction she had gone to Sir Lancelot as he left the cave to discreetly follow her from a short distance. And Lion not far behind him.

It was a beautiful summer morning and the little girl had slept well, but she felt uneasy this morning for some reason and she wanted time alone to sort it out. As she had been doing she once again headed down the path that led closer to the edge of the woods rather than the one that headed deep into the woods. She loved hearing all of the birds singing so early in the morning as they greeted the day and she was noticing the different things that grew this time of year in the woods that were different from the flowers of early spring. There were a lot more ferns and even some areas of English primroses; both of these loving the shade.

As she got near the area where she had bid farewell to Elsie the Keeper of the Hearts she sat down on a huge rock and simply stared at the path that Elsie had taken to leave the woods. It was different than the one the little girl had taken when she first arrived. She wondered how Elsie and all of the orphans were doing and hoped that they were happy.

She thought about how she was feeling. She was definitely feeling more at peace and safer than she ever had in her life and was actually having a lot of fun with her cave mates. This has been one of the best summers I can ever remember she thought to herself. We have played, camped, swam and gone exploring and generally have simply had a grand time. So, why this uneasy feeling inside and why did it show up so strong this morning? She thought back to the past couple of days and realized that it had started the evening before when her friends were telling her that they loved her. It was not that she didn't believe them but their kind of love sure seemed to be different than how she had experienced it in her family. At the thought of her family the little girl looked at the path leading out of the woods again and felt a kind of a shudder remembering that they were still out there. "But," she said to herself, "so is Elsie, the orphans, and Officer Gilbert." With a huge sigh she got up and headed back to the cave arriving in time for breakfast.

"Did you enjoy your walk?" asked P.J.

"I did little one, thank you for asking," answered the little girl.

As they ate breakfast everyone was busy making their plans for what they were going to do that day. During all of this the little girl was rather quiet.

"So, what are you going to do today?" asked Beethoven looking at the little girl. She didn't answer as she was far away in her thoughts.

"Earth calling the little girl, earth calling the little girl," said Fast Eddie. At the same time Bright Eyes took the little girl's hand which brought her back around.

"And where were you little lady?" asked the Prince.

"Oh my," said the little girl, "I'm sorry. I was thinking about Elsie, the orphans, and Officer Gilbert just wondering if they were all doing well."

"Is that all my little lady?" asked Sir Lancelot.

She looked at him for a long time before saying, "No. I was also thinking about my family."

"Are you feeling scared?" asked P.J. snuggling closer.

"No," the little girl answered, "I'm not exactly sure what it is that I am feeling."

Very softly and gently Lion said, "Maybe it is time for you to face some of these people again."

"What!" exclaimed the little girl as panic set in. "Why would you want me to do that? I mean, what purpose could that serve?"

"Maybe that's what you need to find out," he answered.

Seeing the need to be gentle with her the Prince said, "We're not necessarily talking about those who hurt you, little lady, as least not right now. Instead, start with those whom you felt close to."

"But so many of them are deceased," answered the little girl.

"That's OK," began Lion, "you can still write letters to them."

"What about those that are living, should I mail those?" she asked.

"If you wish, but you don't have to," he answered.

"What should I write?" she asked.

"Just start and see what happens. You may end up telling them what they meant to you in your life as you never really have had the opportunity to do that," he said.

"But what if they don't want to hear what I have to say or maybe they don't even remember me?" she asked.

The Prince smiled, "It's a risk that we all take when we put our feelings out there little lady."

"And remember," added Lion, "you aren't doing this simply to get a response; you are doing it because you have things that need to be said. If you do it with any expectations, positive or negative, it won't work. These letters must come from your heart."

"OK," she said, "I'll give it a shot."

All of her cave mates promised to help.

"No," warned Godzilla, "This is something that she must do herself. We can be supportive by listening, by helping her with her chores, and sometimes even by leaving her alone and staying away. But, that's all. You all know the rules." They all nodded.

That very day the little girl sat down and started to write her letters.

She wrote the first letter to her grandmother who had already died; a grandmother that she loved dearly. She had spent time with the little girl teaching her about flowers and plants and always baked special treats for her. The little girl remembered her as gentle, loving and patient. She also cried a little as she wrote this letter as she felt the loss of this special lady.

She then wrote to aunts and uncles who were still living and who had been very special in her life; supportive, caring, and non-judgmental. As she wrote she remembered them as beacons of light in the dismal darkness of her childhood.

She wrote to neighbors that had been kind to her and allowed her to play with their dog; to the priest who had encouraged her and brought the comfort of God during really difficult times. And she wrote to her sister whom she missed. She mourned all of their deaths and actually cried a few tears of loss and healed a little more.

Over the next few days she wrote to her brother whom she hadn't seen in a long time and to her teachers who had given her such a love for learning, for books, for music, for sports, and for God.

She also wanted to write to some of her friends but it had been so long that she had a hard time thinking of them at first. It was so long ago and they seemed so far away since she had come to the woods. She asked the Father for help remembering, which was unusual for the little girl as she didn't like remembering things from long ago. Then she thought of one, Golden Pockets. Then there was Storyteller and Barrister.

"Wait a minute," she said out loud.

A few of her cave mates that were nearby all turned to see who the little girl was talking to, but didn't see anyone.

"Is something wrong my little lady?" asked Sir Lancelot.

"Could you ask Snowbear, Shawn O' Leigh, Nicely, Nicely the Bow Tie Bear, Miss Evelyn, Snowflake, Rudy, Rudy Red Nose, R. Rabbit, Topo G., the Winged Lady of the Snows, Bogie, and Bacall to come and see me please?"

At this point Godzilla poked his head out of the kitchen, "Is everything OK?"

"I think so," answered the little girl, "But I think I just remembered something."

Pretty soon all of the critters she had asked to see were gathered around her. "Rudy, Rudy, when we first found you by the stream you said that two of your friends had told you that Mr. Bear Claus might be found in these woods."

"Yes," he answered, "Sir Galahad and Dancing Girl."

"And Bogie and Bacall, the note on the package that you arrived in at Christmas said that Golden Pockets wanted me to have you, is that correct?" she asked.

"Yes," they said together.

"And our friends who arrived on Christmas day," she began, "Nicely, Nicely you were sent by D.W.?"

"Yes," he answered.

"And I was sent by Junior," said Snowflake.

"I came from Choo-Choo," said Sean O'Leigh.

"I am from Pudie," said Miss Evelyn.

"And Mademoiselle sent me," said Snowbear.

To R. Rabbit and Topo G. she said, "And you both know Barrister and Storyteller?"

"Yes," they answered.

"And you are a friend of Lil Angel's?" she asked the Winged Lady of the Snows. The swan delicately nodded that she was. The little girl became very quiet for a few moments.

"What is it?" asked Godzilla.

"All of those people you mentioned used to be friends of mine when I was little," she answered, "But I had forgotten about them and couldn't remember their names until just now."

"We know," said Bogie and Bacall together.

"And they are still your friends," said Rudy Rudy Red Nose.

"They are?" asked the little girl, "But how could they be? They don't live here."

"They live just on the outskirts of the woods," said Snowbear.

"They really aren't that far away," added Sean O'Leigh.

"Maybe you should write them letters too," offered Miss Evelyn.

"That's exactly what made me remember them," said the little girl, "And yes, I will write to them. But do you think they would remember me or want to hear from me?"

"Yes," said R. Rabbit, "remember, some of us were sent by them."

"And yes again," added Topo G.

So the little girl went back to her letter writing.

With each letter she cried a little as she remembered the rough times and she cried a little as the old feelings of love from these people were finally allowed in. The defensive walls were breaking down after all of these years and with each letter she healed just a bit more. And her cave mates, her new friends were beside her through the entire process.

She decided to take a huge step and to mail the letters to those who were still living knowing that she may not hear back from any of them, but as Lion and the others had said it was a risk that it was time for her to take.

ANN'S STORY
Chapter 7
The Letters

Ann wrote the first letter to her Grandmother Rose who had already died; the grandmother that she loved dearly. She was the one who had spent time with Ann teaching her about flowers and plants, and always baked special treats for her. Ann smiled as she remembered her as gentle, loving, and patient. She also cried a little as she wrote this letter as she felt the loss of this special lady.

She then wrote to aunts and uncles who were still living and who had been very special in her life who were supportive, caring, and non-judgmental. As she wrote she remembered them as beacons of light in the dismal darkness of her childhood.

She wrote to neighbors that had been kind to her and allowed her to play with their dog and to the priest who had encouraged her and brought the comfort of God during really difficult times. And she wrote to her sister whom she missed. She mourned all of their deaths and cried a few tears of loss and healed a little more.

Over the next few days she also wrote to her brother whom she hadn't seen in a long time, and to her teachers who had given her such a love for learning, for books, for music, for sports, and for God.

And to her friends who had always been there for her, many of them since her childhood: Tom, Marie and D.J., Maggie, Don, Lynn, Fred and Barb, J.R., and Randy.

With each letter she cried a little as she remembered the rough times and she cried a little as the old feelings of love from these people were finally allowed in. The defensive walls were breaking down after all of these years and with each letter she healed just a bit more.

And her stuffed animals and dolls were beside her through the entire process.

She decided to take a huge step and to mail the letters to those who were still living knowing that she may not hear back from any of them, but as Dr. Pete had said it was a risk that it was time for her to take.

Tom had checked in with her a couple of times just to see how she was doing and if she needed anything. But other than that, her sessions with Dr. Pete and attending Mass she pretty much kept at it with a few breaks spent on her back deck just to clear her head, to think about letters to be written and process those she had already written.

She talked with Dr. Pete about the letters she had written to her deceased relatives and friends and how all of that had felt. She found herself really enjoying telling Dr. Pete about these special people in her life.

But what really surprised Ann were the first telephone calls that she received from her friends telling her how much not only her letters, but she herself, meant to them.

Marie said, "You know Ann, so many people say they love you and usually act like it, but to actually see it written in words and the reasons why I am special to you really touched my heart. I will treasure this letter always."

Ann found herself fighting the tears back.

Tom shared with her that he had decided to do the same thing, "So often we really do not let the people in our lives know just how much we care about them."

Even Don the computer geek said, "Ann this was just such an awesome surprise to receive this in the mail amid all of the advertisements and bills."

She also heard from a couple of her aunts and uncles who told her how special she had always been to them.

And from an older neighbor who was hoping that they could visit sometime soon. She also heard from a couple of teachers and childhood friends that wanted to renew their old friendships with her. They were all so anxious to hear about everything she had been up to and looked forward to corresponding either by snail or e-mail. Not that she heard from everyone or that all of them wanted to renew their friendship, but Ann still couldn't believe she had heard from so many and was becoming aware that she was starting to feel more life inside of herself.

As fall approached Ann was feeling good. Her work on the research book was going really well as were her sessions with Dr. Pete and even the support group. As upsetting as it was to sometimes hear the stories of the other women she did find it helpful to eventually share what had happened to her, and how it had and in some ways was still affecting her.

In one of the groups when Ann had mentioned this Dr. Pete asked, "In what ways do you still see it affecting you?"

Ann thought a long time and reflected on some of the events of just the past couple of weeks and making a huge sigh said, "I think I am still angry."

Dr. Pete smiled as he asked, "Still?"

Ann noticed the other women smiling and she herself smiled as she answered, "Okay, I guess I am just now noticing that I am angry."

All of the women cheered. Ann could feel herself blushing.

Dr. Pete then asked, "And how is your anger showing itself?"

"Well, a few weeks back I noticed that my voice had an edge and shortness to it when interacting with my friends. They noticed it too and that I had become withdrawn," she answered.

"So, are you still doing that?" Dr. Pete asked.

"No," she began, "well I guess maybe I have still been just a little withdrawn while I was working on the letters you had me write, but I have been very, very conscious of trying not to be short with anyone."

"So, how is it being expressed?" he asked.

"I just seem to be so impatient with everything," she said, "like if my computer is running too slow I find myself yelling at it."

"Yelling's not so bad," offered one of the women.

"Actually," Ann responded, "if I am going to be honest I am screaming at it! And I've become aware that I am slamming doors and drawers over the littlest things."

"Like what?" asked Dr. Pete.

Ann thought a moment, "Well, like the other day, the postal person was a bit later in delivering the mail and I was really upset about that and slammed the front door after getting the mail. I mean after all we pay these people good money, you think they could be on time is what I was thinking."

"But you didn't say anything to the postal person?" asked Dr. Pete.

"No, they were long gone," answered Ann, "And then when I was preparing a meal the other day it was taking forever for the water to boil on the stove and I started yelling at it and slamming cupboard doors."

"Do you ever get upset with yourself?"

"Yes, more and more," she began, "and over the littlest things, like hitting the wrong key on the keyboard when I am typing."

"Ann," said Dr. Pete very seriously, "You are angry. Now, tell me why."

Ann sat there thinking for what seemed like an eternity to her before finally answering, "I am angry at the people who hurt these wonderful ladies when they were just little girls. In fact, I think I am angry at anyone who would harm a child."

"What about those that hurt you when you were a little girl? Are you angry at them too?" Dr. Pete asked very gently.

"Oh I don't know," began Ann, "it is what..."

But Dr. Pete stopped her, "No Ann, it is not that simple. Are you angry at them? And if you are it is okay. No one is going to judge you or hurt you for saying so."

Ann was quiet again and then finally looked at Dr. Pete as she said, "Yes," she almost whispered.

"Yes, what?" he asked prodding her.

"Yes, I am angry at them," she said, but quietly.

"Good," he said gently, "You should be."

As the group was ending Ann apologized for taking up so much of the groups' time but as one lady responded, "No need to apologize. It's about time you took your turn and talked about how you are feeling because it helps us too." Dr. Pete nodded in agreement.

As she left, Dr. Pete said, "We will talk more about this in your session next week. In the meantime, be gentle with yourself and do something fun over the weekend." Ann promised that she would.

When she arrived home Ann gave Tom a call.

"Hey," she said.

"Hey back," he said, "how's it going?"

"Okay."

"Just okay?"

"Kind of an intense group session tonight, so I'm a little bit drained."

"Yes, you sound tired."

"If you are not busy on Saturday I was wondering if you would like to take a day drive up north as the colors are supposed to be really good already."

"Did you see that report on Channel 5 last night too because I was thinking the same thing?"

Ann chuckled, "I sure did."

"Let's leave really early, like about 5 a.m., then we can stop on the way for breakfast and be in the North Country by mid morning."

"It sounds great to me. Do you have an area in mind?"

"Yes, I was thinking of taking the country back roads up ending up in Springbrook."

"Isn't that where they have a number of art and craft stores?"

"Exactly, and they will still be open. So maybe we could also shop a little, have lunch, and then head east to take the main road back."

"I think it sounds great!"

"Great. I will see you at 5:00 a.m. on Saturday and don't forget your camera!"

"I'll have it charged and ready."

It had been a while since Ann had really done anything with any of her friends and she found herself really looking forward to Saturday. She felt comfortable with Tom, even if he asked about how therapy and that type of stuff were going. And, if she didn't feel like talking about it, he was accepting of that too.

It turned out to be kind of overcast on Saturday morning and thus was still darker when Tom picked her up.

"It's not going to rain is it?" she asked while getting into the car.

"No," just overcast for part of the morning and then the sun is to come out. But that's great for photo taking, or so they say."

"Why is that?"

"Supposedly when it is overcast the colors on the trees pop out more."

"Interesting, as I have always enjoyed taking photos of trees where the sun is shining through the leaves."

"I guess it works both ways then."

As they drove Tom shared much of what he had been involved in with his philanthropic work. Ann had always found this so extremely interesting. He then asked how her new book was coming and how therapy was going. She decided to share with him that she had gotten in touch with some anger.

He laughed as he said, "It's about time."

"I'm beginning to think that I was the only one who didn't know I was angry."

Tom laughed again, "Yup, usually the last to know as they say. So, how are you dealing with it?"

"Dr. Pete said that we will start working on it in our sessions next week and in the meantime he told me to have some fun this weekend," she answered.

"So that's why you called me?" Tom asked joyfully.

"Exactly. You told me that anytime I needed a play date to give you a call."

"I'm glad you did."

The rest of the day nothing else was mentioned in terms of Ann's background or her therapy. They simply enjoyed the day together. Both of them were amazed at how glorious the colors already were up north. Ann hadn't remembered seeing so many reds, bronzes and oranges as this year, and of course the yellows.

"It is like God threw different colored paint all over the countryside," she said at one point.

Tom said, "Yes, only He uses a different medium than paint."

"It reminds me of the old Petula Clark song, 'Color My World.'"

Tom started singing one of the lines.

Ann smiled.

Around every curve it just seemed to get more and more glorious and they couldn't take enough pictures trying to capture it all.

As they pulled into Springbrook Tom said, "Now that we have viewed the work of the Master we can look at the works of us His creatures, as we try to express the beauty that is His alone, always falling short with often beautiful yet poor imitations."

Ann was struck with the poetic beauty and truth of Tom's words to the point that she said nothing in return, but rather held them in her heart.

They saw any number of incredibly beautiful items that talented artists and crafts persons had made, but nothing that they couldn't live without. Eventually they made their way to a restaurant for lunch. Not only was the meal delicious, but their conversation about God, creation, beauty, and the marvels of it all was so engaging that they weren't aware of time slipping away.

"Let's continue this conversation in the car," Tom said.

On the way out of the restaurant Ann poked her head into their little gift shop and spotted the loveliest vase she had ever seen. It was done in all of the shades of the colors they had seen that day and embossed all over it were different shapes of leaves such as oak, maple, and birch.

"Oh," Ann said, "What a beautiful memento of this glorious day."

There was still a few hours of bright daylight left so they took advantage of it by taking numerous more photos. As the sun began to set they found a turnout which gave them a wonderful clear view of the sunset.

"I am always in such awe of sunsets," Ann said clicking away on her camera.

"And sunrises," said Tom, clicking away on his own camera.

And then the sun was gone. They drove for a few miles in silence watching the last glow of the sun over the horizon and the first stars leading their way into the dark of night. Tom put on some gentle classical music and each were left to their own thoughts of the day, their lives, and God.

They did stop for supper closer to home but the conversation was kind of mundane compared to the glories they each had experienced that day. Not that the conversation isn't good, Ann thought to herself, but it's like we are gently floating down from an incredible spiritual high that she personally did not want to end.

As Tom dropped her off at home Ann said, "What a grand gift God gave us this day."

"Yes He did," answered Tom. "It's kind of difficult coming back to the real world."

"It sure is, but thanks Tom for sharing it with me."

"And thank you."

Ann flicked the front porch light and waved as Tom pulled out of the drive and honked his horn. Ann immediately set her new vase on a shelf in the family room where it would catch the rays of the sun. And even though she was a little tired, or maybe relaxed would be a better term, she decided to download all of her photos from the day onto her computer as she was anxious to see how they had turned out. There were a few that were very simply awful, but a couple that were even more splendid than Ann had hoped for. She ended up staying up later than she had planned getting all of the photos organized into an album on one of the sites that was designed for that and then sending the link to Tom with a note thanking him for the day.

About five minutes later came a note from Tom with a link to the site where he had put his album together. Ann laughed as she wrote back, "I guess we will be seeing each other at the 10 a.m. Mass tomorrow!"

He wrote back, "Save me a place in the pew."

Ann grabbed Godzilla and Sir Lancelot and fell into a deep, restful and peaceful sleep.

At her session with Dr. Pete that following week he suggested that it might be time to begin to face those that had hurt her. Ann wanted to ask, who do I start with? but she already knew the answer, she would start with the easiest, her father.

Dr. Pete said, "I think that is a great one to start with, even though he is already deceased you can still write him a letter. Are your parents buried here?"

"No, after they retired they moved down south to South Carolina to be near one of my mother's sister and husband that they were close to. And that's where they died."

"Where your uncle that molested you now lives?"

"Yes."

"Are the aunt and uncle still living?"

"Yes, they are one of the ones who were thrilled to hear from me."

"It's too bad they are so far away."

"Actually, I have been thinking of going to see them and to visit the graves of my parents."

"Why don't we talk about that after you have finished the letters to them. Do you plan on seeing your uncle that molested you?"

"No," Ann said emphatically, "with the way that I feel right now I couldn't guarantee that I wouldn't deck him."

Dr. Pete tried to hide a giggle, but when he couldn't he said, "It's good to see the feisty side of you Ann. Just please don't act on it, okay?"

Ann promised that she wouldn't.

"Will you mail him the letter you are going to write to him?" he asked.

"I don't know. I'll have to wait and see how I feel about it after it's finished."

"Please remember that I will be praying for you Ann as you work on these letters."

She thanked him.

Ann absolutely dreaded having to write these letters, but she knew that it was necessary. Again, she decided to first do some work on her research book to kind of clear her mind to work on the three letters. So, come Saturday morning she was ready to begin. Coffee in hand and her stuffed animal friends at her side she sat at the computer and began, "Dear Dad..." "Better get a new box of tissues," she said to her stuffed animal friends. She worked on the letter to her father the better part of the day. She was surprised to find that she had actually reached a place of understanding and forgiveness towards him even though it wasn't total. And she found herself remembering some of the good times they had had together and the things that she appreciated about him not just as her father, but simply as a man and even felt sorry for him that his disease of alcoholism had never been diagnosed. It turned out to be a very freeing and healing letter for her to have written.

A couple of days later she started on the one to her mother which turned out to be much more difficult and not one that flowed as easily as the one to her father. She also found that she could only work on this letter for short periods at a time; there was just so much emotion attached to it that her mind couldn't keep up with them. So, in between she did other things and when ready would go back to the letter. Dr. Pete assured her that this was all perfectly normal and that she wasn't in any kind of a race to get her letters finished before anyone else. Ann laughed at his last comment. Besides, she told herself that they would soon be into the holiday season once again and she didn't want to ruin any of it by having all of these emotions stirred up and running all over the place. She also prayed that God would help her to keep all of that in check. But what if He doesn't? she asked herself. She could hear Father Jack's voice telling her to trust God;

that He knew what was best for her. "Even if I don't agree!" she said to her stuffed animal friends.

ANN'S STORY
Chapter 8
The Fall Holidays

Ann remembered one of her elderly relatives telling her when she was a child and complaining that Christmas was never going to get here, that when she got older time would go so fast she wouldn't believe it. "I think I have arrived at older," she said to her stuffed animals one morning. "Where has this past year gone? And I haven't even started my Christmas shopping yet!"

As she was having her morning coffee the phone rang; it was Randy.

"Hi Ann, how's it going?"

"Going well," she answered, "how about with you?"

"Really good. Actually, it's going great!"

Ann shared how happy she was to hear that.

"Did you know that I started chef school?" he asked.

"Yes, I had heard that. How is it going?"

"I just love it! Which is part of why I am calling. I would like to host Thanksgiving dinner this year."

"Wow. I bet we will all be in for some real treats."

"Well, I don't know about that, but I will give it my best shot."

"Are you going to have room in your apartment?"

"Actually, the building has a large social hall with a kitchen that I have reserved for the day."

"So, you will be able to do the cooking and baking there?"

"Some of it, but the bulk of it I will do in my apartment as that will be easier. However, I was wondering if you happen to have a roaster that I could borrow?"

"Gosh Randy, I'm sorry, but I don't. I think Marie and D.J. have one though."

"Yes, I've already talked with them, but I am going to need more than one. I've decided that using the roasters will be the best way to keep things like the turkey, mashed potatoes, dressing, and vegetables warm."

"Great idea."

"My mother has one, so all I need are two more."

"Is there anything you would like me to bring?"

"If you wouldn't mind, could you bring a centerpiece for the table? I saw the one you put together for Tom at Christmas last year and you have a real talent for arrangements."

"Thank you, I would be happy too. But is that all?"

"Well, Marie and D.J. are going to bring a veggie tray, Fred and Barb are going to her parents so won't be there. Tom is bringing the wine, Lynn is to bring some cheese and crackers and J.R. said that he and Maggie would provide napkins, utensils, cups and paper plates. And I figured that Don could handle relishes. So, I think that everything is covered."

"That still leaves a lot for you to prepare."

"I know, but I really want to do this for all of you. Plus, much of it I can prepare in advance."

"Well, please know that if you get stuck at the last minute just give me a call."

"I promise."

As soon as she hung up from talking to Randy she called Tom. "Hey sunshine," he said when he heard her voice.

"I just talked with Randy," she said.

"About Thanksgiving?"

"Yes and I think I have a great idea for a Christmas gift for him."

"A roaster?"

"Yes. A large one can be a little expensive so I was thinking that maybe you and I could share the cost and give it to him early."

"What a great idea! Should we go get it today?"

"Let's! I will bring along some Christmas wrapping paper and a large bow so we can wrap it and deliver it today too."

Ann then ran around getting dressed, grabbing paper, tape, ribbon, and a gift tag. She also took another gift tag and wrote on it "OPEN IMMEDIATELY."

The store clerk was gracious and allowed them to wrap the gift on the counter which made it so much easier. They then headed over to Randy's apartment.

"I wonder if he's still home," said Tom.

"I think he had today off, which is why he was making his phone calls," answered Ann.

Ann liked Randy's apartment complex. Each apartment was two stories, with the bedrooms upstairs and everything else on the first floor. Also there weren't a large number of units and most of them faced a center garden area. Tom quickly put the package down in front of Randy's door, rang the doorbell and then ran around the corner to hide with Ann. Right away Randy came to the door, looked at the package, looked around trying to locate who might have left it, and then kind of stood there just looking at it as if trying to decide what to do with it. Ann could hardly stifle her giggles. Finally Randy looked closer and saw the tag addressed to him with Ann and Tom's names on it, so he picked up the package.

Just then Ann and Tom jumped out and yelled, "Surprise!"

Randy was so startled that he tripped on the step and almost dropped the box.

"Oh my gosh! You two scared the living day lights out of me!" Randy said. "What are you up to and what is this, and come on in."

When they got inside Randy again asked, "What is this?"

"An early Christmas gift from Ann and me," answered Tom.

"Go on, open it," encouraged Ann.

Carefully Randy took off the large bow and gently separated the paper from the tape.

"It's too nice to rip," he said apologetically. When he saw the picture on the box he said, "Oh my gosh! You two! Oh this is so great! I can't tell you how often I will be using this! I don't know what to say!"

Tom laughed, "I think you are expressing yourself quite well."

"Oh thank you both of you," Randy said giving each of them a hug.

"Now, not only do you have your own, but also you only have to find one more for Thanksgiving," said Ann.

"Actually," he began, "my mother called this morning and one of my aunts has one that I can borrow. So, now I am definitely all set."

They visited for a while listening to Randy's stories of everything he was learning in school. Ann was absolutely fascinated, not just by the stories, but also by Randy's enthusiasm.

On the way home Ann mentioned Randy's excitement.

Tom said, "I noticed it too. It is so wonderful when someone finds what they are passionate about."

"Well, our friend Randy has definitely found his passion," Ann answered.

After she got home Ann thought about what she was passionate about. There were so many things that she enjoyed doing, but she was not entirely sure passionate was a word that she would apply to any of them. "Hmm," she said aloud to her stuffed animal friends, "I will have to think more about that one. But right now I want to start working on the gift list for my friends." As she wrote the names down she thought about what each of their passions might be. "Like with Randy, his passion is cooking," she said to her stuffed animal friends, "so we got him a gift to do with that. I think that is what I will try to do with each of my friends this year."

Ann researched most of the afternoon on the internet, gaining ideas and actually finding gifts that she thought her friends would enjoy. When she had a good basic list of ideas she laughed, "I think I have found my passion!" All of the gift ideas that she had come up with for her friends were BOOKS! "Duh," she said aloud as she looked around her office at the shelves filled with books, "and then there's my library room!"

Ann really liked to shop locally whenever she could, so the next day she telephoned her favorite Catholic Book and Gift store in the mall where she had purchased the majority of her gifts last year. Her special angel clerk was working and greeted Ann warmly. Ann shared with her that she was looking for some special books. The clerk recommended that Ann email her the titles and authors, which would make it a little easier as there were customers in the store at the time. Ann also told her that there was no hurry on her response as these were gifts for Christmas. The clerk expressed her gratitude for shopping early. Ann laughed, "One of my quirks."

Ann then sent off the email with the list of books that she was looking for. Within a couple of hours the clerk had emailed Ann back saying that she had all but two of the books in stock; one she could order, the other was not in stock through any of her regular distributors, but she recommended an independent book store that might have it. Ann emailed in return, first thanking her for all of her work and then asking her to set aside the books she did have for her and order the one she could.

Ann then called the independent book store and they did have the remaining book. Ann went by and purchased that one right away.

About a week later the clerk from the Catholic Book and Gift store called and said that the book she had ordered was in. Ann said that she would be in that day.

While at the store she decided to also purchase the Catechism of the Catholic Church and the U.S. Catholic Catechism for Adults for her brother. While the clerk was getting everything checked out and in bags they chatted. Ann again thanked her for the icon and shared just some of her journey this past year. The woman was so supportive and sympathetic offering her continuing prayers for her that Ann became a little embarrassed and wondered to herself why she had told pretty much a perfect stranger what had happened to her.

As she left the store Ann thought to herself how incredibly easy her Christmas shopping had been this year. She had decided not to send gift cards to her nieces and nephews as they were all young adults now and working. Plus, she never heard from them to even let her know if they received her gifts let alone any kind of a "thank you." As she placed her purchases in the car she thought to herself, I think I'm just simply at a place in my life where I am no longer going to beg people to be a part of my life. Either they want to be or they don't.

Ann decided that she would start wrapping her purchases right away. Another habit she had developed so that she could better enjoy the Advent and Christmas season. As she laid all of her purchases on the table she noticed an additional book. It was a Catholic spiritual book on healing from childhood sexual abuse. Inside there was a piece of paper with a hand written note from the clerk. "So that you may continue to heal."

"What an incredibly generous woman that clerk is," Ann said to herself and decided right then and there to do something special for her for Christmas.

As Ann wrapped each book she thought of the faces of her friends and her brother praying for each one and hoping that they really enjoyed her choices.

Ann continued her work on her research book and was glad that she had set aside her children's book and working on the difficult letters to her mother and the uncle until after the holidays. Not that she didn't think about them and formulated some ideas that she would occasionally jot down, but she really was much more comfortable keeping all of those emotions at bay. Dr. Pete didn't entirely agree with her, but understood and accepted her choice.

As she told him, "Hey, Thanksgiving and Christmas come only once a year and I want to enjoy them. All of that stuff has been there for years and it can wait another month or so before I have to re-visit all of it."

Of course she kept attending the group sessions and was still amazed at how differently each woman had been affected by her molestation. The major problems however appeared to be relationship issues with those that were close to them; intimacy issues with husbands and lots of trust problems, that is, being able to trust anyone.

But she didn't want to think about it too much outside of the group. This was her favorite time of the year and she was going to keep it that way! So, she went to work on the decorations for Thanksgiving Day. She decided that for the centerpiece she wanted to use as many natural items as she could. So, one morning she set out early for the nursery just to get some ideas. And she came home with more than ideas; almost the entire back of her SUV was filled with flats of flowers. She had found some very small, almost miniature individual fall mum plants in so many colors that she was able to get enough different colors for every person who would be at the dinner. They ranged from white to pink to lavender to purple to yellow to copper to orange to red to burgundy and even a green one! She got three of each color; a large white pumpkin and two smaller ones plus ribbon. Whatever artificial items she needed she knew that she already had at home.

Cleaning out the centers of the pumpkins was the biggest mess and she was very glad that she had decided to do that part in the kitchen. Plus, these needed to dry out a bit before she did anything else with them.

The next day as she continued her work on the Thanksgiving decorations she played classical music and even danced now and again with various members of her stuffed animal family. "I wonder what the neighbors would think if they could see me," she said to Godzilla as they twirled around the room. But actually, she didn't really care what they would think as she was thoroughly enjoying herself.

Ann was so happy with the decorations that she could hardly wait for Thanksgiving Day; so she was doubly thrilled when Randy called and asked if she could actually come over the evening prior to get everything decorated because as he put it, "It is going to be one crazy day on Thursday!"

When she arrived at his apartment complex Randy already had plastic tablecloths on the table that were of a pale orange color.

"Oh Randy," she said, "this color is going to be perfect!" She then set the centerpiece in the middle of the table at which time Randy began "oohing and aahhing." "Oh Ann, it is perfect!" he said. Ann had to agree. She had set ten of the small mums inside the large white pumpkin and added a few artificial leaves of the fall colors, but what really set it off was the strand of battery operated twinkle lights she had placed throughout the display. Just about then Maggie and J.R. arrived with all of the paper goods and began to set the table. They also had found fall colored paper goods and utensils. In the meantime Ann set up the two smaller pumpkins on the food table. They were identical to the large one only they had just five each of the small mums. She had also put matching ribbon around the remaining ten plants and placed them by each place setting as a memento for each person to take home.

Randy had even put together a free standing menu board and had written on it what the menu of the day would be.

"That is a really special touch," Ann said.

"And look at all of those fancy names," added Maggie. "I feel like I am in a five-star restaurant."

Randy began to blush a little, "I just hope that my cooking stands up to the fancy names."

J.R. said, "Hey dude, I just know it's going to be great!"

Everyone then decided to leave to allow Randy to get back to his kitchen.

Ann then asked, "Hey, J.R. did you get moved yet? I never heard that you needed help."

"Yes," he said, "I decided to hire movers because Maggie and I jointly like the majority of the furniture that was already in my house. It made it so much easier on the two of us."

"And," Maggie said, "the person buying my house is also purchasing the appliances and most of my furniture. There are only a couple of items I am taking to the new house like my grandmother's cedar chest. In fact, we have already moved most of my stuff over there."

"Wow," said Ann.

"Yeah," said Maggie, "It has been kind of a whirlwind. I am just so glad that you and I spent that day getting all of the decorations ready for the wedding. Otherwise I would be going bonkers right now with the wedding only a week away."

J.R. added, "Maggie is such a good planner. Right now we have nothing left to do for the wedding except to get dressed!"

Maggie and Ann laughed.

"Well, I do have to get my hair done too," added Maggie.

"And we will all get the church decorated on Thursday," added Ann.

"Anyway, Father Jack suggested that Maggie and I take a day and just go away. We are not to talk about the wedding at all, but rather are to simply enjoy each other's company and remind ourselves why we are getting married," said J.R.

"What a great idea," said Ann.

"So, we are going to do that on Monday," said Maggie.

"By the way," asked Ann, "Are you going on a honeymoon?"

"Yes," they both said together.

J.R. continued, "This is so amazing. One of my uncles owns a cabin in Vermont and they offered it to us for our honeymoon."

Maggie added, "I've always wanted to go to Vermont and we both love to ski, so this was perfect."

"Plus," said J.R., "they are there over this long weekend and told us not to worry about anything because they will get everything prepared."

"Including food," said Maggie. "They asked us what foods we didn't like or might be allergic to and his aunt said that they would have the refrigerator stocked and in the freezer she would put meals for us that we simply had to pop into the microwave. Can you believe it?"

"Are they coming to the wedding?" asked Ann.

"No, they can't," answered J.R. "so they want us to pick a night while we are there so they can take us out to dinner. I told them that they didn't have to that the cabin was more than enough of a wedding gift."

"And that's the other thing," added Maggie, "J.R.'s parents and mine split the cost of the airline tickets and the car rental as our wedding gift. We are so incredibly blessed."

Ann smiled, "I really think that Heaven is in charge of this match."

Maggie hugged J.R. and said, "I agree." J.R. kind of blushed.

As Ann left she told them that she would see them at Mass in the morning.

Ann thought about Maggie and J.R. as she drove home and it wasn't that she didn't feel excited and happy for them, but things sure did seem to going perfectly for them. "Definitely not the way my life has been," she said aloud. Then added, "I think a little green-eyed monster just slipped into the car. And what was it that someone said not long ago? Ah, yes, 'The next person's pain is no greater or lesser it is simply different.' And I really don't know what has been painful for either Maggie or J.R., and I definitely don't know what the future is going to bring for them or for me for that matter." Ann said a quick prayer that God remain with Maggie and J.R. and bless them abundantly.

Father Jack's Thanksgiving homily was particularly poignant as far as Ann was concerned. He talked about the need to be grateful for not only the good things in our lives, but also for the trials that come our way.

"Many of the great saints were thrilled that they were able to share in the physical suffering of our Lord," he began. "However, most of us will be thrilled to simply be saints with a small 's.' Personally, I am hoping that I can sneak into Heaven when the Lord isn't looking." The congregation laughed. "But seriously," he continued, "if we look at the challenges we encounter in our lives, however small or great they may be, and offer them back to God not only for our own sins, but also for the sins of those we love, whether living or deceased, then our suffering is not in vain." He let that thought sink in before he added, "Also think about what gifts you may have gained from the suffering and challenges you have encountered. Are you a stronger, more courageous person because of something you had to endure? Do you appreciate something you gained, whether it is a job, an education, or a better relationship because you had to work hard for it? How has what you have been through being used to help others who have encountered the same thing? And finally, ask yourself, how have my struggles, my pain, my suffering, my losses, and my disappointments drawn me closer to God?"

Ann could hardly concentrate on the rest of the Mass as Father Jack's words echoed in her mind and found their way to her soul. She almost wished that she didn't have to go to the gathering, instead wishing that it was a hot summer day and she could just float on a rubber raft in the middle of the lake letting Father Jack's words wash over her like the waves and the sun and become a part of her forever. Instead, she forced herself back to reality and as she left Mass she was at least able to say to Father Jack, "Powerful!"

He smiled as he answered, "It was the Holy Spirit." Their eyes met at that moment and Ann knew that Father Jack knew that the sermon had touched her soul. "Have a most blessed Thanksgiving Ann," he said nodding.

"You too Father, you too," she answered.

As Ann arrived at her car she realized that it was only a little after 10 a.m. and that she didn't need to be at Randy's until 11:30 thus she could have at least a half hour by the lake so off she sped. Getting a car with a sun roof was something that Ann had thoroughly enjoyed having and today was one of those days. Even though the air was crisp, with even a hint of snow in it, the sun was bright and felt warm through the window.

As she pulled into a spot by the lake she noticed that there was a bit of a wind that was causing some pretty good sized waves. "I guess floating on the lake today wouldn't be quite as relaxing as I imagined," she giggled to herself. As she reflected on Father Jack's words she knew that it was going to take her awhile to absorb all that he had been saying and how it applied to her, but for the moment she was happy to be able to recognize that it did apply to her. Her next step would then be, "What to do with it?" she said aloud. She prayed for guidance and after a few moments it came, "Thank you God. I may not totally accept nor understand what I went through or what I am going through today as a result of it, not yet anyway, but thank you. May I draw closer to you because of it." Ann felt a peace come over her that was different than anything she had ever felt before in her life and somehow she knew she was going to be okay.

She arrived at Randy's just as Tom did who immediately asked, "Where did you take off to?"

"Just had something to take care of," she answered.

"Well, I don't know what it was, but you are glowing," he said. She laughed.

Randy had really gone all out with the food as the aromas coming from the social room were incredible. And a number of fellow tenants poked their head in the door on their way out and said, "I wish we were staying here for dinner."

Or, "The smells from your apartment have been driving us nuts for the last two days; I hope there will be leftovers." Randy was in his glory.

He had also finished his huge chalk board showing the menu for the day:

Hors d'oeuvres
Fromage et Craquelins ala Lynn
Legumes et Trempette ala Marie et D.J. et
Petit Patricia

Wine
Vin Blanc du jour ala Tom

Main Course
Roast Turkey du jour
Pommes et Crème
Sauce de giblet
Dressing ala Fruits et Noix
Braised Vegetable Medley
Croissants
Sauce aux Canneberges
Relishes ala Don

Dessert
Mom's Pumpkin Pie

Environment
Arts de la Table (Dinnerware) ala Maggie et
J.R.
Ambience ala Ann

The rest of the gang arrived and there were many "ooohs" and "aaahs." Even little Patricia clapped her hands as she walked in.

"I didn't know you knew French," said J.R.

"Not really," answered Randy, "the internet is a great resource sometimes." Everyone laughed.

Marie and D.J. had brought Patricia's high chair so she was able to sit at the table with everyone. Randy asked Tom to lead the prayer and as everyone folded their hands so did little Patricia. Marie whispered, "She's just learning how."

"Dear Father," began Tom, "we thank you for the many gifts you have bestowed upon each and every one of us. We thank you for this abundance of food and for the gift of the chefs who prepared it. We ask you to be with those who do not have enough to eat this day. We thank you also for the gifts of friendship and family; please bless those here today and those who could not be with us. And in a very special way we thank you for the gift of Your Son and our faith in our lives. Amen."

Little Patricia said something that kind of sounded like "Amen" and then clapped her hands.

Marie shook her head, "It is something that D.J. taught her."

D.J. laughed, "The priest chaplain at the college I attended used to do that before each meal."

After they had all gotten their food and were seated at the table Randy said, "While we are eating I would like us to go around the table and just mention one or two things that we are grateful for from this past year."

It didn't take long for Maggie and J.R. to come up with what they were thankful for; "each other" and "Our new home," added J.R. "And the sale of our previous homes," added Maggie.

D.J. said that he was grateful for his beautiful wife and daughter and that he had a job that he loved.

Marie was also grateful for her family, "And all of you," she added.

"I too am grateful for all you," began Don, "and for my sister and for also having a job that I love."

Lynn giggled, "I too am grateful for my brother and all of you, but also that we live in a country like America. Not that it is perfect, but it so much better than many other places."

It was Ann's turn, "I am grateful for the support, friendship and love of all of you; more than you know. But I am also especially grateful this year for the gift of my Catholic Faith."

Tom too was grateful for the friendships and his Faith, but also that God had blessed him so that he was also able to help those who are in need.

Randy finished with, "I am grateful for all of you, that I got into chef's school and that I was able to get this meal on the table without too many mishaps." Everyone cheered and of course shared with him how incredibly delicious everything was.

As they were eating dessert, Lynn said, "Don and I were talking this past week, and as my apartment building also has a social room like this, he and I would like to host Christmas this year for whoever is not going to be with family."

"I've already checked with Fred and Barb," said Don, "and because they are at her parents for Thanksgiving they will be going to his parents Christmas Day. So, they won't be here."

"Gosh," said Marie, "same with us. We will be with D.J.'s parents Christmas eve and my parents Christmas day."

"I can be there," said Randy, "as the restaurant will be closed Christmas day."

"Me too," said Ann.

"Count me in," added Tom.

Maggie looked at J.R. as she said, "I'm afraid that we won't be able to make it either. We decided that for now Christmas Eve is for J.R. and I so we have to hit both parents on Christmas Day. Gratefully my parents are eating early and J.R.'s parents not until evening."

"I already feel fat just thinking about it," said J.R. Everyone laughed.

"So, there will be five for dinner," said Lynn. "I think I can handle that in my apartment."

"Just let us know what you would like us to bring," said Randy.

"Okay," said Lynn, "Don and I are still kind of working on the main part of the meal."

"Yes," said Don, "I wanted us to get through Thanksgiving first. Hey, I just had another great idea!"

"Another idea," teased his sister.

Don scowled at her just a little. "Yes," he continued, "Because so many are going to be busy on Christmas Day itself, why don't we also have a separate evening like we did last Christmas just to exchange gifts. We could do that in the social room at my condo building as it will already be decorated."

"But, isn't that a lot of work for you and Lynn to host both events?" asked Ann.

"No," said Don, "I was thinking that we could do it after dinner one evening and I would just have drinks and desserts. You know simple things like Christmas cookies from the bakery, coffee, soda; you know that kind of thing."

"You know," said Lynn, "that IS a good idea!"

"It won't be fancy, but at least we will all be together," Don added, "and I will get in touch with Fred and Barb tomorrow."

"You know," said Randy, "I would be more than happy to bake the cookies."

Then Tom said, "And I can bring some of that hot cider I made last year."

"Do you think anyone will want coffee?" asked Marie. "Because we have a little larger coffee maker."

"And it's my turn to bring paper plates, napkins and cups," said Ann.

"I think we've just planned two Christmas gatherings," laughed Lynn.

"Just so all of you don't forget the wedding next week," laughed J.R.

They spent the rest of the day simply enjoying each other's company, telling stories, and laughing. Of course, after the meal little Patricia was ready for a nap so Marie lay her on the couch that was in the room and covered her up. "She can sleep through anything," J.R. said.

At the end of the afternoon everyone pitched in and helped Randy to take everything back up to his apartment. "At least there aren't many dishes because of cooking ahead as I just did the dishes as I went," said Randy. "Now, I'll just basically have the roasters to do."

Ann reminded everyone to take one of the little mums as that was their memento for the day. She also left the two smaller pumpkins with Randy for his apartment.

"This was such a great idea," said Marie, "And I am sure you saw which color that Patricia chose."

"The yellow one," giggled Ann.

As soon as everything was all cleaned up and the cars loaded there were hugs all around and of course great compliments to the chef Randy. Ann noted that he was still beaming from ear to ear as everyone pulled out to head home. She made a mental note to write him a very special "Thank You" note using the photograph she had taken of him standing next to his menu board.

"This was one of the best Thanksgivings ever," she said to all of her stuffed animals as she came into the house. "Thank you Lord for this day, for my friends, for my Catholic Faith, and my life," she said aloud.

ANN'S STORY
Chapter 9
An Elegant Wedding

Ann was really getting excited about Maggie and J.R.'s wedding. They had had snow that week so the ground was covered and looked beautiful, but all of the streets and sidewalks were all clear. "Beauty without the mess," she said to her stuffed animal friends.

The bridesmaid dress and small cape hung over her closet door and the white muff was in a special plastic bag on top of her dresser. Red had never been one of Ann's favorite colors to wear, but this dress was so elegant that she felt even she looked good in it. She could hardly wait to see the guys in their tuxes. If men, and women for that matter, only knew how good they looked all dressed up, she thought, instead of running around half dressed as most of them do these days. She then chuckled to herself, "I think my age is showing."

The dress rehearsal went really well and with all of them pitching in, including Sally the lady responsible for the environment at the church, they were able to get all of the decorating of the church done quickly. Earlier in the day they had all gone over to the reception hall and completed the decorating there. Even with all of the overhead lights on at both places Maggie was so pleased, and so was J.R. on how all of it had turned out.

"And with all of the lights subdued and the candles lit or turned on, it is going to add an elegance to everything," said Sally. "Also, I don't want you to have to worry about all of that so I will be here to make sure everything is all set."

"Oh Sally, how can we ever thank you?" asked Maggie.

"I am happy to do it," said Sally.

The next morning Ann, Lynn, Maggie, and her sister all had hair appointments at the same time and as part of her thank you gift, Maggie had also arranged for all of them to have manicures.

"I feel so pampered and spoiled," said Ann. Maggie then shared that J.R. had also arranged for the guys to get trims, shaves, and manicures too.

"I won't recognize my brother," Lynn laughed.

As Don was driving his sister to the wedding Tom offered to pick Ann up. After Ann finished dressing she stood in front of the long mirror in her room. "Not bad for a gal who loves to wear blue jeans and flannel shirts," she said to the mirror. "Even my mother would faint at this sight," she added. "And what do all of you think?" she asked of the stuffed animals in her room as she turned and did a little curtsy. "Elegant you say? Charming? Lovely? What? Beautiful? Oh, Godzilla and Sir Lancelot you are such charmers," she said. Just then the doorbell rang.

As she answered Tom said, "Wow. You look gorgeous!"

"A little different than blue jeans and flannel shirts," she answered.

"That's my Ann," he smiled. "Just say thank you."

So Ann did a little curtsy and said, "Thank you my lord. And might I add that thou is looking rather dapper this evening."

With that Tom made a bow as he answered, "Why thank you my lady."

Ann did feel like a very elegant lady that evening and was hoping that was really how she looked. Being feminine was never one of her strong suits, but when Tom held out his arm for her to take she felt a little more feminine. When they got to the church J.R. and Randy were already there and Ann got to peak at them as they went into the side room where they were to wait. Tom escorted Ann to the room where Maggie and the bridesmaids were gathering and then went to join the men. Don and Lynn arrived shortly thereafter.

Of course there were last minute things like getting the roses pinned onto the fur muffs and the wrist corsages on the mothers. Maggie looked absolutely radiant and ravishing. Ann asked her if she was nervous.

Maggie smiled, "J.R. asked me the same thing last evening and, as I told him, we have talked about this, we know this is what we want and more importantly are confident that this is also what God wants us to do, so there is nothing to be nervous about."

"Beautifully put," answered Ann.

"J.R. feels the same way," Maggie continued. "I'm just concerned that I am going to trip or do something colossal like that."

"Well, didn't Father Jack say that at least one thing would go wrong?" Ann asked.

"Oh and it did," Maggie said, "The florist forgot my bouquet and had to run back to the shop to get it."

"So, there you are. The one thing has already happened," Ann answered.

Pretty soon it was time for them to go to the vestibule for the entrance. Maggie and J.R. had opted for the same procession in as had Barb and Fred at their wedding as they really liked the symbolism of walking in with their parents and meeting at the half way point of the aisle; then finishing the walk to the altar together.

Don and Maggie's younger sister went first; then it was Ann's turn to meet Tom at the half way point. She said a silent prayer that she wouldn't trip. She was so focused on how she was walking and keeping her eyes on Tom she didn't look to see where their friends were sitting. You could almost hear an audible sigh of relief as she took his arm for the final walk to the altar. Once she was there she then was able to look around a bit. The church was incredibly beautiful with the candles down the aisle and in the windows. There were just no words to describe how elegant it was. Ann also spotted Marie, D.J., Fred, and Barb. They had decided to leave the children home so that they could have a 'date night' of sorts.

Finally J.R. with his parents and Maggie with her parents came to their respective doors. Ann had never seen J.R. looking so handsome and of course Maggie was glowing.

The music and the readings all spoke of Maggie and J.R.'s relationship as they had personally chosen both. And, as always, Father Jack did an outstanding job on the homily. It was all simply beautiful.

When they got to the reception Ann again couldn't believe how beautiful the hall looked with the lights subdued. It was a continuation of the elegance that had been in the church. The glass sleigh centerpieces with the battery candles and the twinkle lights just glistened. Ann felt a moment of pride at having been able to be a small part of that with Maggie.

As their entire group is not huge drinkers the only alcoholic beverage that was offered was wine at the tables. Ann was grateful because so often people get drunk just to get drunk and then simply act stupid ruining an otherwise elegant and special occasion. They had also opted for a small quartet to play background music during dinner and some dance music for only an hour or so after dinner. Their feeling was that you could celebrate and be joyful without a 'party bash' kind of atmosphere. Plus, they had a plane to catch in the morning to Vermont for their honeymoon. They had also rented a room at a hotel near the airport that they kept confidential.

As Tom was driving Ann home he said, "That is one of the most beautiful weddings I have ever seen." Ann agreed. "It was simple and yet so very elegant," he added.

"And I thoroughly appreciated that we only had wine with dinner and that it wasn't dancing half the night," Ann answered.

"Me too," said Tom, "It's gotten so that if I am invited to a wedding that I will only stay for the dinner. I really do not want to spend my evening watching people act stupid. And sometimes I won't even go to the dinner preferring to be there for the most important part, the wedding itself."

"Me too," she answered.

As Tom unlocked the front door for Ann he said, "Ann, I've never seen you looking lovelier."

She started to say something smart but caught herself, "Thank you," she answered simply.

"And it's not just the dress, but something that is coming from inside of you," he said.

Again she simply answered, "Thank you."

"Anyway," he continued, "I know that this has been a really rough year for you and you've done a lot of hard work to heal and I just wanted you to know that it shows."

"Thank you Tom, that means a lot."

Tom blinked his car lights as he left and Ann flicked the porch light back at him. She placed the rose from her muff in the refrigerator and then on a whimsy she put on some music and took turns dancing with many of her stuffed animals. It had been a magical night and she didn't want it to end. So, after she finally turned off the music and headed to her room she started singing one of her very favorite Broadway songs, "I Could Have Danced All Night."

Ann fell asleep with a smile on her face.

ANN'S STORY
Chapter 10
A Fun Christmas

The next couple of weeks seemed to literally fly by. Maggie and J.R. had already returned from their honeymoon and were trying to get settled in their new home in between working and doing a little decorating for Christmas. Maggie was so excited about her first Christmas with J.R.

The group had decided that every year they would try to set the Friday evening prior to Christmas as their gathering night, unless of course it was Christmas Eve and then they would do the week prior.

"At least this way we can all have it on our calendars," said Tom, "and still leave Christmas Eve and day open for family events." Everyone thought it a great idea. They also decided that it would not involve a meal, but rather just dessert and drinks.

Ann continued with her group and individual sessions, but right now the individual sessions were used more in trying to understand some of the things that were discussed in the group. Dr. Pete knew that Ann preferred that the focus be on the others right now because she wanted to try to enjoy the holidays. As he had already told her he didn't necessarily agree with her, but allowed it also understanding that each person needs to progress at their own pace. Plus she was learning a lot about how abuse and molest affect a person. Ann had been particularly struck by one woman's story surrounding the birth of her first daughter.

"I was so overly protective, even for a new mother, almost to the point of being neurotic," she shared. "I wouldn't let my husband be alone with her. And I began having nightmares about children being hurt. This was all before my memories of being molested myself surfaced."

Ann did share with the group the experience she had had with little Patricia on the camping trip.

"Same thing," said Dr. Pete. "For someone who has been molested there are pretty clear 'trigger' moments in that person's life when the memories both recovered and not rise to the surface and can create problems. Of course this depends on the age the girl was when she was molested, but generally speaking the events that serve as triggers are first, when the girl begins dating for the first time; second, when she gets married and has physical intimacy with her husband for the first time; third, the birth of her first daughter; and lastly, when her daughter gets to dating age and then marries."

"It sure can mess up her relationships," commented one woman, "I know it did with me. Thank God that I have a very patient husband who loves me as neither of us understood why I was having so many problems with our sexual intimacy. I am just grateful that I have finally discovered the reason and we have been able to work on it together."

Another woman said, "I almost pushed my teenage daughter away completely because I had been so overly protective for much of her life that she didn't think I trusted her. And this was even with me knowing what had happened to me! But I hadn't worked on any of the issues until I got into therapy. Only then was I finally able to explain to her that I did trust her but I was afraid for her and just didn't want her to be hurt as I was. It was a good talk and we both cried."

"The difficult part for me," began another woman, "was that I did not want to tell anyone, not even my husband, what had happened. So when we were at one of my family's gatherings and the relative was there who had molested me I would not let my daughter leave my side. And when that got to be too difficult to do if I knew that person was going to be there I said that we simply were not going. Of course neither my family nor my husband could understand and simply thought I was being snobbish. I was finally able to tell everyone what had happened."

Dr. Pete said, "As painful as this is for all of you, we can also see how it has affected those around us too; from our children, to our immediate and extended families. As we heal we are better able to balance our own fears with good common sense."

"I think what bothers me," said Ann in one session, "is that from listening to the women and you Dr. Pete it appears this becomes a lifetime of therapy sessions and personally I don't know if I want to sign up for that."

Dr. Pete smiled, "I know it seems that way, but it's not. What many clients do after the initial, more intensive sessions is that when they reach one of those milestones, or something in their lives triggers reactions that they know are not entirely normal, they come back to therapy for a time to deal with it. It may be only one session."

"I am really glad to hear that," said Ann.

So far this had been a really good holiday, or as Father Jack liked to call it, "Holy Day" season. Thanksgiving was wonderful and that weekend she had been able to get her entire house inside and out and decorated. First it was the wedding and now Christmas.

As she prepared her large basket filling it with all of the gifts for everyone for their evening together she thought about what she was going to wear. Don had said, dress comfortable. For Ann that had usually meant blue jeans and a large flannel shirt but being so dressed up for the wedding had done something for her. "Not to mention the therapy sessions," she said to all of her stuffed animal friends in the family room. "Dr. Pete said that I was trying to hide my body and my femininity as a way of protecting myself. Not to mention that I didn't think too highly of myself anyway," she continued. But last week on a whim she had stopped at a store in the mall that had some very pretty Christmas sweaters in the window. Some of them were very fancy, more for dressy occasions but a couple of them were just nice casual sweaters with Christmas trees or winter items embroidered on them. Ann found a wonderful vest that was done in blocks of white, green, and red with each block having a contrasting colored tree, snowflake, heart and other seasonal symbols, and she decided that it would look great with a white blouse and dark green corduroy pants. Plus, she had found some dark green socks with symbols of the holiday. She was actually kind of excited over her finds as it was so different from her usual attire.

Ann left a little early to go over to Don's condo because she was bringing the cups, plates, and napkins and thought that she should arrive before the food and drinks did. Don was already in the social room and Ann thought he seemed a little nervous, "Hey Don, excited about hosting your first gathering?" she asked.

"I sure am. I think this will be fun," he answered.

Pretty soon everyone else arrived and of course Randy had outdone himself with the cookies.

"Oh Randy," began Marie, "these are too beautiful to eat."

D.J. laughed, "Patricia and I will have not problem." Marie gave him a gentle elbow in the ribs shaking her head. When they set little Patricia down she immediately headed for the gifts under the tree.

"She moves so fast these days," said Marie as she took off after her.

Of course everyone wanted to hold John Paul. "He has grown so much just since his baptism," said Ann. "It's hard to believe that he is four months old already. And what a cutie."

John Paul gave her a huge smile as she held him.

"I think he likes you," said Barb.

Ann smiled, "Hello handsome boy. Yes you. Such a precious boy." John Paul gave her another smile.

As soon as everyone got their drinks and were settled Don offered to play Santa. Ann was so excited for everyone to open the gifts she had chosen for them. She enjoyed that more than receiving gifts. Even as a kid it was a big joke in her house that she would give so many "hints" as to what she had bought that her family had already guessed what she had gotten them long before Christmas Day. I would just get so excited, she thought to herself.

Fred and Barb asked that their gifts be handed out first as they were all the same. It was a beautiful 5x7 photo of their family in a frame.

"We just wanted to share our beautiful boy with everyone," said Barb.

D.J. laughing then said, "You can do the same with our gift." It was also a 5x7 photo of their family.

"I think we are doing it again," said Marie, "all thinking alike." They had a separate photo for Tom and Ann of little Patricia by herself as her gift to them as her godparents. She was holding one of her stuffed animals and looked just as cute as a button.

"Our turn," said Maggie, "and yes, hand all of these out first and these second."

J.R. was shaking his head as everyone opened the first gift from them. It was a 5x7 photo of the wedding party.

"Great minds and all of that," said J.R.

"And now for something different," added Marie.

Everyone opened their second gift from them. Each couple and then individuals received one of the glass sleigh candle holders from their wedding.

"Oh Marie and J.R.," said Lynn, "What a special gift."

"We wanted all of you to have a memento of our wedding," said Maggie. "I also planned to have four extra as we are hoping that the Lord will give us at least four children."

"So, when they get to be adults they each will receive one also," added J.R.

"What a wonderful idea," said Ann.

Don then handed out his gifts which was a gift certificate to the Catholic book and gift store in the mall. Tom also gave out gift certificates to everyone, but it was to a major book store.

"I will definitely have fun in both of those places," said Ann.

Then Lynn passed out her gifts which were different for each person. Ann received another gift certificate but to the craft store. "You are so talented in that area that I thought you might really enjoy getting more supplies," Lynn said.

"I definitely will," answered Ann.

Randy also gave out gift certificates, but they were personally made by him on his computer. His gift was a meal prepared for each family or single for up to eight people in their home. Of course, everyone loved it.

Randy blushed a little as he answered, "It's a good way for me to practice."

Ann's gifts were the last to be opened as she had arrived first and the basket had been shoved back under the tree.

Randy received his first saying, "But you and Tom already got me the roaster."

"This is just a little something that reminded me of you," answered Ann.

It was a book and Randy read the title, "'The Brother Lawrence Collection'. Is this the same St. Lawrence who is the patron of chefs?"

"No," answered Ann, "this is a different Lawrence who was a simple monk, but his work in the monastery was in the kitchen. From his writings one can see what a holy man he was." Randy thanked her.

Fred and Barb opened theirs next. It was the same book on Catholic parenting that she had given to Marie and D.J. last Christmas.

Barb said, "I had planned on asking Marie what the title of that book was."

Ann also gave John Paul a cloth book about the first Christmas.

For Maggie and J.R. she had chosen one of Christopher West's books, "Heaven's Song," which explores the "Song of Songs" from the Bible along with the "Theology of the Body" talks given by Pope John Paul II.

"Oh Ann, this is wonderful," said Maggie, "We had his 'Theology of the Body' talks as part of our Marriage Preparation classes and really wanted to learn more."

Lynn's book was on the life of St. Catherine of Alexandria, who is one of the patronesses of secretaries, as Lynn worked as an Administrative Assistant. "It's not very long as not much is known about her so I also got you one of her medals," said Ann.

As D.J. is an attorney, Ann had gotten him a book by St. Thomas More, "The Sadness of Christ," as he is one of the patrons of attorneys. And for Marie an unusual book about the Gospel writers by Robert K. McIver. "He's not Catholic, but the title and the book looked really interesting and I thought you, as a storyteller yourself, would enjoy a book on the most famous story writers of our faith."

"Oh Ann," said Marie, "This looks fascinating. You always choose such interesting gifts for us."

She gave little Patricia a children's book of saints that included the lives of her patron saints: St. Patricia of Naples, St. Jane Frances de Chantal, and St. Michael the Archangel. "I know that she is still a little young, but I wanted to add to her library," Ann said.

Tom opened his package next and found two books by Blessed Mother Teresa "No Greater Love" and "A Simple Path."

"Oh Ann, I am such a great admirer of hers, how did you know?" Tom asked.

"With all of the wonderful work that you do, I just knew that she must be one of your favorites."

Don was the last to open his. As he picked it up he laughingly said, "Gee, I wonder what this is?" His book was "The Etymologies of Isidore of Seville." "The patron saint of computers," said Don, "it's perfect."

Don then went around and refreshed everyone's drinks. Once he was settled he looked over at his sister and she nodded and whispered, "Go ahead."

Don cleared his throat, "I have a bit of an announcement to make. After much thought, a lot of prayer, and driving Father Jack nuts for the past few months I've decided that God may be calling me to the priesthood so I will be entering the seminary right after the first of the year."

At first everyone was a little stunned and so didn't respond. Finally J.R. said, "Wow dude, I had no idea!"

"Me neither," said Randy and Fred together.

Tom got up and went over to Don and gave him a hug saying, "You are going to make a wonderful priest."

By then everyone else had also regained their composure and were congratulating him.

"So, how did this come about?" asked Tom.

Don began, "I had sort of thought about it in high school, but was into dating and computers, so just kind of put it aside. But, last year when I received the icon of St. Donald of Olgivy from you Ann it got me thinking about my faith and how I wished that I knew more. So I first checked to see what I could find out about my patron and discovered that he had been married with children, but when his wife died he began leading the life of a religious. That intrigued me. After doing a little more reading and some research online I finally decided to go and talk with Father Jack; which I have now done many times since. I so admire him and very much would like to be a priest just like him."

"So how did you make the final decision?" asked Marie.

Don turned to Lynn and they gave each other a smile. "Well," he began, "Sis and I had gone shopping and out for lunch and we just got talking about life and how neither one of us was married yet even though we had dated and so we were just kind of wondering what God had in mind for us. Then suddenly, out of the blue Lynn said to me, 'Have you ever considered the priesthood?' I about fell out of the booth, but because I didn't want her to know that I was considering it I simply asked back, 'So, have you ever thought about joining a religious order?'"

With that Lynn chuckled, "And I told him that when I was younger I had, but that now I didn't feel God calling me to that. And then I added, but, you didn't answer my question. Don looked me straight in the eye at that point and I knew, I just knew..."

"So then what does she do?" interrupted Don. "I'll tell you what she did. She said loud enough for people over in Johnsville to hear her, 'You're going to be a priest aren't you?' I felt like the entire restaurant was looking at me."

"They weren't," Lynn chided, "I was just so excited."

"So are we," said Ann.

"So have you told your parents?" asked J.R.

"Not yet," began Don, "I will be doing that Christmas Eve."

"Gosh, the first of the year is not that far off," said Marie.

"Actually, it will be more like the middle of January," he answered.

"Well that's good as we will want to give you a 'Holy' send off," laughed Randy.

"What are you going to do about your condo?" asked Fred.

"Well, that has turned out to be something providential too," began Lynn. "My lease is up the end of January and I have been putting aside some money so I was thinking of moving out of my apartment and maybe purchasing a small house or a condo, just to get into the equity market."

Don jumped in again, "So Lynn is going to buy out half of my condo, which will help me with tuition costs, and we will own it jointly. That way I also have a place to come when I am home."

"Without having to stay with Mom and Dad," added Lynn.

Don added, "That too. Plus, it's a large condo with two bedrooms and a third smaller one that I have been using as an office and library room, so there is plenty of space for the two of us."

"It's also going to help me to not only build up some equity, but to also save money for a house as my monthly payments will now be lower. It really is working out great."

Tom then said what was on everyone's mind, "Well, I don't know about the rest of you, but this is the best Christmas gift I have ever received." All agreed.

Everyone wished Fred, Barb, John Paul, Marie, D.J., and Patricia a "Merry Christmas" as they would be going to an earlier Mass on Christmas Eve, while the rest of them would be attending Midnight Mass, including Maggie and J.R. Tom of course offered to pick Ann up for the Mass and she was happy that they were continuing their "tradition."

When Tom picked Ann up for Christmas Midnight Mass he commented once they were in the car, "You seem excited tonight."

"It's Christmas!" she replied, "I'm always excited at Christmas."

"But not like this," he responded.

"When I was a kid I would get so excited that almost every year I had to walk out of church at some point because my stomach would get so upset."

"Really? Wow."

"For a while after I began this 'memory journey' I was afraid that maybe it hadn't been excitement, but more fear of what kind of fight my parents were going to get into. But, then one day I sat outside and just thought about it and went over all of the memories and the feelings and what I came up with was that it really was because of Christmas. I love the music, the decorations, the subdued lighting, being in church, the snow, the cold, and most of all the overall feeling of love and peace that seems to envelope the world at this time of year."

"Me too."

Don and Lynn were already in the pew and had saved enough spaces for everyone. Maggie and J.R. sat with them and then Randy came in from the other side and sat next to Ann.

Once again the church was decorated beautifully. Maggie and J.R. had donated the battery candles that were still among the greens in each of the windows as well as a few of the poinsettias and the battery operated twinkle lights. But now, there were also the tall evergreen trees and the Nativity set added up front and only a few of the overhead lights were on at the moment. Just before the procession was to begin the lights were turned off as Father Jack had done before. But, this year instead of the church slowly regaining light as they came down the aisle there was instead one lone server with a candle who was walking next to a young girl who was carrying the Baby Jesus and all was silent.

When they arrived at the Nativity scene the two of them stood there, and from the back of the church they could hear Father Jack's voice, *"In the name of the Father, and of the Son, and of the Holy Spirit. Amen. Grace to you and peace from God our Father and the Lord Jesus Christ."* The people responded, *"And with your spirit."* Then at the ambo they saw a little light go on and a male voice began chanting: *"The Twenty-fifth day of December..."*

As the cantor continued, Ann thought back to the Midnight Masses of her youth and how holy they all seemed. She hoped that the children attending this Mass would feel the same way.

"The nativity of Our Lord Jesus Christ according to the flesh."

As the cantor finished the last line the little girl placed Jesus in the manger and the choir began singing "Silent Night" while the rest of the church lights slowly came on and servers lit the candles in the sanctuary as Father Jack and the rest of the servers processed in. Ann felt a tear trickle down her cheek and for the remainder of the Mass she felt herself transported back in time to a stable.

Father Jack's homily carried through with the theme of the darkness of the world and how Jesus was born to bring us light; not just 2000 plus years ago, but also today.

"We are encountering very dark times in our present day society with abortion, embryonic stem cell research, couples living together without the benefit of the Sacrament of Marriage, and homosexual's wanting to change God's definition of that Sacrament, just to name a few. I have heard so many say 'Our world is in trouble' or 'What a mess we are in' and then usually add, 'I wish someone would do something.' Well, somebody did and His Name is Jesus. He showed us how to live and what we need to do, but most of us don't do it or sometimes we forget what we are supposed to be doing, but it's time to change that. Right here and right now make yourself, your family, your friends, and God a promise that you are going to start doing things differently. Start small. If you only come to church on Sunday once a month, make it twice a month and then build from there. If you don't pray, then try saying an 'Our Father' at least once a day and increase from there. If you have been meaning to volunteer, then do it. If there is something you don't understand or even that you don't agree with as relates to a teaching of the Church, then do your homework. Find out exactly 'why' the Church teaches what she does. I am sure the answers will shock you. If you are always working late so that your family has dinner without you, then make the commitment to be home at least one night a week to eat with them. These are your priorities, God, family, work and everything else follows. If all of you make those commitments then be prepared;

be prepared for the world to change. Jesus did what God the Father called Him to do and now it is our turn to do what we were called to do too. Merry Christmas everyone! Jesus loves you and so do I!"

"Wow," Ann whispered to Tom.

"I'll say," answered Tom.

The rest of the Mass included familiar Christmas hymns. Ann thought how wonderful to hear everyone singing. And then the recessional "Joy to the World" could not help but make one feel incredibly uplifted.

As they were walking out Ann could see that it had started to snow. "Thank you God," she said in silent prayer.

When they got to Father Jack Ann said, "Wow, I really, really feel like I have been to church! Everything was just so beautiful, uplifting, and inspiring." Father Jack thanked her.

Then Tom said, "Boy, you sure hit all of us where we live with that homily!"

"I hope I was gentle enough," Father Jack replied.

They wished him a Merry Christmas and were on their way.

"And God once again gave you His personal gift, SNOW!" Tom said to Ann.

"I am so very blessed," answered Ann.

As Tom dropped Ann off at home he offered to pick her up for dinner the next day. Ann was really appreciative because she had volunteered to bring a vegetable tray and would feel more comfortable holding it on her lap.

Once inside Ann wished all of her stuffed animals a "Merry Christmas." Then got changed into her pajamas, made herself some hot chocolate, and opened the gift from her brother. It was a small book on the life of St. Ann.

She decided to call him, hoping that their "Midnight" Mass at 10:00 p.m. was also concluded. "Merry Christmas," he answered.

"Merry Christmas," she said in return. "I am so glad that I caught you at home."

"Actually, we are on our way home from Mass. I only have a cell phone now."

"Well, I won't keep you," said Ann, "I just wanted to wish you a Merry Christmas and thank you for the wonderful book on St. Ann. I can't wait to read it."

"I know how you love books," answered her brother, "and I already opened mine too. The catechism book is perfect as a number of questions have been coming to mind."

"I'm glad. Have a Merry Christmas."

"Wait a minute I'm just pulling into the parking lot at Jenny's place." Ann could hear him turning the car off.

"Ann, we were at Jenny's parents tonight for dinner and after we opened gifts I asked her to marry me and she said yes!"

"Oh my goodness! That is so exciting! I am so happy for you!"

"Would you like to say hello to her?"

"Of course."

They talked for a couple of minutes before her brother got back on the phone, "Gotta go. Merry Christmas sis. I love you."

"Love you too. Merry Christmas," Ann replied.

Ann sat drinking her hot chocolate and thinking about her kid brother and was so grateful that he had not only found his way back to the Church, but that he had also found the person that apparently God wanted him to spend the rest of his life with. Ann said a number of silent 'thank you's' to God before crawling into bed.

She could hardly wait to tell Tom the good news about her brother when he came to the door to pick her up. Tom was excited too for Ann's brother.

Even though it was a bit of a smaller crowd for Christmas dinner it was really enjoyable. The food was delicious and then, because they had already exchange their gifts, Lynn had picked up a Bible game for all of them to play. It was challenging, but a lot of fun.

At one point Lynn kiddingly said "Boy Don, am I ever glad that we are playing this game before you enter the seminary because after you have been there awhile none of us would have a chance."

Don laughed, "Even after I have been ordained, if God so wills it, I think that the playing field will still be pretty even."

"You know," began Randy, "playing this game has made me realize that there is a lot I don't know about the Faith."

"Me too," added Ann.

"Ditto," said Tom. "I know that Father Jack wants to start some Adult Faith Formation classes and after playing this game I am glad he is."

"That's great," said Lynn.

"I agree," said Don, "as all of you know that was part of the beginning of my search as I realized there was a lot I didn't know. But, if you think about it, it only makes sense; even if we attended a Catholic School from Kindergarten through 12th grade that is where the education of our Faith ended. And for those who attended Religious Education classes only, their understanding of the Faith is diminished a bit because of not being exposed to it all day long."

"Attending a Catholic college or university helps, but again, if you are not majoring in theology or religious studies the knowledge is again going to be limited," added Tom.

"It sure does make sense," said Ann. "The only reason that I have learned a few things is because I have always been so curious about everything; so if I hear something in a homily or a story about a saint, for example, and I want to know more I have simply gone and done the research. But even in that I am very limited and not everyone has the research bug like I do."

"You can say that again," Tom said teasing her.

"Not changing the subject," said Lynn, "but before I forget, I am going to host a little 'going away' party for my brother in the social hall at his, well, our condo on Saturday, January 13th for all of his friends and our family, as he will be leaving for the seminary that Sunday. We are going to have it starting at 11a.m. with a simple lunch. I thought I would make a big pot of chili, but if all of you could bring something that would be a huge help." Everyone stated what they would bring.

"Also," began Don, "no gifts, please. I will be living in a very small room so there won't be space. I just want you to come and celebrate with me the beginning of this new chapter in my life. And also, to attend 4pm Mass with me that day. Father Jack said that he would have pews reserved for us if we wished."

The rest of the day was simply spent visiting, laughing and singing Christmas carols.

On the way home Tom said, "It was a small group, but still fun."

"Yes," said Ann, "but I really missed the rest of the group too."

"I know what you mean. It seemed like a big chunk of us weren't there and it left a hole."

Even though it had been a good Christmas Ann was glad to be home and get snuggled into her p.j.'s for the rest of the day as she felt tired. She lay on the couch with Sabrina, the stuffed kitty, and Father Charlie, the stuffed bear with the lace collar, close by and before she knew it, she had fallen asleep and there she stayed the entire night.

When she awoke the next morning at first she felt a little disoriented until she figured out where she was. "Wow, I don't think I have ever done that before," she said to Sabrina and Father Charlie, "I must have been really tired." The rest of the day she spent straightening up the house and doing a little more work on her research book, but also knew that it was now time to get back to her children's book and eventually the letters.

THE BOOK
Chapter 6

It seemed like only yesterday that the little girl and all of her cave mate friends had been running around playing the games of summer, going camping and swimming and now here they were all snuggled into the cave with the snow swirling around outside. It had been a beautiful fall with the colors of the trees more glorious than anyone ever remembered. They had gone on many long walks collecting leaves and other items for decorations in the cave for their Thanksgiving. It had rained that day, but everyone still had a good time sharing not only a wonderful meal, but also all of the things that they were grateful for. At the top of the list, everyone was grateful for the Father and for each other. It had been a good day.

After that everyone got really busy collecting and storing things they would need for the winter. All helped from the smallest to the largest. A crew of them even collected more new evergreen branches in case they needed extra ones for the door at the front of the cave. Branches, twigs, and logs were collected for firewood. Berries, honey and other wonderful treats from the forest were also gathered. So, by the time the first snow fell the cave was well stocked with everything needed for the winter.

And now of course they were into the little girls' very favorite time of the year, Christmas!! And for some reason this year seemed to feel even more joyous. The little girl wasn't sure why, but she was definitely enjoying it. As soon as there was enough snow she took whoever wanted to go outside to go tobogganing down the hill in front of the cave. There were so many of them that they had to take turns. Godzilla, Raspberry Sundae and Cotton Candy also took turns riding down with a group and hauling the toboggan back up the hill. Whoever was not on the toboggan at the time started working on a snow man and others were making snow angels.

Of course when they were ready to come in Godzilla and his kitchen crew had snuck in early to make hot chocolate, hot cider and some kind of treat. The cave was filled with laughter and giggles as everyone re-lived the adventures of the day in the snow around the warm fire. And as was natural for this time of year the conversation turned to Christmas and all of the excitement that came with it; how they would decorate the cave this year; when would they go and get the tree; and gifts. It was decided that if the weather was good the next day that whomever wanted to go would venture out and collect new items for decorations. They still had a lot from the previous years, but could use some new berries to string and maybe a few more pinecones and whatever else they came across.

It turned out that everyone wanted to go. Godzilla decided that it would be good to take the toboggan for the smaller critters so they wouldn't get tired trying to keep up with the larger ones. Right after breakfast everyone bundled up and got ready for their hike into the woods. "Let's take a different path this time," said Godzilla as he headed around towards the back of the cave and down that little hill. The little girl had never been down this path and felt a little nervous, but knew that all of her friends were with her and they wouldn't let anything happen to her.

They did come across a patch of berry bushes and the smaller critters began picking as many as they could. "Remember to leave some for the birds that are still around," Godzilla said. A little while later they came across an area that looked like it might be a marsh during the warm weather and growing beside it were some tall grasses that were an off white color and had wispy plumes on the top. The Prince said that it was from the Pampas Grass family. The little girl thought it would look nice in tall containers in the main room of the cave. They also found some red-twig dogwood bushes and took a few branches of that to mix with the grass.

Little Jeanette remarked that it was too bad that snow melted because each snowflake was so beautiful and would look lovely on the tree.

"We could make paper snowflakes," said Bacall.

"If we had some paper," added Bogie.

Everyone looked at the Prince, "Of course we do," he said smiling.

They also found pieces of white birch bark and even a feather or two dropped by different birds here and there, and different sizes and shapes of twigs that could be made into wreaths or swags or whatever they wanted, plus, of course, the pine cones. It had been a very successful outing.

The next day everyone got busy with different craft projects. The Prince provided white and light blue paper, scissors and even glue and glitter so that some of the critters could make cut-out snowflakes. And just like with real snow, each one turned out different from the one before and the one after. Over the next few days they worked on their projects and began a little decorating here and there. Many of their decorations were being made for the tree so they were stored off to one side of the room. While working they shared stories or sang Christmas carols. It was a very joyous time in the cave.

One evening after almost everyone had gone to bed the little girl approached the Prince and asked if he had any construction paper left that was of an off white color. He said that he did. She was also looking for some different colored felt pens that she could do some artistic style writing with and some colored ribbon.

Of course the Prince had all of these, "Is my little lady working on a special project?" he asked.

She gave him a little smile as she said, "You know better than to ask questions like that around Christmas." He laughed.

She then asked if there was a little room hidden away somewhere in the cave where she could work and not be bothered. He led her upstairs and to the far back part of the cave to a room that was actually hidden from the main hallway. "This is perfect," she said.

The next day she headed up to the room and hung a sign on the wall nearby that read:

PLEASE DO NOT DISTURB

She worked most of the day on her project and was not bothered by anyone. She had brought a huge basket with a lid that she could place everything in and then tied it with some twine. That way no one might be tempted to peak.

About a week or so before Christmas it was decided that it was time to go and find a tree. A little more snow had fallen but it was still manageable for most of the critters.

As the rest of them were getting ready Godzilla took the toboggan outside thinking to himself, "I don't know how we are going to fit everyone plus the tree on this one toboggan."

Just then the Prince came out hauling two more toboggans, "Will these help?" he asked.

"How in the world...?" Godzilla began to ask and then stopped himself saying, "I know, I know, you have your sources."

The Prince laughed, "Raspberry Sundae and Cotton Candy have both volunteered to pull these two; so I think that we are all set."

Pretty soon the rest of the critters came out all bundled in hats, scarves and mittens and piled onto the toboggans. Godzilla, Lion, and Sir Lancelot led the way and Front Porch the Buffalo Bull, Moose Bear, and Van Gogh brought up the rear. Everyone else was on the toboggans. The little girl had chosen the second toboggan so that she could ride in the middle of all of her friends.

They headed down the middle path eventually meeting up with the path that kind of went through the middle of the woods. All the way they would stop and look at different trees to see if any of them were the right one. Not finding anything they decided to turn left at the middle road and head the way which took them to the road that Elsie the Keeper of the Hearts had used to leave the woods. As they got closer to that point they noticed a beautiful tree up ahead that just might be the one.

As everyone got off of their toboggans to give the tree a closer look Jacques said, "Look, there's two envelopes on the tree."

They were a little higher on the tree so Godzilla reached for one of them, "It's addressed to the little girl," he said and grabbing the second one added, "and so is this one."

"They look like Christmas cards," said Kris.

"I wonder who they are from," the little girl said.

"Why don't you open them?" suggested R.T. Cold Nose III.

The little girl thought a moment and putting the cards inside of her jacket she said, "I think I will wait until we are back at the cave." Everyone thought that was a good idea.

All seemed to like the tree and were about to make the decision that this would be the one when Shawn O'Leigh said, "I don't know. I mean someone thought it was a good place to put cards for the little girl so it must be a special tree."

"Yes," added Snowflake, "And maybe others will want to leave cards there too."

"Those are some good thoughts," Godzilla said.

"Hey," yelled little Arp from somewhere off the road, "Here's one."

All of them made their way through the evergreen trees to where the sound of Arp's voice had come from and there it was, kind of standing all by itself.

"Oh it's beautiful," said the Winged Lady of the Snows. Everyone else agreed.

Artie J. and J.B. Bear had brought the saw and they worked together to cut the tree down. But, before they did, everyone had to look to make sure that the trunk was straight.

Once the tree was loaded on the front toboggan and everyone had piled back into their places they headed for the cave. As they crossed the place where Elsie and the little girl had said good-bye, the little girl looked down the path that led out of the woods but as she didn't want anyone to see her doing that, which of course they already had, she started singing the song "Over the River and Through the Woods."

It didn't matter that it was really a Thanksgiving song because everyone only knew the first couple of verses anyway. Before long they were back at the cave. Godzilla shook even more of the snow off the tree and propped it up against the outside wall. In the meantime everyone else had headed inside to get their wet things off, a fire going and some treats from the kitchen.

Pretty soon they were all having their hot drinks and cookies around the fire.

"Do you feel like opening your cards now?" asked P.J.

All eyes were on the little girl and when she noticed that she said, "I guess I could."

The first card had a beautiful scene of Bethlehem on it with the star shining over the manger and wise men approaching from the distance.

"Oh my," exclaimed the little girl as she opened the card.

Little Jacques so much wanted to ask who it was from, but his mother had already given him a look that said, "Don't do it!" The little girl read everything on the inside to herself first. Then looking around at her friends they could see she had a tear in her eye as she said, "It is from my friend 'Golden Pockets.'"

"I thought that was his handwriting," Bogie whispered to Bacall.

"Me too," she whispered back.

"What does he say?" asked Lord Percival.

The little girl took a deep breath before answering, "He says that he received my letter and that it was so wonderful to hear from me. He had been worried about me and had wondered where I had gone. He then says some things about what a good friend I have always been to him."

"Aren't thou now glad my little lady that thou wrote to him?" asked Arthur.

The little girl nodded that she was. As she went to open the second one she noticed a note on the back of the envelope that read, "We knew you lived in the woods, but we didn't know where. We hope you come to this tree sometimes."

The little girl noticed R. Rabbit and Topo G. winking at each other, so she asked, "Do you know who this one is from?"

Before they could answer the Winged Lady of the Snow said, "We think that it is from the family that sent the three of us to you."

On the front of the card was another beautiful picture of Mary, Joseph, and the Baby Jesus in the manger. As she opened it, the little girl smiled at R. Rabbit, Topo G. and the Winged Lady, "You were correct. It is from Storyteller, Barrister, and Lil Angel. They too received my letter and were so happy to hear from me and to know that I was OK. They are hoping that I will come for a visit sometime."

The little girl looked at the cards without saying anything and then gently put them under her pillow. In the meantime all of her cave mates were secretly smiling and winking at each other.

A couple of days later Godzilla brought the tree in from outside the cave and got it all set up with help from Raspberry Sundae. They let it get settled for a few days before decorating it. And what a party that was. Of course the kitchen crew got busy popping the popcorn to string plus making a few snacks to enjoy while decorating the tree. The young ones set at stringing the berries. P.J. had to keep Lord Percival and the other little bears from eating more than they were stringing. Once the popcorn and berries were strung they were hung on the tree; then the decorations from Christmas' past and the pyrite from last year. Finally, they put on all of the paper snowflakes that they had made.

As they stood back to admire their work the little girl exclaimed, "Oh, it is the most beautiful tree ever!" All of her friends agreed.

It seemed that Christmas was approaching rapidly so everyone in the cave was off in their own rooms working on various things. That included the little girl in her hiding place on the second floor. With so many friends to make gifts for she knew she was running a little short on time, but she also didn't want to hurry too much because each of the gifts had to be perfect. A few evenings she would go back to her room after dinner and work late into the night and yet, she would be up early the next morning. She so loved what she was doing that she didn't feel tired at all.

Pretty soon it was Christmas Eve. After dinner everyone gathered around the fire for their annual reading of the Christmas story. This year Lion read the story by Luke (2:1;6-7;20)

> *In those days a decree went out from Caesar Augustus*
> *that the whole world should be enrolled...*

Everyone was listening intently as the story unfolded.

> *While they were there, the time came for her to have her child,*
> *and she gave birth to her firstborn son...*

All of the way to the end.

> *Then the shepherds returned, glorifying and praising God*
> *for all they had heard and seen, just as it had been told to them.*

Then Amelia and Beethoven began gently singing "Silent Night" and the rest of the cave mates joined in. Afterwards everyone gave each other a hug and whispered "Merry Christmas," before quietly going off to bed.

Before climbing in her sleeping bag the little girl stole upstairs to retrieve her basket that was filled with the gifts she had made for her friends and set it by her bed. Just as she was getting ready to crawl in Pumpkin-Pumpkin came to her side and motioned for the little girl to follow her. They went to the entrance of the cave where Raspberry Sundae and Cotton Candy had pushed back the door as wide as it would go. The view took the little girls breath away. It was SNOWING! Sabrina, R.T. Cold Nose III, and Pumpkin-Pumpkin all snuggled close to the little girl and whispered, "Merry Christmas."

The little girl looked up and said, "Thank you Father."

After watching it for a few minutes they closed the door and all hustled off to bed as the little girl said, "Hurry, we need to be asleep before Santa gets here."

The little girl crawled into her sleeping bag and lay there waiting until she was sure that everyone was asleep and then she carefully hung the gifts for all of her friends on the tree.

Of course the young ones were up early as always and as in years past Godzilla was already busy in the kitchen.

"Shall we run through the cave yelling 'Merry Christmas' like we did last year?" asked Jacques.

"I like that tradition," said little Arp.

"We've only done it once," protested Jeanette, "so how could it be a tradition?"

"If we do it again, it will then be a tradition," Sure to Go gently offered.

By then P.J. and Lord Percival had joined them in the kitchen. "Are we going to do what we did last year?" asked Lord Percival.

"That is what everyone is currently deciding," answered Godzilla.

They all looked at each other and then said together, "Let's do it!"

So first they went around and quietly woke up the rest of the younger critters and headed for the back of the cave. All at once pandemonium broke out as they came running through the cave knocking on all the doors and yelling, "Merry Christmas Everyone!"

Pretty soon everyone started coming out of their rooms and gathered near the fire. Rudy, Rudy Red Nose and Mr. Bear Claus were the last to join them both rubbing their eyes.

"Wow, look at all the gifts," said Lucy the pink bunny.

"I have never seen so many," said In No Rush, the green bunny.

Everyone settled into their spots as Mr. Bear Claus and Kris started passing out the gifts. This year most of the critters had made gift certificates for each of their cave mates. For example, Barely Bear gave Miss Louise a certificate that offered to take her place in fixing a meal. In fact, he gave each of the kitchen crew that same certificate. Miss Evelyn gave certificates to each of the young critters promising to read each of them a story. And so it went, each offering a gift of themselves to their friends.

P.J. then noticed the gifts hanging on the tree from the little girl. "Oh look," she began, "These are beautiful. Who are these from?"

"They are from me," answered the little girl, "but you will have to see if you can find the one that was made for you. You will see that each hanging paper has just one, or maybe two initials that represent your name and that it is done in what I hope is your favorite color."

Lucy the pink bunny found hers right away, "A beautiful 'L' done in pink," she said.

"Here's mine," said Pumpkin-Pumpkin, "Two 'P's in orange."

"I'm going to hang mine over my bed," said Little Teresa.

"Me too," added Jeanette.

Everyone loved their special initial ornament and the little girl was happy.

Santa Claus had brought each of them new scarves, hats and mittens in so many different colors that after they were all unwrapped it was like a rainbow in the room. There were still two gifts under the tree. Little Kris crawled under and got the first one which was for Godzilla from Santa. It was pretty heavy but Kris was finally able to lift it to hand to the big bear.

As he opened it Godzilla began laughing; it was a big jar of honey, "Which I of course will share with all of you."

The last item was addressed to the little girl and was from Lion. It was a wonderfully hand carved wooden box.

"Oh, it is beautiful," said the little girl.

Lion said, "I found this on my travels and thought that you might like it to keep your letters and cards in."

"What a wonderful idea," she answered, "Thank you."

"In fact," he began, "I went for a walk very early this morning and I found these on the tree by the crossroads."

With that he handed her five more envelopes that looked like they might also be Christmas cards.

The little girl looked at them for a few seconds and then said, "I don't know about you, but after opening all of those wonderful gifts I am kind of hungry and I know that Godzilla and his kitchen crew have made us a delicious breakfast. So, why don't we eat first and I can open and read these later."

Even though her friends were anxious to see who the cards were from they agreed.

"Thank you," said Godzilla, "as I don't want the hot food to get cold nor the cold food to get warm."

With that there was a lot of scurrying about as wrapping paper and gifts were cleaned up and put away; the table set and the food placed on it.

The little girl asked if she could lead the prayer that morning.

Dear Father,
Thank you for the gift of Jesus.
Thank you for the gift of Christmas.
Thank you for the gift of my dear, dear friends.
Thank you for the gift of this food and for the talents of those who
prepared it.
Please be with those who do not have food, shelter or friends this
day.
Amen.

After breakfast and getting everything cleaned up P.J. asked, "Are you going to open your cards now?"

"I guess I could," the little girl answered.

Immediately everyone came and gathered around her. As she opened the first one Snowbear and Snowflake held hands as they thought they had recognized the handwriting on the front. Sure enough, it was a card from Mademoiselle and Junior. They had received the little girls' letter and they too were very happy to hear from her as she had always been such a good friend and they missed her. "Hope we will see you soon," they had added at the end.

After she opened the next one she turned to Nicely, Nicely the Bow-Tie Bear and said, "This one is from your friend D.W."

Nicely, Nicely clapped his paws, as he said, "How is he?"

"He is well," answered the little girl.

"And what does he say?" Nicely, Nicely asked.

"He says that he was so glad that I had written to him because he missed me and was now hoping that we could at least continue writing and maybe even visit each other," she answered.

The next card was from Sir Galahad, Dancing Girl and Lil Man.

"Lil Man?" questioned Rudy, Rudy Red Nose, "There must be a new member in their family."

"Yes," answered the little girl, "That is what they say in their note. They are also wondering if you found your way here and hope that you are well and happy. They would like for you and I to come for a visit sometime as they miss seeing both of us." The little reindeer broke out in a big smile.

Miss Evelyn wanted to ask if the next card was from Pudie but she was way too polite to do that.

The little girl sensed her curiosity so the minute she opened it she said, "Miss Evelyn, this is from Pudie." Miss Evelyn smiled. "She is doing very well," the little girl continued, "and was very, very happy to hear from me and hopes that I will continue to write to her as she wants to hear everything about my life."

"Well then," said Shawn O'Leigh, "I am hoping that this last card is from Choo-Choo."

"It is," said the little girl smiling.

On the front of the card was the picture of a beautiful Nativity scene that was set up inside of a church. It looked very familiar to the little girl.

"I think this is in my church," she said. "Choo-Choo said that he is doing well and was very happy to hear from me as he has some news to share." She was quiet a moment as she finished reading and then she said, "He is going to study to become a priest!" Everyone cheered. She continued, "He is asking us to pray for him. He hopes that someday he and I can see each other again." After she finished reading the little girl just sat there for a moment.

Finally Sure to Go said, "Wow. I am so glad that you heard back from your little friends." The little girl nodded in agreement.

"So, do you think that you will go and visit them?" asked Charlie.

"I'm not sure," answered the little girl.

"It is something to think about though isn't it?" asked Rudolph Valentino the Heart Nosed Bear.

"Yes," answered the little girl, "something to think about, but not today. It's Christmas and there is snow outside. Who wants to go play in the snow?"

Of course all of the younger ones yelled, "We do!"

Some of the critters stayed indoors and worked on preparing the Christmas dinner; others, like Mr. Bear Claus decided to take a nap and the rest bundled up and went out into the snow to play.

It was a wonderful Christmas Day, but by the end of it the little girl felt very tired and shortly after dinner she fell fast asleep by the fire. She looked so comfortable that no one disturbed her but simply covered her with a blanket and let her sleep.

The next morning she awoke very early and for a moment wondered where she was. She knew that this would be a good morning to take a walk, so she bundled up and snuck out of the cave while it was still fairly dark. Of course, Sir Lancelot followed at a discrete distance as did Lion.

The little girl headed for the crossroads where she had bid Elsie good-bye and stood there for a long time looking down the road that her friend had taken to leave the woods.

The next few days in the cave were not the best. The little girl seemed to be upset about something and once again she was not sleeping well. She began waking up in a state of panic and during the day she seemed to be short tempered and even yelled at some of her cave mates. She would always apologize saying that she didn't know what was wrong and then would go for a long walk trying to calm down and to figure it out. But, nothing seemed to help.

THE CRITTERS
Time for a Trip

One time after Ann had once again become upset, slammed a couple of doors and then left for a walk, Godzilla called a meeting.

"What is happening to Ann?" asked P.J.

"Yes," said Sure to Go, "she seems to be upset and even angry at times."

"And she is not sleeping well," added Lord Percival, "I can attest to that!"

"So can Bright Eyes," added P.J. "because he has been snuggling closer to me during the night." Bright Eyes nodded yes.

"Is our little lady having more memories?" asked Arthur.

"That may be part of it," answered Godzilla, "but I am suspecting something else is going on. Lion?"

The Lion stepped forward and began, "Ann knows that it is time for her to face more people and is afraid to."

"Even the ones that have already died?" asked Nicholas of the North Pole.

"Especially those," answered the Lion.

"What can we do to help?" asked Amelia and Tali together.

"It is time to coax her, but in a supportive way," answered Lion.

"Can you explain what you mean?" asked the Prince.

"She seems almost ready to see her friends again, so I think that we should support her in doing that," he began, "Then, after that, we can push her, but in a gentle way, to face the more difficult people and memories."

"But what if she gets angry at us? I mean, she has been yelling at us when we haven't done anything. What will she do when we suggest these things?" asked Raspberry Sundae.

"Good point," answered Lion, "I will do the talking then, but I expect all of you to be there backing me up."

They all agreed that they would.

ANN'S STORY
Chapter 11
New Year, Secrets and Farewells

The next couple of nights Ann did not sleep well coupled with a lot of tossing and turning. Then during the day she simply felt cranky and irritable. She didn't even want to answer the phone when it rang and Tom had mentioned that she sounded a little out of sorts. She held Godzilla in her arms one morning and said, "What is wrong with me now?" As she lay there she tried to sort it all out and was able to admit that there was still some fear and obviously some anger, but what to do about it. She wasn't going to see Dr. Peter again until after New Year's as he had taken the week between the two holidays off to spend with his family. "Okay," she said aloud to all of the stuffed animals in her room, "What would he say?" She didn't have to think about it long, "I know what he would say. It's just that I don't want to hear it; not yet. He will want me to face more people from the past and I am just simply not ready."

As she fixed her morning coffee she talked to the stuffed animals in the kitchen and family room, "I'm wondering if part of this is because I am also kind of keeping a secret from my friends. What am I afraid of? I've told Tom, Marie, and D.J. and they have all been supportive. But I do have to admit that I got uncomfortable when they all said how sorry they were that stuff happened to me. I wonder why. What do you think?" she asked Fuzzy Wuzzy Woof Woof who was sitting on the window sill. He seemed to smile back as if to say, "Why do you think?" Ann then sat at the counter drinking her coffee and eating her bowl of oatmeal and thinking.

"Why do I think it is such a secret?" she asked Bogie and Bacall the two stuffed puppies Tom had given her last year. She then suddenly remembered her uncle saying to her, "This will be our secret." "Wow," she exclaimed, "well that explains some of it. But, I don't have to keep it a secret anymore. However, there is still something else," she pondered out loud. She thought about Tom telling her a long time ago that she always seemed like she needed to be the strong one; that nothing affected her. Again talking out loud, "Dr. Peter has explained that that was how I protected myself as a little girl and kept myself from being hurt again as there were no adults to take care of me. It was how I survived, but now because I am an adult myself that is not really needed anymore. So what else is going on?" She thought about the night she told Marie and D.J. about the molest and how she was afraid of what they would think of her as if it was her fault. "Hmm," she said aloud, "I think that is why I am keeping this huge secret from the rest of my friends because I am afraid that they will think badly of me and how unrealistic is that?! I guess I know what I need to do about that."

With that she got on the phone and invited everyone to a Rose Bowl Game gathering on New Year's Day even though none of their favorite teams were playing this year. "I know it's last minute, but I thought it would just be a good time to be together."

She told Tom and Marie that she planned on telling the rest of the group her "secret" after the game was over. They both felt that it was about time as there was absolutely nothing for her to be ashamed of, nor to hide any longer.

And as Tom said, "Ann the only one you are protecting is your uncle."

As Ann hung up the phone from talking to Tom she said to herself, "He's right! And why would I want to protect him!"

Ann thought that ordering a 3 foot sub for the group would be the easiest and most fun. Tom offered to bring beer and wine; Maggie and J.R., chips; Don and Lynn, soda and water; D.J. and Marie, some other kinds of snacks; Fred and Barb the paper goods; and gratefully Randy said he would bake some cookies.

Ann cleaned up her house New Year's Eve Day. It was still fully decorated for Christmas as she seldom took anything down until at least after the Feast of the Presentation so basically she only had to do a little dusting, clean the bathrooms and vacuum. She did put a tablecloth on the table in the Family Room and made sure there were enough standing trays for everyone to sit their drinks and food on. She had also put pillows and blankets rolled up on the edges of the bed in her spare room for the two little ones to be able to take naps safely.

New Year's Day she went to Mass and the only one from the group that was there was Tom as everyone else had attended the vigil Mass.

Afterwards he said, "Are you nervous?"

"I have to admit that I am," she answered.

"I think that everyone is going to be supportive, just like Marie, D.J. and I were."

"I sure hope so. I mean, I think about Fred and Barb and I don't want them to worry about John Paul around me."

"Ann, they have seen you with little Patricia and how good you are. Not only that, but how she responds to you. You are the first one she always wants to go to and she wouldn't do that if you had hurt her in any way."

"True. Even now, the thought of being around my uncle upsets my stomach."

"It will be fine and would you like me to come over early to help you get everything set up?"

"I think I am pretty well set, but come early anyway."

On the way home from church she picked up the huge sub sandwich and was grateful that she had a refrigerator that would accommodate it if she cut it in half. She changed into comfortable clothes and then turned on the TV to watch the Rose Bowl parade while she put together some dishes of pickles, olives and other relish type of items. "I wonder if my brother is there again," she thought out loud, "One of these years I will go."

Tom arrived about a half hour early and got the beer and wine put away. "You do such a beautiful job decorating for Christmas. I always feel like I have entered a winter wonderland when I step into your home. It has such a peaceful feeling."

"Thanks," said Ann, "but once the game starts I think that will end."

"So, who are you rooting for?"

"Well, I'm not necessarily an Iowa fan, but I have never been a USC fan and we are in Big Ten country, so I guess Iowa."

Tom laughed, "I love how you arrived at that."

Ann laughed too, "Hey, I love football so I will simply enjoy the game."

Pretty soon the rest of the gang arrived. John Paul was still asleep so Fred lay him on the bed in the spare room, but little Patricia was as active as she could be and Ann had forgotten how quick they could be. Pretty soon Ann had placed all of the breakable stuff up and away from the little one's reach. It was decided that to make the game a little more fun the girls would cheer for Iowa, seeing as how that was the team Ann was going to go with and it was her house, and the guys would cheer for USC. However, as the game got going it was clear that everyone wanted Iowa to win. How little John Paul slept through the first half was nothing short of a miracle. He stayed up for most of the second half and then everyone could tell he was getting sleepy as he kept rubbing his eyes, so Barb went and lay him down again. Shortly thereafter it was little Patricia's turn to fall asleep.

After the game was over everyone sat around talking and sharing their stories of their family Christmases. "I think we are going to have to get a bigger house," said Fred, "with everything that the grandparents and godparents got for John Paul!"

"It will taper off," D.J. assured them.

Finally, there was a bit of a lull in the conversation so Ann took a deep breath, "I have something that I would like to share with all of you."

Of course all eyes turned towards her which didn't help her nerves, but Tom reached over and took her hand and that helped to calm her a bit.

Then Marie said, "It's okay Ann, we are your friends."

"What's going on?" asked Lynn, "Are you okay?"

Ann smiled, "Not entirely, but I am getting there. Tom knows, and so do Marie and D.J., and I decided that it was time to tell the rest of you."

"Ann, please, whatever it is we are here with you," said Maggie.

Ann took another deep breath and said very quietly but firmly, "I am an abuse and molest survivor."

At first no one reacted as they were adjusting to their own shock, but gratefully Don said, "Oh Ann, I am so sorry."

"You will make a good priest," Ann said giving him a weak smile.

Then Maggie jumped in, "Oh Ann, my head is spinning with so many questions and yet I don't want to pry, but I do want to know, are you okay?"

"I have been going to therapy for a while now and a support group for women who were molested plus I have met with Father Jack. All of this has been a tremendous help along with my faith, and believe it or not, all of these stuffed animals that all of you brought into my life. And I can tell you that I am not totally healed and don't know that I ever will be, but I am so very much better than I was."

Tom added, "I can vouch for that."

"I know that I am kind of new to this group," began Barb, "but is there a reason that you didn't tell us?"

D.J. then jumped in, "She just told us a little while ago."

Ann continued, "At first, I didn't know what was wrong, so there was nothing to share. Then when I started having nightmares and then memories, it was so painful for a while that I didn't know what to do as I was just trying to deal with all of it. Then when the memories of the sexual abuse came I felt embarrassed and ashamed, so I didn't want any of you to know."

"You blamed yourself didn't you?" asked Fred.

"I did," answered Ann.

"I have read that that often happens to victims because the perpetrator will say things about you really enjoying or wanting it," he said.

"Yes, and it takes awhile to sort all of that out to know what is real and what is not," said Ann.

"But we are your friends Ann," said Randy.

"I know," said Ann, "and please do not be offended that I didn't tell you earlier. Keeping it a secret is also part of the damage that is done. We think that we need to keep all of it inside for a lot of different reasons. Some victims blame themselves for it happening, others have been threatened or their family members threatened if the perpetrator finds out they told anyone, or they feel ashamed or are also told that no one will believe them."

"That is really, really sick," said Lynn.

"Yes," said Tom, "they are very sick individuals who do these things."

"Did you know your attacker?" asked Don.

"Yes, the one who physically abused me was my mother and it was an uncle who touched me inappropriately. I am one of the fortunate ones in that it wasn't full intercourse," she answered.

J.R. finally said, "Ann, I am just so stunned and there is a part of me that wants to go and confront your uncle and your mother."

"Well, my mother is deceased so that might be a little difficult," answered Ann.

"So, the uncle is still alive," asked J.R., "good, because then if we ever meet I can punch him!"

"J.R.," said Maggie.

"I know, I know," answered J.R., "I probably wouldn't but I sure do feel like it."

"I did too when I found out," said D.J.

"Were the letters you wrote us part of your therapy?" asked Lynn.

"Yes, sort of," began Ann. "I was to first write to people who had meant something to me in my life and of course all of you are definitely on that list. And once I started writing them I found that there had been a longing inside of me to let each of you know how special you were to me that I had never before expressed. And what that helped me to do was to also write letters to those who had hurt me, which I am just now beginning to do."

"Will you mail them?" asked Marie.

"Some of the people, like my parents, are deceased and the rest of them I'm not sure yet. It is something that my therapist and I will sort out when I get to that point," answered Ann.

"How do you feel at this moment?" asked Tom.

Ann looked around at her friends, "First of all I feel grateful; grateful for each and every one of you as I can see the care in each of your eyes and because you have allowed me to share this with you. Second, I feel as if a weight has been lifted as I no longer have to keep this huge secret I have been carrying around with me. Not that I am going to tell the world, but at least I am not keeping it from those who mean the most to me. So, thank you for listening and hopefully for not judging."

"What do you mean, 'hopefully for not judging,'" said Maggie, "why on earth would we judge you?" The others agreed with her.

"We love you," added Don and the rest agreed with him.

They talked for a while longer about the problem of child abuse and molest in the world and most especially in the United States, but the conversation steered more towards support and love for Ann and the courage she had shown in facing all of this.

As everyone left and gave her a hug, assuring her again of their love and support it was almost too much for Ann to take in, but she did her best. After they all left Tom stayed and helped her to clean up.

"Are you tired?" he asked.

"Absolutely bushed," she answered.

"I know that was hard for you to do, but I also noticed that it was almost harder for you to take in and accept how much your friends love you," he said.

"I think you are correct. I will add it to my mental list of things to talk with Dr. Pete about this next week."

After Tom left Ann was barely able to get into her p.j.'s and crawl into bed. She grabbed Godzilla and Sir Lancelot and was asleep immediately.

Ann hadn't been up long the next morning when her front door bell rang. It was the florist with a dozen red roses. The card read, "I am so proud of you. Love Tom." "What a good, good friend he is," Ann said as she set them on the corner of the kitchen counter where she could admire them with her morning coffee.

Two hours later, the doorbell rang again and once again it was the florist, "Is today your birthday?" he asked.

"No," answered Ann, "I just have some really good friends."

This was a beautiful arrangement of all different kinds of flowers from D.J., Marie, and Little Patricia. The card read, "We love you!"

That afternoon the doorbell rang again only this time it was a different delivery person with an edible arrangement. This was from Maggie and J.R. and the card read, "Be good to you as you heal. We love you." Ann could not believe all of the wonderful fruits the arrangement was made from and gratefully it was one of the smaller ones.

The next day she received a beautiful card from Barb, Fred, and John Paul with a gift certificate to get a massage. The card told Ann how special they thought she was and they hoped this helped her to heal. They also told her that they planned on inviting her to dinner soon. "Oh my gosh," she said to her stuffed animal friends, "I have never had a massage in my life."

She also received a card from Lynn and Don with another gift certificate to her favorite ice cream shop. "For those rough days," the note read followed by, "We love you and we are praying for you."

And then while she was running errands Randy dropped off a huge plate of different kinds of his homemade cookies with a beautiful card letting Ann know how much he cared about her.

Thank goodness everything had not arrived on the same day as then she was able to call Tom, Marie, and Maggie the first day and Barb, Lynn, and Randy on the second day. Ann was feeling overwhelmed by all of their caring actions, but little by little the acceptance of the thought and feeling that she actually was loved was creeping in. Still, it was hard and she was very grateful that the phone did not ring at all that day nor did anyone come to the door so she was able to work on her research book and not have to think about all of this other stuff. It was definitely going to be a full session with Dr. Pete the following week.

"Happy New Year," said Dr. Pete as he welcomed Ann.

"And to you too," she answered.

"How are you?"

"Are you ready?"

"Always," he said smiling.

"It has been quite a ride since I last saw you," she began. "Christmas was wonderful between church, being with friends and a couple of announcements." She then told him about her brother becoming engaged and another friend who has decided to enter the priesthood. And, also that she had had some responses to the letters she wrote to friends, relatives, and former neighbors.

"But then after Christmas," she began, "my sleep was restless and I just started feeling cranky. At first I thought it might just be the let down of my favorite Holy Day having passed, even though we as Catholics and especially me, celebrate Christmas much longer.

However, after a lot of thinking and praying I decided that it must be something else."

She then shared how she thought it might have to do with the other letters she knew that Dr. Peter wanted her write that she wasn't ready to, but then how her awareness grew that it might actually have to do with not having shared her secret with her closest friends. She then told him about the New Year's Day gathering and how they all reacted.

"How are you feeling about it?" he asked.

"I am glad that I told them, as nervous as I was to do so, but..." she paused.

"But what?" he asked.

"I am feeling really overwhelmed with their responses; the flowers, the cards, the gifts."

"Do you have any idea why?"

Ann thought a moment, "Well, first of all I really don't like all of the attention being directed towards me. I feel uncomfortable. And second, I am much more comfortable giving than receiving; I don't think I do that very gracefully."

"It sounds to me like you were very gracious in your response to their care and their gifts. After all you called each of them and you said that you also plan on sending them notes of appreciation," he responded.

"I suppose."

"But let's look at your first reason. Why do you think that you don't like to be the center of attention?"

"Other than performers and politicians do you think anybody does?"

He laughed a little, "You have a good point there. But, do you think that is really all that it is or may there be something else?"

"Hmm," she pondered, "I guess that I am going to have to think about that."

"Let me ask you this then, how do you feel when you are the center of attention besides uncomfortable?"

Ann thought before answering, "I guess that I don't like all eyes being on me. If I were involved in the theatre, for example, I would much rather be doing something behind the scenes rather than on the stage. I guess I'm a little shy that way."

"Okay, but you weren't on a stage. You were with a small group of your friends and they were showing you that they love you and care for you and because of that you wished you could run away and hide. Isn't that correct?"

Ann didn't answer for a moment keeping her head down then slowly she raised it and looked at Dr. Pete as tears formed in her eyes, "I just realized that I am uncomfortable with their care and the fact that they love me."

"But why would that be?" Dr. Pete gently asked. "Is how your friends are showing you that they love you the same way that your parents and your uncle said they were showing you love?"

"No," Ann said softly.

"I bet they said things like, 'I am doing this because I love you,' or 'this is for your own good,' or in the case of your father, his alcoholism didn't allow him to show you much affection right?"

Ann nodded in the affirmative as she answered, "But that wasn't really love they were showing me and I know that."

"You know that now as an adult but that little girl inside of you still doesn't. It is something that she is going to have to learn all over again; what a healthy love is and you are going to be the one to teach her."

"Great!" said Ann kind of sarcastically.

Dr. Pete laughed, "Actually, you have already started to do that by the ways that you are learning to take better care of yourself emotionally, physically, and spiritually, plus using that bright mind of yours to understand on that level what happened to you and how you are to go about healing. Ann, you are doing great, you just don't know it yet."

Ann laughed, "I guess not."

"Now, that being said," Dr. Pete began.

"Oh no, here it comes," laughed Ann.

"Yes, you know what I am going to say. It is time for you to face more of the people from your past; the ones that hurt you. I would like you to begin working on those letters," he said.

Ann groaned.

Dr. Pete laughed, "It's hard work, I know, but you do want to heal right?" She nodded that she did. "Well, this is part of that. We not only have to face the angels of our past, but also the demons. And as always, please know that I will be praying for you as you do this," he added.

"So, once they are completed, then what?"

"Write them first and we will then decide."

Ann's head was spinning as she left Dr. Pete's office. "I wish I could just run away to a cabin in the woods somewhere where no one could find me," she said to herself as she started her car. She sat there for a moment trying to decide what she wanted to do; she was just feeling so out of sorts she wasn't sure which direction to go to help her to feel better. She already had flowers and comfort food at home so she didn't need to get flowers or cookies. Another stuffed animal? "No, as I am beginning to have problems remembering all of their names as it is," she said to herself. She thought about a drive along the lake but that felt like too much energy so she simply decided to head for home. To get there however, she had to drive by her church. "That's it!" she said aloud. The church was totally empty; no one to be seen nor heard and the only lights were a few vigil candles that people had lit. She sat in the pew for a long time just trying to soak in the silence and the... "what is that other feeling?" she said to herself. She talked to God in her mind, asking Him to help her sort all of this out, to give her the strength to write the letters and for healing. Pretty soon she was aware of a calm that was coming over her, a feeling of peace. Ann smiled.

When she arrived home she fixed herself a light lunch that included some of the fruit from the edible bouquet. She was so happy that it had included watermelon, which was her absolute favorite; especially at this time of the year.

After lunch she decided to go back and double check her letter to her father and the little bit that she had written in the letter to her mother. However, as she re-read the letter to her father she became very aware of feelings of loss and grief. She missed her father and so was able to add that in the letter plus mentioning that she wished he had done more to protect her from her mother and that she wished he had known about what her uncle had done to her.

She did feel good about having finished the letter to her father and this helped her to realize that the other two letters needed to be done also. However, as all of this was so emotional for her, Ann also decided that for the other letters she wouldn't try to write them all in one day, but rather would write a little bit each day over how many ever days it took. This turned out to be a good decision as by the end of this first day she was exhausted and went to bed early.

Ann had been so busy between the letters, her research book, appointments, and groups with Dr. Pete that before she knew it January 13th was upon her. Even though Don had said 'no gifts' Ann wanted to at least give him a gift of money and had found a perfect card to put it in. As Ann was bringing crackers to go with the chili she decided that she had better be there a little before 11 a.m. A few of Lynn and Don's family members had already arrived, including his parents and they seemed to be simply beaming. Ann helped Lynn where she could in getting everything set up and gratefully she had put out a basket to place cards in.

"That was a good idea," said Ann.

"Thanks," answered Lynn, "I know my brother said 'no gifts', but I also know this group!"

"You were right!" answered Ann as Tom also placed his envelope in the basket.

It was a fun gathering. His father had put together a slide show about Don's life from birth, actually before birth, to today. Don was embarrassed, but all of them loved it. Then there were the stories from not just his parents and Lynn, but also cousins and of course, his friends.

The afternoon passed by so quickly that before everyone knew it, it was time to leave for 4:00 p.m. Mass.

As they were getting ready to leave, Don stopped Ann, "I have been thinking," he began, "have you talked with Father Jack about receiving the Sacrament of Healing? You know, it's not just for physical ailments and I would think that what you have been through would definitely qualify."

"I hadn't thought about that," answered Ann. "I did ask God for healing the other day. Maybe this is His answer. Thanks Don," as she gave him a hug.

It was nice to have the pews up front set aside for Don, his family, and friends. He sat in the front pew with his parents and Lynn; the rest of the family was in the next pew and then his friends. After the homily Father Jack came to the middle of the steps and said, "I bet there are more than a few of you who are curious as to why this group of people is sitting in reserved seating today." Pointing to Don and Lynn's parents he continued, "How many of you thought that maybe it is this couple's wedding anniversary?" About half of the congregation's hands raised up. He then asked, "And how many of you thought that maybe this young lady is getting ready to go on some type of mission trip?" A few hands were raised. "Well," he said smiling, "it's neither one of those things." He then asked Don to step into the middle aisle with him. Father Jack continued, "This young man is feeling God calling him to the priesthood and so he has decided to enter the seminary and will be leaving tomorrow morning."

With that the entire congregation started applauding. Ann could tell that Don was feeling a little embarrassed but he handled it well. Father Jack continued, "And we are going to give him a special blessing this morning. So, if all of you would extend an arm in blessing as I pray:

Oh dearest Jesus,
Infant of Prague and patron of vocations,
You tenderly love us and your greatest joy
is to dwell among us and to bestow your
blessings on us.

Though none of us are worthy, this young man
feels drawn to you in a special way.
Bless, protect and guide him in knowing what
Your Holy Will is for him.
If You are calling him to the priesthood,
help him to have the courage
to follow that call.

We pray to you, most Holy Infant,

*in the name of your Blessed Mother Mary
who cared for you with such tenderness,
and by the great reverence with which
St. Joseph carried you in his arms.
We ask this in Your Name. Amen.*

He then made the Sign of the Cross over Don and asked the congregation to pray in a special way for him. Once again, everyone applauded and the Mass continued.

After Mass Don, Lynn, and their parents were going out for a special meal together so the rest of the family and friends had to say good-bye at the church. Of course a great number of parishioners came up and promised Don their prayers too.

"Boy, I sure hope that I can live up to their expectations," Don said at one point.

Tom answered, "You do not have to worry about their expectations, only God's, and if you listen, He will let you know what He wants."

"Thanks Tom, I needed to hear that," answered Don.

Ann found it a little difficult to say good-bye but managed to do so saying, "We'll see you on your visits home."

Ann was glad that no one had suggested they go somewhere for a bite to eat as she was feeling tired from all that had been happening in her life over the past couple of weeks. Time alone in her p.j.'s on the couch and maybe watching a movie would be more than enough for her that evening and maybe even all day Sunday.

THE BOOK
Chapter 7

When the little girl returned from her walk all of her friends were gathered in the main room waiting for her.

She looked around at all of them and then said, "I know I have been a little cranky lately and I really am sorry, but I don't know what is wrong."

Lion stepped forward, "I think you know if you thought more about how you are feeling."

The little girl was able to admit that there was still some fear and obviously some anger, but she didn't quite know what to do about it.

"I think you do know," answered Lion gently but firmly.

"I don't want to write more letters yet," she answered almost a little panic stricken. P.J. fought the urge to snuggle close to her.

"What about your childhood friends?" asked Lion.

"What about them?" asked the little girl a bit defensively.

"Didn't they say in their Christmas cards that they would like to see you?" he asked.

"Are you trying to get rid of me?" she answered with another hint of panic in her voice.

P.J. could stand it no longer, "No! Oh no! We love you and we are just trying to help."

The little girl gave her friend a hug and said, "I know."

"Are you afraid of your friends?" asked Sure to Go.

"No," answered the little girl.

"They didn't hurt you, did they?" asked Bear Buns.

"No, not at all. We used to have a lot of fun together," she said.

"Do they know what happened to you?" asked Van Gogh the Sheep Dog.

The little girl shook her head no.

"Are you scared to tell them?" asked Sabrina.

"Yes," answered the little girl.

"But why my little lady?" asked the Prince.

"Because maybe then they wouldn't like me," she answered as tears rose in her eyes.

Bright Eyes came over and hugged the little girl as tight as he could.

"I think that he is trying to tell you what I and others have felt once we found our way here," began little Teresa, "you accepted us just as we were. It didn't matter what condition we were in or where we had come from or what we had been through. You took care of us and helped us to heal."

"Yes," added Barely Bear, "Just like Arthur did for me."

"Don't you see?" asked Sabrina, "Many here you did not know and yet you helped them."

"And friends, good friends will help more," added Pumpkin-Pumpkin, "you just have to give them a chance."

"Will all of you go with me?" the little girl asked.

"That would not be possible as this is something you must do on your own," began Lion. "However, I think an exception could be made and one of the smaller critters may accompany you."

Of course all of them wanted to be the one chosen. Godzilla suggested that their names be placed in a basket and Lion would choose one. Before picking out the slip of paper Lion really mixed all of the names up and closing his eyes placed a paw in the basket and drew out one slip of paper and handed it to Godzilla who said, "The critter accompanying the little girl on this adventure is…P.J."

Of course the rest of the little critters were disappointed but they congratulated P.J. and told her they knew that she would do a great job. It was decided that the little girl should first send a letter to her friends inviting them to meet her at the edge of the woods in the park for a picnic in the park building in one week.

As this was not going to be a long trip there wasn't much to prepare, however the little girl did decide that she wanted to make some of the ornaments for each of her childhood friends like she had for her cave mates for Christmas. So she got busy at those right away. Godzilla and the kitchen crew put together some snacks and drinks for the journey and also some items to share at the picnic.

Before she knew it the day to leave on her journey had arrived. The little girl was nervous and also was very, very happy that Lion was allowing P.J. to accompany her. There were lots of hugs and wishes for a good time and safe travel. Then Lion and Charlie gave P.J. and the little girl a special blessing.

Jacques then asked, "Can some of us please travel with her to the crossroads?"

"Oh yes, please?" asked Arp.

All eyes turned to Lion and Godzilla who looked at each other and then said together, "Yes."

Lion added, "But just to the crossroads and only if Sir Lancelot agrees to go with us."

"I would be honored," said Sir Lancelot, "but I suggest that we take one of the toboggans as that way R.T. Cold Nose III can go along too."

Pretty soon everyone was ready to go. The little girl had a special back pack that she placed P.J. in so that she wouldn't have to walk. Then Jacques, Jeanette, Arp, Kris, Lord Percival, Barely Bear, Sure to Go, Bright Eyes and a few others got on the toboggan with R.T. Cold Nose III sitting right up front. Lion walked behind the toboggan.

After walking a few steps the little girl turned around and waved at the rest of her cave mates who were gathered at the entrance of the cave. She kept doing this until she could no longer see them.

When they got to the crossroads the little girl let P.J. down so that she could give Lord Percival a hug. Then of course all of the other critters had to give the little girl and P.J. hugs too.

Finally Sir Lancelot said, "My dear little lady thou is only to be gone for a day and if thou dost not hurry thou will be late in meeting thy friends."

So off the little girl and P.J. went down the path that Elsie the Keeper of Hearts had taken. As with her other cave mates every few steps she turned around and waved at the group until she could no longer see them.

Then it was just her and P.J. on the path. They talked a little bit with P.J. asking her if she was nervous and telling her that everything was going to be OK. Before long they could see the clearing up ahead and it looked like someone was standing there and waving. It was Golden Pockets!

"Hello," he was yelling.

The little girl waved back. Then she could tell that he was saying something to someone else. Pretty soon she saw more people gathering. There was Storyteller and Barrister and Lil Angel; oh how she had grown. Also, Mademoiselle, Junior, D.W., Choo-Choo, and Pudie. Then she spotted Sir Galahad and Dancer Girl who was holding their new addition, Lil Man.

"Oh P.J.," she said, "they are all there."

"I am so happy for you," answered P.J.

Pretty soon the little girl was at the edge of the woods and Golden Pockets was giving her a huge hug. And then there were hugs all around and comments about how good she looked and how great it was to see her.

Storyteller said, "And you still have P.J. I am so glad that you brought her so that our Lil Angel can meet her."

They then headed off to the park building for their indoor picnic. There were long picnic tables inside and even a fireplace with a fire going.

Everyone had brought something to share; Golden Pockets, Choo-Choo and Pudie had brought drinks; Mademoiselle and Junior, chips; Galahad and Dancer Girl, the paper goods; Barrister and Storyteller some snacks that went well with the snacks that the little girl had brought; all of them had shared the cost of a huge sub sandwich and D.W. had made some cookies that were the best the little girl had ever tasted. So they sat around eating and sharing stories and even played a few games together. The little girl really felt good being with her friends again.

"So why did you move to the woods?" asked Barrister.

"I'm not really sure," she answered.

"Is it because of what happened to you?" asked Storyteller.

"What do you mean?" asked the little girl.

Golden Pockets answered, "We all know what happened to you."

"You do?" she asked, "and you are still my friends?"

"Of course we are," they all almost said together.

"That's how really good friends are," said Golden Pockets.

They all had a great time visiting and playing different games the rest of the day.

Then the little girl suddenly said, "I almost forgot, I made something for each of you."

With that she gave them each the initial ornaments she had made for them.

"What fun," said Storyteller, "You used the initials of our nicknames from when we were kids."

"And our favorite colors," added Pudie.

"I can't believe you remember all of this," said D.W.

The little girl felt confused at Storyteller's comment but tried not to let on, but rather quickly said, "It's starting to get late so we had better get going."

Everyone agreed.

"This sure was fun," said Dancing Girl, "We'll have to plan to do this more often."

As the little girl and P.J. left the building Storyteller said, "Stay in touch."

The little girl promised that she would. "I'll be praying for you," said Choo-Choo.

Everyone gave her a hug and then Golden Pockets walked her to the door and said, "I know that it must have been a little hard for you to meet with all of us but please know that we all love and care about you."

"Thank you," answered the little girl.

As he gave her a hug he said, "It was really good to see you Ann. Have a safe and most blessed journey."

The little girl had to fight running out of the door, across the park and back to the path into the woods. It was what she wanted to do, but didn't want to appear that she was eager to leave her friends, because she wasn't, she just felt confused. Besides, she felt exhausted. Finally, she was at the path and decided to turn around and look and sure enough there were all of her friends in the window of the park building waving at her. She waved back and then headed into the woods.

After she went around a curve and could no longer see the path leading out of the woods, she stopped and grabbed P.J. from her backpack saying, "Oh P.J., I am so glad you are with me."

P.J. hugged her and said, "I am glad too."

"I don't understand why Storyteller said that I had used their nicknames and then Golden Pockets called me Ann and come to think of it, you didn't say anything while we were there."

P.J. gave the little girl another hug and said, "They can't hear me; only you can. And as for the rest, we will have to ask Lion what he makes of it."

"OK," said the little girl, "Let's go home."

P.J. gave her a third hug and said, "I love you." The little girl smiled and gave her friend a hug back and she didn't put her in the back pack rather she carried the little bear in her arms.

It felt like they had been walking a very long time and of course, once they were in the woods it did get a little darker.

"I wonder why it always seems longer getting home," the little girl said. P.J. just snuggled closer to the little girl. All of a sudden off in the distance she thought she saw someone waving.

"Who is that?" she asked P.J.

"It's Sir Lancelot!" P.J. replied. As tired as she was the little girl began running until she almost fell into Sir Lancelot's arms.

"Oh my little ladies thou both seemest so very tired," he said as he hugged both of them. "I am therefore quite happy that I have brought with me the royal sled."

It was only one of the toboggans but, there were a couple of blankets and even a pillow. He got both of them snuggled under the blankets and tucked in tight so they wouldn't fall off. The little girl then looked up at him and said, "Thank you so much for meeting us."

He patted her on her head and said, "Let us then go home."

Sir Lancelot did not even have the rope tightly in his hands before his two little passengers were sound asleep. They never even woke up when he pulled them into the cave. Gently he lifted both of them off of the toboggan and placed them in the little girl's sleeping bag.

"It must have been a hard journey for her," said Pumpkin-Pumpkin.

"For both of them," added Lord Percival.

Both of them slept through the night and late into the morning. They were definitely surprised to find everyone up and moving about.

"Well good morning sleepy heads," said Lord Percival.

"Morning?" asked P.J. and the little girl together.

"Yes," everyone responded, but not too loudly.

"As soon as you all get cleaned up breakfast will be served," said Godzilla.

Of course everyone was very anxious to hear about the little girl and P.J.'s outing. The little girl started by sharing that it had been really good to see her friends again and that they had had a good time talking, playing games, and eating.

"I bet they were glad to see you again too little lady," said the Prince.

"Yes," she answered, "they seemed very glad and even said that they would like to get together again."

"And that you should stay in touch," added P.J.

The little girl laughed, "And that too."

"Did they like the gifts you made them?" asked Ada B. Green.

"Yes," answered the little girl, "but Storyteller said a curious thing."

"What was that?" asked Sabrina.

"She thought it was great that I had remembered and used their nicknames," the little girl answered, "which I wasn't sure what she was talking about."

"What do you think it means?" asked R.T. Cold Nose III.

"Well," began the little girl, "if those are their nicknames, then they must have real names and either I don't know what they are or I don't remember them."

"That is some good insight my little lady," said Arthur, "maybe the Prince and I can find a book that has their real names in it."

"It's worth a try," said the Prince.

"So do you think you will visit them again?" asked Fuzzy Wuzzy Woof Woof.

The little girl thought for a moment before answering, "At first I didn't think that I would, but after a good night's sleep I think that I would like to visit and play with them again."

Joan said, "Maybe I can go along with you the next time too." Of course the rest of the critters jumped on that bandwagon.

"One more thing," began the little girl, "As I was getting ready to leave Golden Pockets walked me to the door, gave me a hug, told me to have a blessed and safe journey, and said that it was really good to see me again."

"What's so unusual about that?" asked Sure to Go.

"Nothing," answered the little girl, "except that he called me Ann."

ANN'S STORY
Chapter 12
Finishing the Letters

Ann kept busy with her research and children's book plus the letters. Having finished the one to her father she began working on the one to her mother. The question that kept coming to mind was "why?"

She found that question coming up in the group session too as the women shared their stories. Why would people, who supposedly loved them, do such horrible things to them? So many had blamed themselves for many years, but therapy and the group had helped them to see that it wasn't their fault; it was nothing they did or didn't do. They also shared their fears of becoming like the parent or the person that had abused or molested them. One woman shared that what she had decided to do was to ask herself what her parents did in any particular parenting situation and then she would do the opposite and it had worked. Her daughter was now grown, married and with children of her own and was very healthy and had a very close and loving relationship with her mother. Dr. Pete pointed out that for each person who has been abused or molested that at some point it does seem to become a choice to treat others as they were treated or not and to get the help they need so that they can overcome it. One woman shared that her father continually said that there was nothing wrong with him and that his behavior was normal. But he was so abusive, especially verbally that he pushed everyone away from him and had no clue as to why.

In her private session Dr. Pete asked her at what point did her mother quit hitting her, if ever?

Ann gave a little smile, "I remember it as if it happened yesterday. I think I was about 13 or 14 and she was yelling at me because I had put a bowl in a wrong place in the cupboard; I apologized and she slapped me across the face. Something just kind of snapped inside and I looked her straight in the eye, because by then we were about the same height and I said, 'Don't you ever hit me again.' I don't know who was more surprised, her or me. But I must have had a look that said I meant it, because she never did hit me again. Unfortunately that was when she began picking on my younger siblings more. I always felt guilty about that."

"But you were just a kid who was trying to protect yourself," said Dr. Pete.

"I know, but I was also the eldest and should have protected my younger siblings."

"Did you try?"

Ann thought a moment, "I guess I did by taking them different places to get them out of the house and trying to get them to behave so that she wouldn't get angry at them. But as soon as I could I left home and left them there."

"And what did you find out about that in your meetings for those from alcoholic homes?"

"That that was pretty normal for someone from a family like mine."

"So, don't you think it's time that you began redirecting the anger that you have against yourself towards those who were really responsible?"

"I guess you are correct."

That very afternoon she went back to work on the letter to her mother and was able to write about not just the hurt, but also the anger. Ann was typing so fast and furious that by the time she finished her fingers and hands both hurt and she was exhausted. She decided to take a warm bubble bath to soak away the day and then ordered a pizza delivered and found a comedy on one of the movie channels to watch. All of this helped her to relax and she slept soundly through the night with a few of her stuffed animals surrounding her.

Eventually she did begin work on the letter to her uncle, which she knew was going to be the most difficult one. Once again, the question "why?" kept coming up. "Why would you do this to me, your stepdaughter and Heaven only knows who else?" As Ann was having difficulties writing the letter Dr. Pete suggested that instead of doing it on the computer that she write it in long hand, even printing and using her non dominant hand as a way of maybe getting a little more in touch with the little girl inside of her. At first Ann thought it was a little silly, but decided to give it a try one afternoon. At first nothing came and then she found herself writing in big letters "I'M AFRAID" over and over and then "PLEASE DON'T HURT ME."

She began to cry so hard that she didn't think she would ever stop. She finally curled up on her bed with as many of her stuffed animals around her that she could get to fit and she cried herself to sleep. When she awoke it was already dark outside. "Great," she said to her stuffed animals, "now I won't be able to sleep tonight!" She fixed herself something to eat and then lay on the couch trying to watch TV and not think about anything. But all that was on the TV were shows about cops, robbers, and criminals or the stupid reality shows. Thank goodness she also received the home improvement channel and watched that until she felt sleepy. Her dreams were of herself as a little girl that night and of being afraid again, but someone always came to protect her only she couldn't see who it was in the dream, but she knew she was safe.

The next day she went back to work on the letter to her uncle and this time she felt a little stronger and was able to write at one point, "I AM LITTLE AND YOU ARE BIG AND YOU SHOULDN'T BE HURTING ME!"

She dreamt again that night of being little and the uncle was coming after her but someone was stopping him and at first she couldn't see who it was, but then her stuffed bear Sir Lancelot came into view and protected her, however she still had the feeling that he wasn't the only one there.

She shared with Dr. Pete the results of the letter thus far, and about the dreams, except she left out the part about Sir Lancelot coming to the rescue. She didn't want him to think she was as weird as she thought she was. He suggested that she ask St. Germaine Cousins to intercede on her behalf asking for strength to face her molester in the letters.

That afternoon Ann sat down to write again and she said a quick prayer to St. Germaine asking for her help. Out loud she said, "I am scared, but I have got to face this. Please Lord, help me." Before long she was writing down her feelings as a child of the fear, the hurt, the betrayal, the guilt, and the lack of strength to fight against him. Again, that night came the same dream only this time not just Sir Lancelot came, but also Lion to protect her.

While working on all of this Ann was very grateful for what she called "blessed distractions;" meal gatherings here and there with friends; helping Lynn to move into the condo; babysitting, which she called "god-parenting" with Little Patricia; and an evening with Maggie and J.R. and their wedding party to look at their DVD of their wedding day and some shots from their honeymoon in Vermont.

As they were leaving Maggie's and J.R.'s place Tom asked, "So, how is it going with the letter writing?"

"I have to admit that this is really tough stuff," she answered.

"Bringing up a lot of old feelings?" he ventured.

"And then some, or so it seems."

"You seem better, but how are you feeling?"

"It's helping, I think; getting all of those feelings that are inside out on paper at least is offering some kind of relief and somehow I am feeling stronger."

"Maybe it's because you have been carrying all of the extra emotional weight around."

Ann laughed, "Yup, it's what Dr. Pete calls 'emotional baggage.'"

"Well, you know everyone else and I are here if you ever need sounding boards."

"I know and I really, really appreciate that, but this part seems to be something that I kind of need to do by myself. Well, except for the help of all of my stuffed animals," she laughed. "You really started something with Godzilla!"

"Who would have known," commented Tom.

"I think the Holy Spirit did," she answered. They gave each other a hug and headed for home.

Even though she was a little tired she made some notes to include in the letter to the uncle that she planned on working on the next day.

That night the dream returned and just when she was feeling the most afraid Sir Lancelot and Lion showed up, but this time so did every single one of her stuffed animals. And Ann as the little girl in the dream was smiling just a bit.

The next morning she felt almost energized to finish the letter to the uncle. And what she wrote really surprised her; not only did she include the feelings of hurt, fear and betrayal but the anger really came out and she wrote cuss words that would have embarrassed a sailor or a truck driver or both! Even she couldn't believe it was her writing. And like with the letter to her mother her fingers and hands hurt by the end of the day and she was worn out and yet..."what is that feeling?" she said aloud. After a few moments she smiled and said, "Happy!"

She wanted to celebrate so she called Tom and said, "I know that it's still a little chilly outside, but are you up for some ice cream, my treat?"

"Always!" he answered.

They decided to meet after dinner at their favorite ice cream parlor which had just opened again after being closed for some of the winter months.

"So what's the occasion?" Tom asked once they had gotten their ice cream.

"I finished the letters."

"So, that's why you're glowing."

"You are such a charmer."

"No, seriously" he protested, "you look...."

"Happy?" she offered.

"Yes! So, any insights?"

"One major one, how really angry I was!"

"You mean you didn't know that?"

"I knew I was angry, but not that angry. You mean it showed?"

"Well, you were a little cranky, actually more than a little cranky at times," he began, "and all of your friends saw that, but we also decided that each of us would have been furious, so a little cranky was more than acceptable."

"That's interesting because furious, is exactly what came out. In fact, I would also add livid. In fact, even I couldn't believe the words I wrote."

"Good girl. Did it feel good?"

"Afterwards, but at the time I felt embarrassed and a little concerned that I was so angry."

"Like it might get out of control?"

"Yeah, but a part of me knew it wouldn't."

"So, now what?"

"Well, I will share all of this with Dr. Pete and the group and we'll go from there. But enough on me, what has been keeping you busy these days?"

They then talked about Tom's volunteer work, the world, politics and anything else that came to mind.

As they parted Ann said, "Thank you Tom for everything, but especially for being my friend and sticking by me."

Tom smiled and gave her a hug saying, "That is what friends are for."

That night she had the same dream again and all of her stuffed animal friends showed up. However, there was someone else who was coming to the rescue of the little girl and she was so surprised that it woke her. "Oh my gosh," she said to her stuffed animals, "It was me as I look now." Ann was really glad that her appointment with Dr. Pete was scheduled for the next morning as she could hardly wait to tell him everything!

She awoke early, showered, had breakfast, and got dressed in record time. She debated as to whether or not she should take the letters she had written and then decided not to, "I think I know what I am going to end up doing with them," she said aloud.

Gratefully Dr. Pete was right on time. "You look like a kid on Christmas morning, what's happened?" he asked.

She then told him about the letters and the dreams, including the stuffed animals in them this time. "And then last night I had the same dream and all of my stuffed animals were there, but so was I, as an adult!"

"Well, you don't have to tell me how you feel about that, because it shows, but what does it mean to you?"

Ann thought a minute, "I think it means that I am really beginning to take care of and protect that little girl that is still inside of me."

"And what do you think will happen as the result of doing that?"

"Well, that she doesn't have to be afraid anymore because she knows that I will take care of her."

"Anything else?"

Ann thought a minute and then said, "Nothing is coming right now. However, after the dream I did make a decision; I think it's time for me to confront these people and so I am going to take a trip the week before Easter to South Carolina."

"I'm proud of you Ann."

"Don't be, I haven't actually made the trip yet."

"So, what are your plans?"

"Well, I can visit my aunt and uncle, who are wonderful and then go to the graves of my parents one day and read my letters to them."

"What about the uncle who molested you?"

"I really do not care to see him. Not that I am afraid of him anymore, but I think there is a part of me that just isn't sure what I would do if I did see him. I mean, as I said before I might just punch him, which I don't think would be appropriate especially because I am now in touch with all of that anger. Plus, there is also a part of me that just doesn't care about seeing him."

"May I make a couple of suggestions?"

"By all means."

"First, be sure to take my telephone number with you and feel free to call any time of the night or day just in case anything unforeseen happens. Second, after reading the letters to your parents you might want to take a container with you that you can burn them in or you can tear them up and throw them into the ocean, if you are going to be near it."

"Kind of a symbolic letting go?"

"Exactly. Now with the letter to the uncle, it would be good if you could find a more or less deserted place where you could read it out loud and pretend that he is standing there and then destroy that letter too. How does that sound?"

Ann thought a moment, "I think it sounds okay."

"But?"

"I don't know. It just feels like something is missing, but I don't know what."

"Would you like to read them in my presence before you leave on the trip?"

Ann looked at him for a few seconds as she thought, "Yes, yes I would; especially the one to my uncle."

"Okay, then let's plan on doing that during the three sessions prior to your departure. We will do one letter a session and you choose the order you want to go over them in."

Ann's aunt and uncle were thrilled that she was coming for a visit but felt bad that they had a small apartment. Ann assured them that she would be just fine in a local motel. In fact, the truth be known, she actually preferred that for this trip in case she needed to hide out and regroup for awhile.

Ann let all of her friends know about her plans. "But you will be back in time for our annual Easter morning brunch together won't you?" asked Tom.

She assured him and the others that she would return the Wednesday of Holy Week and so would be there for all of the beautiful services.

"So, Passion or Palm Sunday as we used to call it, you will be going through your own passion?" suggested Marie.

"I never thought of it that way, but yes, and then I will be home for hopefully, my resurrection," she giggled.

Ann had also decided to spend a day before she left on the trip walking and driving around her town; a sort of mini trip back to her childhood. The day she decided to do it was a really nice late winter, early spring day. At the last minute she put Sir Lancelot in the passenger seat, "For moral support," she told him. She first went by the Catholic grade school she had attended and then into the park where she had played as a child. She sat in the parking lot allowing her mind to drift back. It was like stepping back in time and yet still trying to keep one foot in the "now." She thought about all of the teachers and nuns who had taught her and laughed, "A couple of 'stinkers,'" she said, "but also some really, really good ones too, like Sister Cecilia." She wondered what had happened to her. She then drove by the other park where she had gone ice skating and sledding in the winter and played different games and sports in the summer. She thought of some of her childhood friends that had moved away and a couple who had died. She then went by her old Catholic high school. Good memories, but also some difficult ones, as she remembered feeling like she never really fit in; it was a very awkward time for her. She let the sadness come and be a part of her without it taking over. She then drove through the old neighborhood past all of the houses where she and her little friends had played 'hide and seek,' 'tag,' 'jump rope' and so many other games. Next she drove by her grandparents' old home, and warm memories returned of her Grandmother Rose. Finally, she arrived at the house she had grown up in. She sat across the street from it letting the memories flood back in. After a few moments a young woman came out that Ann recognized from church so Ann got out of the car and greeted her. The young lady recognized Ann too.

"I didn't know you lived here," said Ann, "this is the house I grew up in."

"Really? Would you like to see what few changes we've made inside?" she asked.

"That would be wonderful," Ann said.

As she entered the house she said a silent prayer asking God to be with her so that she could stay calm. Gratefully, the young couple had made a number of changes so it really did not look much like the house that Ann had lived in.

"You have done some wonderful things with this home," Ann said. "I really like it."

The woman smiled with pride, "My husband and I have been doing much of the work ourselves. It was a good house, it just needed some updating."

Ann thanked the woman for her time as she left.

Once back in the car she thanked God for that little pleasant surprise. "Life does move forward," she said. On a whim she decided to see if she could find the house where the uncle who molested her had lived with his family. Not much had changed on the house and as she drove by she felt uncomfortable, but she also knew she was okay. She said a prayer for her cousin Lucy that she too would heal.

On the way home she stopped in the florist shop that her family had shopped at while she was growing up.

"Well, what a pleasant surprise," said the owner, "it's Ann isn't it?"

"I can't believe you remember," she said.

They then talked about the old neighborhood and how many were deceased or had moved away and also what the various members of their families were doing. Ann bought a large bouquet of fresh cut flowers and headed to the cemetery. She visited the graves of her neighbors, her grandparents, and other relatives and friends who had already died. At each grave she remembered, she thanked them, prayed for them and left a few flowers.

Once back in the car she sat there for a moment simply reflecting on the day and she realized first how healing it had all been. "Healing!" she said aloud, "I think I will see if Father Jack is available." So, she gave the rectory a quick call and he was in. When she told him what she wanted he told her to come right over.

Driving over she realized something else, "I missed lunch!" She laughed.

Father Jack explained to Ann that most people think that the Sacrament of Healing or The Anointing of the Sick is only for those who are at risk for dying, but that is not the case.

"There are other grave illnesses as well as surgeries where the individuals can benefit from this Sacrament and I include emotional illnesses as well, especially in a case such as yours," he said.

"I am glad," said Ann, "I need all the help I can get."

Father Jack smiled as he continued, "This Sacrament also involves the forgiveness of sins and as you are able, I would suggest that I hear your confession first."

Ann agreed and then asked for a few moments to examine her conscience.

After her confession Father Jack then prayed over her and this was followed by some special readings. He then made the Sign of the Cross on her forehead and each of the palms of her hands with the blessed "Oil of the Sick" saying, *"Through this holy anointing may the Lord in his love and mercy help you with the grace of the Holy Spirit. May the Lord who frees you from sin save you and raise you up."*

They talked for a few moments and Ann shared with him the plans of her trip to South Carolina.

"I will be praying for you Ann," he said. "In fact, after Mass this weekend before you leave come and see me and I will give you a special blessing for your journey." Ann thanked him for everything.

It had been a full day and as hungry as Ann was she really didn't feel like going out for dinner, alone or with anyone and yet she didn't feel like a pizza either. She finally decided to grab a double burger from her favorite place and head for the comfort of home.

As she laid Sir Lancelot on her bed she said, "Thank you dear friend for your support today."

The day of her departure was only a week away. Ann felt a little nervous, but by and large was really doing okay.

As she was thinking about this the telephone rang, "Hey," Tom said.

"Hey back," she answered, "how are you?"

"I am good and you?"

"Good."

"Ok, now that we got all of that settled," he said laughing, "how about a quick pizza with the gang after 4 p.m. Mass on Saturday? We all want to see you before you go, but we know that you are also going to be busy packing and all of that good stuff."

"That's a great idea."

"Good, then it's all set. How about I pick you up for Mass?"

"Sounds good to me."

The Gospel for that Sunday was from John and dealt with the grain of wheat that has to die in order for fruit to be produced and how it related to the impending death of Jesus.

"All of us go through trials like this in our lives at one time or another," said Father Jack. "In fact, it begins with our birth. In order for a child to live and thrive it has to let go of the comfort of the womb. In order for us to learn and grow, we have to leave the comfort of our homes as little children to attend school or even as a teenager to attend college. And sometimes entire families have to move across country so that a parent can accept a job. And most of us know how hard it is to diet and exercise; we have to give up something so that we can obtain the greater good of good health. And how many of you gave up chocolate this Lent? Not easy! And hopefully you set the money aside that you would have spent to give to a charity so that you learn the good that can come from sacrificing. And sometimes it is even more subtle than this; maybe it's a personality trait like anger or impatience that we want to get rid of. To do so means dying to oneself; not doing the thing that comes easiest to us but rather that which is the hardest; to control our reactions to situations. One of the hardest things, however, sometimes has to do with letting go of the past so that we can move forward. Has someone hurt you or your family? Was it a slight, a word or an action? If you remain in that hurt you will simply stay stuck and won't be able to move forward with your life remaining a victim of your past. So, what is the answer? Forgiveness. Forgive that person, not just because it will help you, but it is what we as Christian Catholics are called to do. It is what God asks of us."

Tom whispered to Ann, "Does he know about your trip?"

Ann nodded yes.

After Mass Ann and the others waited for Father Jack in their pews.

Eventually he made his way back down the aisle and stopping by Ann he said, "A blessing for your journey, right?"

Ann nodded in the affirmative as she said, "But I think you gave that to me in your homily."

He laughed, "Not much gets by you does it? Actually, you were part of the inspiration for that homily because of all of the hard work that you have already done."

"Really?" said Ann totally surprised.

"Yes, really, now let's give you a blessing."

Father Jack then asked all of her friends to surround her and to extend an arm of blessing towards Ann. Just before she bowed her head Ann noticed that little Patricia was extending her little arm just like her mother and that brought a smile to her face. After he blessed her, Father Jack gave her a hug and said, "Drive carefully and if you need anything while you are away, just give me a call."

"Thanks Father," Ann replied.

Over pizza everyone talked about a lot of different things, but interspersed were questions to Ann about the trip; "How she was feeling?" "Where would she stay?" "How long would it take to drive?"

Lynn said, "It's too bad that you have to go by yourself. I wish I could go with you."

Ann smiled, "Thank you, but I know that this is something that I need to do by myself."

"All of us will be with you in spirit," said Maggie.

"I know you will," answered Ann.

"And prayer," said Tom.

"I'm counting on that," she answered.

"And if you need to talk, just call. Patricia and I are usually home all day," said Marie.

As they got ready to leave there were a lot of hugs and a few tears.

"Don't worry," she began, "if things get tough I will just picture all of you around me with your arms raised in blessing and I know that I will be okay. And please know that I will carry each and every one of you in my heart."

"We will miss you," said Randy.

Both of them were quiet on the way to Ann's house lost in their own thoughts. Tom walked her to the door and gave her a hug saying, "We all love you Ann."

Ann thanked him and gave him a hug back, "I'll be home before you know it."

She flicked the front porch light and he flicked his car lights and was gone. Ann stood in her living room feeling very much alone, but just for a moment, because she knew that all of them were with her in the Spirit.

The next couple of days Ann laid out everything on the bed in the spare bedroom that she wanted to pack for the trip; checking things off of her list as she did so. She then went to bed early Tuesday night planning to leave as early as possible the next morning.

ANN'S STORY
Chapter 13
The Trip

Once she had the car packed she looked around at all of her stuffed animals and said, "I wish that all of you were going with me." She went around and gave each of them a little hug or a pat on the head. At the last minute she decided to take Sir Lancelot. "After all," she said, "every damsel needs a knight to protect her no matter how strong she might be."

After buckling him into the passenger seat she started up the car, made the Sign of the Cross and her journey began.

She had packed a number of her favorite CD's and a few snacks so that she didn't have to stop except for gas and to stretch. She was grateful that the weather was good. It was overcast but that made it easier on the eyes for the long drive.

She did decide to stop for lunch even though she had done a fast food drive-through. There was a rest stop nearby and it was just enough of a break to rejuvenate her.

She sang along with the music or drove in silence just thinking about where she had been just a few years ago and now where she was headed and was about to face. She prayed and thanked God for this journey and for the aunt and uncle whom she would soon see. And the time passed quickly.

She was glad that she had told the motel that she would probably be a late arrival as it was evening by the time she pulled in. And she was very grateful that there was a restaurant right on the grounds as she could then get something to go. She called her aunt and uncle when she got to her room and let them know she had arrived safely. They suggested that she come over for breakfast in the morning.

She then called Tom. "I was hoping this was you," he said.

They talked of the drive and how she was feeling. He then told her that they already had a "system" so that everyone would be informed that she had arrived there in one piece.

After dinner, Ann unpacked and watched a little TV before calling it a day. Surprisingly, she slept very well that night with Sir Lancelot in her arms.

She was up early the next morning as the excitement of seeing her aunt and uncle wouldn't let her sleep a minute longer than absolutely necessary. They saw her pull into their apartment parking lot and were waiting with the door wide open.

Both of them hugged her at the same time because as her uncle said, "We were arguing over who was going to get to hug you first."

Ann laughed. It felt so good to be with these two special people. They shared some wonderful memories over breakfast; some things that Ann had forgotten about and others that got all of them laughing.

After they had finished eating her uncle said, "I know that you mentioned that you have a couple of things to take care of while you are here, but here are our thoughts. We would like to show you around the area today just so you can kind get the lay of the land, maybe go by the cemetery where your parents are buried, and then tonight we would like to take you out to one of our favorite restaurants."

"Sounds good," said Ann.

"Now tomorrow," he continued, "and Saturday we have other commitments so you would kind of be on your own."

"That's perfect," said Ann, "as that will give me the time I need to take care of the other items."

"Wonderful," said her aunt, "we were a little worried."

Her uncle continued, "Sunday, Mass of course and brunch and then our daughter Mary and her family live not too far from here and have invited us over."

"Oh gosh," said Ann, "I haven't seen them since my parents' funerals."

"On Monday," her aunt continued, "We thought maybe a little sightseeing of some of the special places in our area."

"That would be good as I also need to get a few souvenirs to take back to my friends up north," she answered.

"Oh I know a great gift shop just for that," said her aunt.

"She knows all of the best places to shop," teased her uncle. And then asked, "Is there anyone else you wish to see while you are here?"

"No," answered Ann.

"You know your other uncle lives down here now too," said her aunt.

"I had heard that, but we were never particularly close," Ann said.

"Then there's Tuesday," started her uncle.

"And I am taking both of you out to your very favorite restaurant that night for dinner. No arguments!" said Ann.

"Okay, Okay," said her uncle.

After helping her aunt clean up everything from breakfast they all got in Ann's car with her uncle in the front and her aunt in the back. They were so excited to show her the town that they had grown to love since moving here and it was a beautiful place. Her uncle still loved to play golf and so had her drive past his favorite courses.

"Maybe we can get in a quick nine on Monday," he offered.

"I didn't think to bring my clubs," said Ann.

They drove by their church which was a beautiful, newer building and then just up and down various streets showing Ann where their grocery store was, the post office, their doctors' offices, and numerous other places that were their regular places to visit.

They did stop for a quick lunch and then went by the cemetery to visit her parents' graves. Ann had not been here since their funerals. She was concerned that everything she had been through the past couple of years and what she was about to encounter would be evident on her face to her aunt and uncle, but gratefully it was not. Ann mentally said, I will be back tomorrow. After dinner Ann dropped her aunt and uncle off at their apartment and headed back for her motel room. After the long drive the day before she was glad to be able to hit the sack a little early again that night.

The next morning she went over to the restaurant for breakfast. Gratefully there was a small booth in the back where she could sit alone and kind of gather her thoughts regarding the day ahead. After, she got Sir Lancelot from her room and the two letters and headed for the cemetery. At the last minute she decided to stop at a florist shop and picked up some fresh cut flowers.

She sat in her car until she felt she was ready. She gave Sir Lancelot a quick hug and took a deep breath as she got out. She stood in front of her parents' graves and decided to read the letter to her father first. It had helped to have read them in the office with Dr. Pete as now she was not hearing them out loud for the first time. She took a deep breath and read the letter.

After she finished she stood there looking at the grave and said, "Dad, when I was a kid, I didn't understand, but now I do. You had a disease and I wish you would have been able to get some help for it, but that is in the past and I have moved forward. I forgive you, I love you and I miss you." Ann started to cry and she just let the tears flow as she placed some flowers in the vase that was in the ground next to his head stone.

She then decided to take a little break and walked over to where the faucet was and got some water for both of the vases. She looked at the head stones of those she passed and wondered what their stories were and what their children thought of them.

She put the flowers in her mother's vase before she began because she started to feel a little nervous. She then pictured all of her stuffed animals there with her and her friends standing around her with their hands outstretched in blessing and she began to read the letter to her mother, but first looked around to make sure there was no one watching or nearby.

When she finished she said, "Mom, I know that you were ill, but why couldn't you see that? Why couldn't you see how much you were hurting your children? I do love you and because I am healing, I forgive you. I don't know that it is a total forgiveness yet, but I hope that someday it will be."

Ann didn't cry, she just felt kind of numb. She prayed for the souls of each of her parents and then tore the letters up and placing them in the metal bucket she had brought set them on fire. When there was nothing left but ashes she poured water over them and then emptied the pail in the shrubs that were on either side of the headstones. "May you both rest in peace," she said and then walked back to the car and sat there for quite awhile. Even though it was lunch time, she wasn't hungry. She felt like she wanted to do something, but didn't know what to do and so prayed asking for guidance, almost at once she knew.

The church was empty but light was shining through the windows, and as always there were vigil candles burning. She knelt in the pew and prayed; thanking God for the gift of this morning, for the gift of her friends, her therapist, her women's support group, her priest, her parish, her Catholic Faith, her aunt and uncle, and for her parents; for the gifts of life and faith and other good things her parents had handed down to her. Slowly she felt life coming back into her. She prayed for awhile longer and then went to the rectory and arranged for a Mass to be said for the intention of her parents.

Then she went back to her motel room and wrote out some postcards to about half of the group saying, "All is well, but wish you were here." She hoped to send the second half out tomorrow after she had gone to the ocean. She made some notes to share with Dr. Pete and then decided to take a walk. It really was a lovely town that her aunt, uncle, and parents had decided on. There were a couple of shops she stopped in just to look around and then she walked through the nearby park. As it was a Friday people were still working and the kids would be in school so the park was pretty empty.

The next morning Ann was up very early again, and after a quick drive-through breakfast she headed to the ocean with her caramel iced coffee in hand. She had noticed on a map that there seemed to be a small park or something not too far off of the main road. She was hoping that it was desolate enough or maybe that she was early enough that she would be alone; at least long enough to finish what she had come to do.

God had blessed her as there were no other cars in the parking lot. She walked down onto the beach with the letter in hand. The sun had just poked up and the sunrise was beautiful. She prayed asking God to help her to read this letter and then she started. In Dr.

Pete's office she had toned down her inflection a bit, especially when she came to the cuss words, but this morning she didn't have to. She yelled them, pretending the uncle was standing in front of her.

Periodically she would stop and look around just to make sure no one had driven into the park and then she would continue. It was a long letter, but she finished "yelling" it in about 15 or 20 minutes. And then she just stood there; she felt tired, but somehow freer too. She searched inside to see if there were any unexpressed feelings still roaming around, but there was just one that she became aware of.

"I have only forgiven you a little bit as there is a part of me that understands and accepts that you are a sick, sick son of a gun; but believe me, I am far from forgiving you totally. I know that I should for my own healing and because God asks me to, but all I can do at this moment is to ask God for the grace to help me to do that. It's as far as I can go at this time. I will pray for you and most especially for your victims, but that is the best I can do."

She stood for a few moments just trying to absorb everything. Finally, she tore the letter into little pieces and burned it in the same pail she had used the day prior. Once it was nothing but ashes she added water from the ocean to it and let it drift away. "You are in God's hands now," she said aloud. She put the pail back in the car and then took a long, long walk along the beach taking her coffee, some snacks and her notebook. It was mid-afternoon by the time she returned to the car. She was a little tired, but also aware that she felt good.

Once back at the motel she took a shower, ordered a pizza for supper and wrote the rest of her postcards to her friends simply saying, "Work completed! All is well! Time for some fun! Wish you were here!" Again Ann slept very well that night.

Ann was grateful that her aunt and uncle's parish had a 9:30 a.m. Mass as then she could sleep in just a little longer. She picked them up and both of them commented on how nice she looked. They liked to sit near the front so after gathering up their palms they headed down the main aisle. Must be a family tradition, Ann thought to herself. As people started arriving Ann smiled to herself as it was very evident that this was mostly a retirement community. A few minutes before Mass began Ann noticed two women come in who sat just a couple of pews in front of them and to the left. The one woman really looked familiar to Ann, but she couldn't imagine why she would know anyone here. But periodically during Mass she would look at the woman trying to place her.

Today was Palm Sunday of the Passion of the Lord which commemorated Jesus entering Jerusalem with glory and honor, but it was also the beginning of Holy Week, the last week of His life, and so the Passion of the Lord was read and this year it would be from the Gospel of Mark. Because the majority of the congregation was elderly the priest had the congregation sit instead of stand for the reading. They had a woman who served as the narrator and a man for what was called the "voice;" the priest read Christ's words and the congregation was of course the "crowd." Ann always found it extremely difficult when it came to the part when the crowd had to say "Crucify Him." In fact, she would often simply not say it.

As the Gospel was particularly long for this day, the priest gave a much shortened homily simply inviting everyone to enter into this week walking with Jesus.

"If you are struggling with something or suffering because of an illness or whatever else might be a challenge for you in your life right now, Jesus knows about it. Or if you have reasons to be thankful and to celebrate, He understands that too. If you are facing something difficult ahead, He has been there. So on Holy Thursday come and celebrate the Lord's Supper with Him when He instituted the Eucharist promising to give us His Body and Blood and the priesthood so that the Eucharist might continue for all ages. A celebration of the Passover with His friends knowing what lay ahead of Him. Be here on Good Friday and place all that you are suffering on the cross with Him. Join us on Holy Saturday as we bless the new fire, Paschal or Easter Candle and the water for this year and feel the blessing of God's new life upon you. Then be here Sunday morning for the celebration when we remind ourselves once again that God is God and through Him all things can be overcome - even death! May each and every one of you have a most blessed Holy Week."

The Mass then continued and Ann was still trying to figure out where she knew the woman from. At the sign of peace the lady turned around to wish those behind her peace and glanced at Ann giving her a smile. Ann smiled back.

After Mass had ended Ann asked her aunt, "Do you know that woman?"

Her aunt smiled, "Yes and you know her too. That's Sister Cecilia!"

"What?" exclaimed Ann, "I can't believe it! I've got to talk to her!"

"Well, you are going to have your chance because she and her sister are headed this way," answered her aunt.

Sister Cecilia put her hands on each of Ann's cheeks and said, "Is this really my little Ann?"

Ann couldn't believe her eyes but was able to stammer a "yes" before the tears started to come.

"Tears?" asked Sister Cecilia.

Ann felt like she was a little girl again as she answered, "I never ever thought I would see you again."

"I know," answered Sister Cecilia. "It turned out that you were correct that last day of school and I was wrong, but I didn't know it at the time."

"It sounds like there is a great story here," said her uncle. "Sister would you and your sister please join us for brunch so you and Ann can get caught up?"

"That would be wonderful," said Sister Cecilia.

When they got in the car Ann thanked her uncle for inviting them.

"She was my very favorite grade school teacher! I can't believe I am getting to see her again."

"Yes," said her aunt, "we were surprised to see her in church one Sunday I guess it's been about a year ago now. Their mother lived down here and she needed some help so Sister Cecilia asked for a transfer here and is part of the Religious Education program. Then her sister decided to retire here and shortly thereafter their mother died. But both of them like it here and so have decided to stay, at least as long as Sister Cecilia's order will allow her to."

All during brunch Ann and Sister Cecilia talked catching up on each other's lives and what they had been doing since they last saw each other. Ann felt as if time had suddenly stood still and all of those years in between had gone away. In some ways Ann was still feeling like that little girl from so long ago, but as Sister Cecilia said, "Now we have to get to know each other all over again as two adult women and develop a new relationship and hopefully friendship."

Ann's uncle then asked about what had happened the last day of school.

"Ann, why don't you start?" suggested Sister Cecilia.

Ann smiled, "Well, first of all it needs to be said that our entire class did not want to see the school year end because we all loved Sister Cecilia so much."

Sister Cecilia said, "Well, I don't know about that."

"It's true!" Ann protested. "We learned a lot from her, but we also had fun doing it. Well, the last day of school arrived and everyone was slow leaving as we all gave her hugs good bye, but I made sure I was the last one. I really did not want to leave."

"Do you remember what I asked you to do?" asked Sister Cecilia.

"You asked me to clean the erasers," Ann answered.

"I can't believe you remember that," Sister answered.

"I remember everything about that day because I felt so sad. And then you asked me to help you carry your things to the convent," Ann said, "and we stood and talked for a minute."

"You were trying so hard not to cry," said Sister Cecilia, "so I asked you what was wrong and you said the most incredible thing."

Ann nodded, "I told you that I knew that I was never going to see you again. But of course you assured me that you would be back in the fall after summer vacation."

"But, I wasn't," said Sister. "I didn't know it, but they decided to transfer me."

"That first day of school that fall was the worst ever," said Ann.

"I thought about you and said a prayer that you would be okay."

Ann felt like she was little again and almost on the verge of tears, but she fought them back and said quietly, "I looked everywhere for you and then asked one of the sisters where you were, and that was when I found out you weren't coming back."

Then Sister Cecilia said, "But here I am! A few years late, but I am here."
Ann laughed, "Yes indeed!"

Sister Cecilia's sister then said to Ann's uncle, "How about I give the two of you a ride home and then these two can visit a while longer?"

"What a great idea," said Ann's aunt, "as I want to change clothes anyway before we go down to see our daughter and her family."

"Would a half an hour be long enough?" asked Ann.

"Why don't you make it 45 minutes?" answered her aunt.

Her uncle then laughed and said, "Knowing your aunt you had better make it an hour."

Her aunt shook her head and said, "45 minutes will be just fine." Ann laughed.

After they had left Ann said, "Your sister doesn't miss much does she?"

"No, she doesn't," answered Sister. "She picked up that I wanted a little time alone with you."

Ann laughed, "And here I was thinking that she had picked up on the fact that I wanted some time alone with you." Sister Cecilia laughed.

Ann then said, "I just want to thank you for all that you did for me that year. I loved you so much. I mean, I had always liked coming to school, but that year I couldn't wait. And I will thank God for the opportunity He has given me to tell you that."

Sister Cecilia smiled, "Thank you. Now, I want to ask you something and you don't have to answer if you would rather not."

"Okay," said Ann.

Sister then asked, "Were things okay at home that year? I always sensed that something was wrong, but I didn't know what to do or how to help, I just tried to be there for you when I could. I was so young myself at the time."

Ann took a deep breath and told her as briefly as she could all that she had become aware of in the past couple of years.

"Oh Ann, I wished I had known, maybe I could have done more to help," she said.

"There was no way you could have known as I kept things pretty well hidden even from myself."

"Do your aunt and uncle know?"

Ann shook her head no, "and I am not going to say anything. After all, my mother and the uncle are siblings of my aunt and I don't want to hurt her. She and my uncle have always been so good to me."

"I understand," said Sister Cecilia, "I will not say anything either."

"Thank you," answered Ann, "but if you wish to tell your sister it is okay with me. We had better get going."

When Ann dropped Sister Cecilia off they promised to write each other and to stay in touch. Then Sister Cecilia said, "And I will be praying for you." Ann thanked her and gave her a hug.

Her aunt was ready when Ann got to their apartment, which of course she teased Ann's uncle about. On the way to her cousin Mary's house, her aunt sat in the front seat.

After they had been driving for a while her aunt said, "Ann, I noticed you were kind of quiet at the cemetery the other day."

Ann said, "Yes, it was the first time I had been back to the graves since Dad's funeral."

Her aunt continued, "Ann, I also know that growing up with my sister as a mother wasn't the easiest. She was an unhappy woman and she didn't have an easy childhood either." Ann didn't say anything so her aunt continued, "Our mother, your grandmother Naomi, had a problem with alcohol and when she drank she became mean. Your uncle and your mother were the two eldest and so they took the brunt of it."

"Gosh," said Ann, "that means that I have alcoholism on both sides of my family."

Her aunt nodded, "Your father right?"

Ann said "Yes. But how did you turn out to be so loving and giving?"

With that Ann's uncle chuckled, "I had to teach her."

Her aunt shook her head, "No, he didn't. Anyway, my father, your grandfather, had finally had enough of it and told her that if she didn't stop drinking he was going to take your mother and uncle and leave her."

"And so she quit?" asked Ann. "Wow!"

"From what I was told," continued her aunt, "it wasn't easy and the only thing that changed is that she wasn't mean. She wasn't happy, but she wasn't mean. It was after she quit drinking that I was born, so I never got exposed to that."

"It sure explains a lot," Ann answered, "Now, I understand a little more where my mother's mean streak came from. Thank you for sharing that with me." By then they had arrived at her cousin Mary's house.

They had a wonderful time. Ann really felt comfortable as if she had known Mary's husband and four children her entire life even though she had only met them briefly at her parents' funerals. And Mary was a wonderful cook. She was having such a great time that she felt sad when it was time to leave.

When Ann dropped her aunt and uncle off they reminded her that the next day they would be sightseeing, "And shopping," added her aunt.

Ann was happy to crawl in bed that night as it had been a pretty full day; all good, but full nonetheless.

After breakfast Ann picked up her aunt and uncle. Her uncle sat in the front saying, "This morning we are going to show you the sights, then after lunch I am going to go and play golf and you and your aunt can shop to your hearts' content." Ann thought it a marvelous plan. This really was a wonderful area and Ann could tell that her uncle enjoyed showing it off, especially the many marinas; a couple of museums and of course the famous golf courses. They stopped at a place near the ocean for lunch and Ann had to admit that the seafood was delicious.

After they dropped her uncle off Ann and her aunt hit the stores. They had a great time. Ann found a beautiful little summer outfit for Patricia that she would give her for her birthday which wasn't that far off. Then they went into an import store that had items from Poland, the Ukraine and a couple of other Slovakian countries. Ann was immediately drawn to the large baskets of the decorated wooden eggs called "Pisanki." She decided that they would be perfect Easter gifts for her friends. Ann picked out a dozen of them as she also wanted to give one to her aunt and uncle, Father Jack, Dr. Pete and send one to her brother, and of course keep one for herself as a memento.

They then went into a Catholic religious book and gift store and Ann found a book for children about the Easter story. So, she got one for Patricia and John Paul. As she was approaching the counter she spotted it and could not hide her excitement. It was the most beautiful statue of the risen Christ that she had ever seen!

"This is gorgeous!" she exclaimed. The sales clerk nodded in agreement. Ann continued, "I mean, I have seen some beautiful states of the risen Christ, but this one is so different. Not only do I love the bronze finish, but the expression on His face I have never seen on any statue before. It is...." She was having problems coming up with the right word, "JOY!" she said loud enough for her aunt to have heard her on the other side of the store and came over to see what she was looking at.

"Oh Ann," she said, "how beautiful! Are you going to purchase it for yourself?"

"I don't know," said Ann, "It's a little more than I am used to spending."

"Okay, let me ask you this, if you knew a good friend would like it would you purchase it for them?" her aunt asked.

"Of course," Ann answered without any hesitation.

"Well then?" her aunt said with one eyebrow raised. Ann was still hesitating. So her aunt added, "Ann, you work so hard and are so giving to so many people; sometimes we just need to treat ourselves too."

"But..." began Ann.

Her aunt stopped her, "And you deserve this." So Ann purchased the statue of the beautifully resurrected Christ.

They went to a few more shops and then stopped for a light supper together as her uncle was going to eat with his golfing buddies. Ann dropped her aunt off and said that she would see them late tomorrow afternoon.

When she got back to the motel she decided to call Tom.

"Hello?" he answered.

"Hey Tom," she said.

"ANN! where are you?" he exclaimed.

"I am still in South Carolina but will be leaving really early Wednesday morning to come home."

"More importantly, how are you? We all got your postcards and it sounded like you were doing okay, but how are you really?"

Ann laughed, "I am well. In fact, I would even say that I am good. It's been an amazing journey Tom and I can't wait to tell all of you about it when I get back."

"I don't know if I can wait that long," he said laughing. "Can you at least tell me if the letter reading went okay?"

Ann laughed, "It was good. Difficult, but healing and good."

"And your aunt and uncle are they well? And are you now having a good time?"

"Tom!" she said, "They are great and I am having a really good time."

"Good. Sorry, but all of your friends are going to want to know when they find out that I talked with you. Now, call me when you get home."

"It will probably be quite late; what time do you go to bed?"

"Usually about 10 p.m."

"Okay, wherever I am at when it is 9:45 p.m. I will call you and then when I get home I'll send you a text so you know that I arrived."

"Okay. Drive safely and we will talk to you sometime on Thursday."

Ann was glad she had called Tom. He had gone through so much of sadness with her she was glad that she could now share some of her happiness with him too.

Ann slept really well again that night. In the morning she lingered in bed just a little longer then went and had a huge breakfast at the restaurant. She spent the rest of the day cleaning out her vehicle, getting the tires checked and filled it with gas. She also picked up a few snacks for the trip home and then got as many things packed as she could. She gave Sister Cecilia a call and they chatted for a while. Ann promised to write as soon as she got home. Then she got cleaned up for dinner with her aunt and uncle. She picked out the Pisanki egg that she thought they would like and wrapped it in tissue paper.

They loved the egg and her aunt proudly displayed it. She had also purchased one for Sister Cecilia and asked them if they would deliver it.

They had a really nice supper and even though her uncle tried to pay for it Ann wouldn't let him saying, "It's the least I can do for all of your hospitality this week."

It was difficult for Ann to leave her aunt and uncle. She had had such a good time with them and at their ages one never knew if they would see each other again. There were lots of hugs and a few tears after she got in the car. She waved out of the window until she could no longer see them.

Ann paid her bill at the motel office knowing that she would be leaving before they opened in the morning. She went to bed early and gratefully slept well as she had a long drive ahead of her.

It was still dark when she finished loading the car and left for home. As soon as it got a little light she stopped at a drive-through for a quick breakfast and some of her favorite iced coffee. She made good time, even with the stops to fill the tank and have lunch. And though she played some of her music she also spent much of the drive just thinking about the past few days.

At 9:45 p.m. she stopped to call Tom and to let him know that she was still about an hour or so away.

Finally, she pulled into her garage. She was home and even though she was tired, she felt good. She was also grateful that her garage was attached to the house so she could just leave everything in the vehicle until morning except for Sir Lancelot of course.

As she opened the door and turned on the light there was a huge banner hanging over the fireplace that said, "WELCOME HOME!" And in front of the fireplace were many of her stuffed animals. As she got closer she could see that all of her friends had written little notes and signed it. Someone had even helped little Patricia write her name. Ann quickly sent a text to Tom and he replied right away. She sent a text back asking if he was still up and that she loved the sign. He replied that he was in bed, but decided to read until she got home. She thanked him and told him good night. A few minutes later her phone went off again and the text read "ANN'S HOME!" Tom had sent it out to everyone. Within minutes she had received messages from everyone. So she sent one back to everyone that simply said that she loved them.

Ann quickly crawled into bed with Godzilla and Sir Lancelot and was fast asleep within minutes.

Ann slept in until mid morning and then slowly moved her way into the day. As soon as she had had some coffee she telephoned her aunt and uncle to let them know that she was safely home.

As she sat eating a light breakfast the phone rang.

"Welcome home," said Tom.

"Thanks," said Ann, "it is really good to be back."

"I'm sure that you have a lot to do today, but I was wondering if you would like for me to pick you up for Mass this evening?" he asked.

"Oh Tom, that would be wonderful. After the long drive yesterday it will feel good to simply ride even if it is only to church."

Ann spent the rest of the day unloading the car, doing laundry, and even took a nap in the afternoon before getting ready for Holy Thursday services.

Tom gave her a huge hug when she answered the door saying, "You look great!" Ann thanked him. "And you look different somehow," he said.

"I do?" Ann answered, "How can I look different? I'm still me."

Tom smiled, "You look happier and you know what, you look younger too."

"Oh there is that charm that I have come to know and love."

The gang was all there except for Don and they were all sitting near each other even having saved a couple of places for Ann and Tom. Of course everyone greeted her and gave her a hug and little Patricia came right to her and stayed with her until she fell asleep during the homily and then D.J. took her back. John Paul slept through the entire Mass not even waking when they rang all of the bells during the "Gloria."

As Father Jack and the servers came down the aisle the group got a special surprise as Don was one of the servers! "He wanted to surprise all of you," Lynn whispered. As Father Jack went by he smiled and nodded slightly in Ann's direction.

For the washing of the feet Father Jack asked for twelve volunteers of all ages. Of course no one was anxious to come forward at first until Tom grabbed Ann's hand

and they both went up. Ann just shook her head at him as if saying, "I'll get you for this." Tom just smiled. Ann was uncomfortable as she was in the limelight and she hated that. But when Father Jack got to her he looked up at her and said, "Welcome home. I can tell it was a good trip." Ann relaxed and almost became mesmerized as this grown man poured warm water on her feet and gently dried them with a towel. Something stirred in her soul. What was it the priest had said last Sunday?

"So on Holy Thursday come and celebrate the Lord's Supper with Him when He instituted the Eucharist promising to give us His Body and Blood and the priesthood so that the Eucharist might continue for all ages. A celebration of the Passover with His friends knowing what lay ahead of Him."

Ann thought silently to herself, Thank you Father for the gifts of the Eucharist and the priesthood. I know that like Jesus I have more struggles ahead of me, but with these two very special gifts and the gift of my friends I know that I will be okay.

At the end of Mass the Most Blessed Sacrament is transferred to a special place and the main tabernacle is left empty and open. It is very solemn and beautiful representing our Lord's entrance into the beginnings of His Passion in the Garden of Gethsemane. As the procession moved slowly around the inside of the church the lights were slowly dimmed so that by the time they had reached the spot where the Most Blessed Sacrament would be placed the entire church was almost totally dark. They had only left a few lights on near the exits and a couple on the side aisles. Everyone was asked to stay and pray for a while and then to leave the church in silence. Ann and Tom stayed for about a half hour before leaving.

On the way home Tom apologized for dragging Ann to the front saying, "I forgot that you don't like to be the center of attention. I just felt bad for Father Jack standing there with no one coming up."

"It's okay," said Ann, "actually I offered it up as an act of humility. Well, at least I tried to. But, to be honest when Father Jack started to wash my feet the rest of the church just kind of went away. It was very moving for me."

"Well, then it appears that it was actually the Holy Spirit who prompted me to grab your hand," he answered.

"Could be," she said.

Ann thanked Tom for driving and said that she would see him at Good Friday services.

Ann lay in bed thinking about the past week, that night in church and whatever else floated through her mind that always seemed to be working overtime. She also thought about the services tomorrow for Good Friday. It's not that they were long, but there would be the reading of the Passion of Jesus only from the Gospel of John this time. Again the words of the priest's homily from last Sunday came to mind,

"If you are facing something difficult ahead; He has been there. Be here on Good Friday and place all that you are suffering on the cross with Him."

Ann decided that this year instead of following along with the reading in the book that she would simply close her eyes and try to be there with Jesus; to take her sufferings and to suffer with Him somehow. She wasn't sure how that was going to work, but she wanted to try it. She grabbed Godzilla and Sir Lancelot and fell fast asleep.

Again, she slept in a little bit on Friday morning. Getting back to her work and a routine next week would be soon enough.

The gang was at church except for Fred. It seems that John Paul had a bit of a cold and so Fred offered to stay home with him and let Barb come to the services. They probably would not be at the Holy Saturday services again either because of him being sick.

"I will really miss being here for that night," Barb lamented, "but it's just how it is right now."

"But we will see you on Easter won't we?" asked Ann.

"I sure hope John Paul is over his cold by then," answered Barb.

Ann was able to close her eyes during the reading of the Passion and to picture herself there with Jesus. Her sufferings seemed to be so minor compared to His, but something told her that He didn't feel that way. When they got to the part where they crucified Jesus between the two others, commonly known as thieves, an image came to Ann's mind that shocked her. Instead of the two thieves hanging there, what she saw were her mother and her uncle. She wondered what it meant but she did not want to think about it right then, but it would definitely be something to talk with Dr. Pete about next week. Ann returned her focus to the reading of the Passion.

During the veneration of the cross Ann's soul was touched as she kissed the wood knowing that she was also kissing her sufferings as well as Jesus'. Something else to reflect upon; how her sufferings had in so many ways drawn her closer to the Church and most definitely to God.

Ann also smiled as she saw Marie walking Patricia up to the cross and the little one mimicking her mother kissing the wood.

It was a powerful service and once again, everyone was to leave in silence. Ann stayed in the church as she had always liked to observe as much silence as she could during the three hours that Jesus was traditionally said to have hung on the cross. Pretty soon even the sacristan had left. Ann just sat there letting the peace flow through her. "Peace," she said aloud, "I'm not sure that I have ever really felt that before in my life." It felt good.

Ann never did much decorating in her house for Easter, but she did usually put out a few spring type items. So on the way home from church she stopped in the nursery and bought herself a couple of the large and one small of the Hyacinth plants that were in full bloom. She put one in the family room, another in the living room, and then the small one in her bedroom. The wonderful aroma filled her entire house. "So what do all of you think of that?" she asked her stuffed animals. They all smiled back at her of course.

Holy Saturday morning was traditionally the day that the food for Easter dinner was blessed by the priest. But as Ann and the group would be going for their special brunch instead, Ann decided that this would be a good time to wrap the wooden Polish Pisanki eggs for each of her friends and the books for the kids. As Holy Saturday was also not only at a later time, but was also a longer Mass Ann felt that an afternoon nap was in order.

Just before she lay down the phone rang and it was Tom, "I forgot to ask you if you wanted me to pick you up for Mass tonight."

"You are such a good guy," Ann said.

"You are just figuring that out?" Tom teased back. After arranging the time Ann curled up on the couch and fell into a gentle sleep.

It's a good thing she had set an alarm as she was sleeping so soundly that she might have slept through to Easter morning. She knew she had been dreaming, but couldn't remember what the dream was about.

As she got ready for Mass she tried to remember the words of the priest from last Sunday regarding this night.

*"Join us on Holy Saturday as we bless the new fire,
Paschal or Easter Candle and the water for this year
and feel the blessing of God's new life upon you."*

"New life," said Ann aloud to the stuffed critters in her bedroom, "I sure hope that is where I am headed."

As always, Tom was right on time. Ann always liked walking in the church on Holy Saturday night as there were only a few lights on here and there so that people could find their pews. For Ann, it was somehow comforting. She and Tom found pews and saved seats for the rest of the group. Pretty soon all of them had arrived except for Fred, Barb, and John Paul. Marie whispered to Ann as Patricia climbed into Ann's lap that Barb had called her, "John Paul is well, but they didn't want to bring him out into the night air yet. They will be at Mass in the morning."

Before he had put on his alb, Don came out and greeted his friends, "It's a busy few days and we haven't had time to talk so I just wanted to let you know that I will be able to go to brunch with all of you tomorrow."

Then he added, "Ann, you look great! Welcome home."

As everything was about to begin Father Jack invited everyone to join him outside to watch the blessing of the new fire and the lighting of the new candle. He also asked them to bring their individual candles.

As Ann wanted to watch this year she handed Patricia back to Marie whispering, "I'll be right back little one." Patricia protested a little until Ann gave her a kiss on the cheek.

Tom went with Ann to watch. Ann was very moved by the ceremony. After the blessing of the fire Father Jack then turned to the new Paschal or Easter candle that would be at all Baptisms and Funerals for the coming year in addition to being lit every day during the Easter Octave. He traced on part of the candle the image of a cross and added the Greek symbols for Alpha and

Omega and then the numbers for the current year between the lines of the cross saying:

Christ yesterday and today;
the Beginning and the End;
the Alpha;
and the Omega.
All time belongs to him;
and all the ages.
To him be glory and power;
through every age and forever. Amen.

Father Jack then inserted five grains of incense into the candle, again in the form of a cross saying:

By his holy
and glorious wounds,
may Christ the Lord
guard us
and protect us. Amen.

He then lit the candle from the new fire as he said:

May the light of Christ rising in glory
dispel the darkness of our hearts and minds.

At those words Ann felt herself touched in a way that was not explainable.

Father Jack then carried the candle to the door of the church and lifting the candle high he sang, *"The Light of Christ,"* and everyone responded, *"Thanks be to God."*

Father Jack then had everyone who was with him light their candles from the new Easter candle instructing them to follow him and as they got to their own pews to light the candles of their family and friends around them. Two of the servers were to come at the end to light the candles of anyone who might have been missed. Father Jack then started down the aisle with this huge procession of light following him. When Father reached the middle of the church he again sang the chant and then a third time when he reached the front and turned around to face the people. By then, everyone was back in their pew and all candles were lit.

The male cantor for the evening then came and sang the Exsultet or "The Easter Proclamation" as their parish does not have a deacon and Father Jack does not feel that he has the voice to do this canting the justice it deserves. He had told Tom once, "I want the congregation to be focusing on the words and not on how terribly I sing." And this night Ann was able to listen closely to the words.

Exult, let them exult, the hosts of heaven,
exult, let Angel ministers of God exult,
let the trumpet of salvation sound aloud our mighty
King's triumph!

Be glad, let earth be glad, as glory floods her,
ablaze with light from her eternal King,
let all corners of the earth be glad,
knowing an end to gloom and darkness.

Rejoice, let Mother Church also rejoice,
arrayed with the lightning of his glory,
let this holy building shake with joy,
filled with the mighty voices of the peoples...
It is truly right and just,
with ardent love of mind and heart
and with devoted service of our voice,
to acclaim our God invisible, the almighty Father,
and Jesus Christ, our Lord, his Son, his Only Begotten.

Who for our sake paid Adam's debt to the eternal Father,
and, pouring out his own dear Blood,
wiped clean the record of our ancient sinfulness.

These then are the feasts of Passover,
in which is slain the Lamb, the one true Lamb,
whose Blood anoints the doorposts of believers.

This is the night,
when once you led our forebears,
Israel's children, from slavery in Egypt
and made them pass dry-shod through the Red Sea.

This is the night
that with a pillar of fire
banished the darkness of sin.

This is the night
that even now, throughout the world,
sets Christian believers apart from worldly vices
and from the gloom of sin,
lending them to grace,
and joining them to his holy ones.

This is the night
when Christ broke the prison-bars of death,
and rose victorious from the underworld.
Our birth would have been no gain,
had we not been redeemed.

O wonder of your humble care for us!
O love, O charity beyond all telling,
to ransom a slave you gave away your Son!
O truly necessary sin of Adam,
destroyed completely by the Death of Christ!
O happy fault
that earned so great, so glorious a Redeemer!

O truly blessed night,
worthy alone to know the time and hour
when Christ rose from the underworld!

This is the night
of which it is written:
The night shall be as bright as day,
dazzling is the night for me,
and full of gladness.

The sanctifying power of this night
dispels all wickedness, washes faults away,
restores innocence to the fallen, and joy to mourners,
drives out hatred, fosters concord,
and brings down the mighty.
On this, your night of grace, O holy Father,
accept this candle, a solemn offering,
the work of bees and of your servants' hands,

An evening sacrifice of praise,
this gift from your most holy Church.

But now we know the praises of this pillar,
which glowing fire ignites for God's honor,
a fire into many flames divided,
yet never dimmed by sharing of its light,
for it is fed by melting wax,
drawn out by mother bees
to build a torch so precious.

O truly blessed night,
when things of heaven are wed to those of earth,
and divine to the human.

Therefore, O Lord,
we pray you that this candle,
hallowed to the honor of your name,
may persevere undimmed,
to overcome the darkness of this night.

Receive it as a pleasing fragrance,
and let it mingle with the lights of heaven.

May this flame be found still burning by the Morning
Star:
the one Morning Star who never sets,
Christ your Son,
who, coming back from death's domain
has shed his peaceful light on humanity
and lives and reigns forever and ever.
Amen.

There were so many lines from this beautiful chant that struck Ann this night...

"Knowing an end to gloom and darkness," and "The
night shall be as bright as day, dazzling is the night for
me, and full of gladness."

But the words that touched her most deeply were:

"The sanctifying power of this night dispels wickedness,
washes faults away, restores innocence to the fallen,

and joy to mourners, drives out hatred, fosters concord,
and brings down the mighty."

Ann felt these words were written just for her personally this night. Of course the rest of the service and the Mass were beautiful especially when new members were brought into the Church which is always such a special moment.

She had brought a small bottle with which to bring home the newly blessed Easter water which she and many, many others filled after Mass. As she and Tom were leaving the church both of them noticed how clear and full of stars the night sky was. Ann felt so full that she thought she might burst but other than 'happy' she wasn't quite sure what the feeling actually was.

Tom walked her to the front door and gave her a hug wishing her a Happy Easter. Ann gave him a hug back, "and the same to you. See you in the morning at Mass."

After Tom left Ann put on her p.j.'s and then went around and blessed her entire house, including all of the stuffed animals with the holy water, leaving her bed for the last.

She crawled into bed between Sir Lancelot and Godzilla thinking about the words of the priest last Sunday regarding Easter Sunday morning,

"Then be here Sunday morning for the celebration when
we remind ourselves once again that God is God and
through Him all things can be overcome; even death!"

New life, Ann thought smiling and quickly fell asleep.

THE BOOK
Chapter 8

It was a busy time in the cave as spring had pretty much arrived and Easter was right around the corner. Everyone had settled into a bit of a routine, which again included the little girl waking up in the middle of the night in a panic. And her extra sensitivity also began to return where the littlest thing would upset her.

Finally, Lion approached her again. "It is time for you to face more people." The little girl wanted to ask "Who?" but she already knew the answer.

She asked all of her cave mates to join her in the main room one night after supper. Once again she apologized for her crabbiness and said that she knew that it was time to make another trip out of the woods. Of course all of her little friends wanted to go with her to help her and to protect her and of course she wanted to take all of them, too. However she was starting to see that there were simply some things she had to do alone, as scary as they might be. Lion also stated that if she really needed assistance she would be able to get word to him and he would be there for her.

The Prince then said, "Arthur and I finished the research on your friend's real names so we can give you that list too."

"I am sure my little lady that they would be honored to help thee if needed," added Arthur.

Great were the preparations for the journey as it would be long and difficult with more than a few people to see and much to accomplish. She knew she would be visiting an aunt and uncle who were very kind to her and she also packed the letters she had written to the people who had hurt her. She had reviewed them with Lion and he felt that she had expressed herself quite well.

Finally, the day of departure arrived. The little girl was filled with many feelings of excitement, fear, anticipation, happiness and sadness, just to name a few.

At the last minute it was decided that Sir Lancelot would accompany her, "After all," said Godzilla, "every damsel needs a knight to protect her no matter how strong she might be." The little girl was very grateful with this decision.

All of her friends decided to go with her to the crossroads and the path that would lead her out of the woods. It was quite a parade; most walked but a few of the little ones, like R.T. Cold Nose III hitched a ride in the arms or on the backs of the larger critters. Of course the young ones were running ahead and then running back to the group.

When they arrived at the crossroads everyone knew this would be a difficult few moments.

Jungle Jane kind of broke the ice by saying, "Be sure to send postcards." The little girl assured her that she would.

"And take lots of pictures," added Nicely, Nicely the Bow-Tie Bear. Again the little girl nodded.

"And write notes about all of your adventures," said Barely Bear.

"Also notes about any new music you hear," added Johann.

"Eat lots of good food!" chimed in Easy Does It.

"And don't take any wooden nickels!" giggled little Donny Williams.

They all had wonderful advice and many suggestions to offer. There were lots hugs and a few tears from all of them. The little girl assured them that she would carry all of them with her in her heart and would return to them soon. Finally Godzilla asked if she had the list of the names of her friends and of course, the letters. She assured him that she did.

But, now the moment of departure was here. With that all of the critters formed a layer of protective circles around her.

"If you feel afraid, just picture us like this in your mind and you will feel safe," said Godzilla.

Then the Winged Lady of the Snows said, "Remember, there is a power greater than all of us that will also keep you safe and offer you guidance."

"The Father," answered the little girl.

They all nodded "yes."

The last to wish her well was Bright Eyes. The hug was long and sweet; no words were needed, the single tear from each said it all.

And then she and Sir Lancelot were on their way. Every few steps she would turn around and wave at her friends until she rounded a curve and could no longer see them. At that point she gave a huge sigh and said, "Well, here we go; just the two of us."

"All will be well, my little lady, all will be well," answered Sir Lancelot.

Before long they were at the park by the woods and Sir Lancelot said to her, "Remember, my little lady no one outside of the woods can hear me talk; only you can."

"OK," she answered.

As they walked more into the center of town they saw Officer Gilbert.

"Hello," he said in greeting, "I haven't seen you for a long time. Do you have another stuffed animal for me?"

"No," answered the little girl, "this one already belongs to someone."

Memories started flooding back as she walked the streets of her home town. There was her church, her grade school and high school, houses where friends had lived, and the house where she had grown up. The place where so much had happened that had been so sad. The house looked the same and yet different. There were also the houses of neighbors who had now died and she felt a sadness that they were no longer there.

Pretty soon she arrived at the home of her aunt and uncle, Artist and Songmaker, and they had a surprise for her. Another aunt and uncle she called the "Parents of Many Boys" were also there to greet her. They were all so happy to see her and they spent the afternoon together visiting and catching up.

On her walk the next morning the little girl stopped in the library to borrow a book to read during her visit and there she saw Golden Pockets.

"Hi. Are you home for a visit?"

"Hi Tom, yes I am," she answered being very grateful that the Prince and Arthur had given her the list of her friends' names.

They talked for a few minutes and then he said, "If you need anything while you are here, just let me know." She promised that she would.

That afternoon as she was walking through the town she stopped to get an ice cream and some of her friends were there. Barrister, Storyteller and Lil Angel were also having ice cream and invited her to join them.

"Hi D.J. and Marie," she began, "and this can't be little Patricia? She has grown so much."

They visited while they ate their ice cream and before she left Marie said, "If you need anything while you are here, just let us know." She promised that she would.

After leaving the ice cream store she stopped into a gift shop and there was Mademoiselle and Junior.

"Well, hello," they both said.

"Hi Maggie and J.R., how are you?" she answered.

"We are well," said Maggie.

"Are you home for a visit?" asked J.R.

The little girl said that she was. After visiting a few moments Maggie said, "If you need anything while you are here, just let us know." She promised that she would.

The little girl then went to the park and there she saw Galahad, Dancing Girl and Lil Man.

"Hello," they greeted. "Are you home for a visit?" asked Dancing Girl.

"Hello Fred and Barb. How are you? And look at how much John Paul has grown already since I saw you last," the little girl answered.

They too visited for awhile and then Fred said, "If you need anything while you are here, just let us know." The little girl promised that she would.

That night her aunt and uncle took her to a restaurant for dinner and there was D.W. working at the chef.

"Hi Randy," said the little girl, "How are you?"

"I am doing really well. Are you home for a visit?" he asked and she answered that she was.

He then said, "If you need anything while you are here, just let me know." She promised that she would.

As they were finishing their meal Pudie walked in. "Greetings," she said, "Are you home for a visit?" The little girl said that she was and then introduced her aunt and uncle to Lynn. Before she left the table Lynn said, "If you need anything while you are here, just let me know." She promised that she would.

She was enjoying her time but she knew that the next couple of days were going to be difficult because they would involve confronting those who had harmed her. She slept with Sir Lancelot very close to her that night. The next morning she decided to stop in the church to pray before she did what she had to do.

As she was praying Choo-Choo came in and greeted her. "Are you home for a visit," he asked.

"Yes Don, I am. It is good to see you," she answered.

"You seem to have something on your mind," he commented.

"Yes," she answered, "I have something difficult that I must do today."

"I will pray for you," he answered, "and if you need anything else while you are here, just let me know." She promised that she would.

And now it was time to do what she had come to do. It wasn't going to be easy and she wished that all of her critter friends from the woods were with her. Sir Lancelot was at her side and she was able to imagine all of them in a protective circle around her. When she did that she could feel their strength and she was able to do what she came to do. Standing at the graves of her parents she told them how she had felt when they hurt her.

And then she went to a deserted place to pretend she was talking to the uncle that had hurt her. She still didn't feel strong enough to do it in person yet. She was able to tell him how angry and hurt she was and how afraid she had been. And in the process of doing this she discovered something wonderful; she was no longer afraid nor did she really feel hurt. All of this was quite a revelation to the little girl and she also noticed that she was feeling something different, but she couldn't quite explain the feeling because she had never felt it before.

However, her journey was not over yet.

As with all journeys of this sort, there is at least one miracle that occurs. And the little girl's journey was to be no exception!

One day near the end of her stay, Sir Lancelot said, "I have a surprise for thee."

"What is it?" inquired the little girl.

"My little lady, if I were to tell thee then it wouldst no longer be a surprise. I will tell thee that we are going on an outing this day."

"I'm not sure I like surprises," answered the little girl.

"Please do trust me my little lady for thou will likest this one," he answered.

They walked until they came to a house that the little girl had never seen before. "What are we doing here?" she asked.

"Please be patient, my little lady and thou will soon understandeth everything." With that he rang the doorbell and then ran around the side of the house.

The little girl was about to follow him when the door opened and there stood the little girl's teacher from so long ago!

The little girl could hardly believe her eyes. She just stood there staring, then, slowly, the tears came.

For hours they sat and talked. It was as if time had stood still and all of those years between had never happened. The little girl was able to share how her life had been since they had last seen each other; the ups and downs, the good and bad, the triumphs and the defeats, the joys and the sorrows. But the little girl was also able to share all of the love and gratitude that she had felt for this dear teacher those many years ago. The feelings just seem to pour out from a bottle whose cork had long been stuck and finally removed. The little girl felt a freedom and a lightness that she had never known before. Or had she? There was a bit of a memory creeping in of knowing that once this was how it had been. But something had changed that.

That evening the little girl and Sir Lancelot talked about the journey. "Has thou completest everything that thou had wished to my little lady?" he asked.

She answered that she had. Sir Lancelot smiled, "Then it is time that we departed for home."

"Yes," she answered, "I can't wait to tell all of our friends about our adventure."

They went to bed early that they might get an early start in the morning.

The next morning the two headed back towards the woods. When they got to the edge the little girl turned around and looked out over the town.

"Is something wrong my little lady?" asked Sir Lancelot.

"No," she answered, "I was just thinking about my friends and family who live here. I will miss them. And yet, my home is with all of you in the cave in the woods, which I love." She made a deep sigh giving the town one last look and then said, "Let's go home."

They headed down what was now becoming a well-worn path. A couple of times the little girl glanced over her shoulder looking back at the entrance to the woods. Sir Lancelot said nothing.

"The woods are sure beautiful right now," the little girl said as they walked, "but they also seem to be darker too. I guess it's because the leaves are now on the trees and hiding the sunshine that came through over the winter." Again Sir Lancelot said nothing.

As they approached the bottom of the hill that led up to the cave the little girl remarked, "It sure looks quiet up there. Do you think they are all out for a hike?"

"I do not know my little lady,"

"I don't even see any of the guard critters, nor the little ones running around. I thought they would remember that today was the day I was returning," she said a little sadly.

Sir Lancelot said nothing.

Then the little girl exclaimed, "Oh you don't think something has happened to all of them do you?"

And before Sir Lancelot could answer the little girl was charging up the hill as fast as she could and ran into the cave. With that everyone jumped up and yelled "Surprise!" They were all there. The little girl was at first very startled then she went around and hugged each and every one of them. "Oh, it is so good to be home," she kept saying.

There were banners, balloons and streamers everywhere, plus a "Welcome Home" sign; music playing and Godzilla had even baked a cake. It was wonderful! The little girl had never had such a marvelous party in her whole life.

Of course, all wanted to hear of her adventures, every detail, so they all stayed up very late listening to her story. Sir Lancelot would interject a reminder here and there. Pretty soon everyone decided that it was getting pretty late, especially for the younger ones. So they all headed off for their rooms, but not before giving the little girl a hug and telling her they were glad she was home safe again and that all had gone well on her journey.

Eventually it was just the little girl and Godzilla sitting by the fire.

"You look different," he said.

"I do?" asked the little girl, "How can I look different? I'm still me."

"Well," he began, "you definitely seem a lot happier, but you also seem more mature and yet younger too."

"You are not making much sense my friend," said the little girl, "but, you know, I do feel different. I feel more like playing or at least doing some fun things and I don't feel so angry or sad and the surprising thing is that I don't feel afraid anymore either. But...", and then she stopped.

"But what?" asked Godzilla.

"I'm not sure," she answered. "It's like a little something is still missing, like an unanswered question. And there's a bit of an emptiness still inside of me and I don't know why."

"Ask the Father to guide you," Godzilla suggested, "but now it is time for rest."

The little girl climbed into her sleeping bag and P.J., Sure to Go, and Bright Eyes all snuggled close. She was soon fast asleep and the dreams began.

She saw herself as she had been so many years ago. It was the happy times with her favorite teacher and it all played out before her like she was watching a movie only it was exactly as it had happened. It was a wonderful dream until she got to the part when it was the last day of school that year. And there it was again, the saddest day of her life ever, or so she felt.

The little girl started to moan a little in her sleep and Sir Lancelot moved closer and put a gentle paw on her head and she seemed to calm a little.

Once again, the little girl was the last to leave the classroom. She tried very hard not to cry, especially in front of her favorite teacher, but suddenly she couldn't help it because she just felt so sad and so very much alone.

The teacher asked her why she was crying and the little girl said, "Because I know that I will never see you again." The teacher smiled gently at her and said, "But you will."

By now the little girl is tossing and moving in her sleep. Sir Lancelot stayed close trying to offer her protection and comfort as she dreamt.

The dream moved on through the long summer as she was waiting for that first day of school. Finally it arrived and off to school she ran. Only something was different this time. As the little girl got closer to the school there was suddenly a crossroad. To the left there was a winding road with the school house at the end, and to the right there was a winding road with the same school house at the end. This was very strange; she had not remembered two school houses before, but she told herself that this was a dream and dreams sometimes do strange things like that. But, which road should she take? It felt as if she had made this decision before, but she couldn't quite remember for sure.

Suddenly, she could hear the school bells ringing in the distance. She would have to hurry or she would be late. Which to choose, which to choose? They both looked identical, so it was very confusing.

Then she remembered the words of her friend the Winged Lady of the Snows, "Remember, there is a power greater than all of us that will keep you safe and offer you guidance."

"The Father," the little girl had answered.

She could feel her friends' circle of protection around her again and then a voice she had not heard before said, "Look again."

So, the little girl looked down the road to the left. There was the school house just as before, but what she could see now is that the road ended there, for right behind the school was a huge mountain. So, she looked to the right and again, it was the same building, but there was a beautiful road that ran beyond it with trees, flowers and beautiful rolling hills. Then off in the distance there was someone waving to her, but she couldn't quite see who it was.

She now remembered that before she had taken the road to the left. Now, it was as if she was being given a second chance, a new start, and a new life. She knew what the road to the left had been like before and she didn't want to go that route again especially because she knew for sure that her teacher was no longer at that school. But, she wasn't sure about the road to the right either; what if it was worse?

Then, the voice said, "Follow your heart."

"But, I am not sure what my heart is saying and what if..."

But, the voice cut her off before she had a chance to finish, "Listen," it said.

Then the little girl could hear children singing; it was coming from the school on the right road. The songs all sounded familiar and then the little girl remembered. They were all of the songs that her favorite teacher had taught her.

She started to head up the road on the right and then stopped, "Maybe it's a trick. Maybe she's not at this school either and someone is just trying to fool me."

Again the voice said, "Follow your heart and trust. You are being guided."

So, the little girl let out a big sigh and continued up the road on the right. She felt more and more nervous and yet more excited the closer she got. She could still hear the singing, which meant there was still hope, but when she got to the school it stopped!

Once again she found herself searching the playground and the halls, looking for her favorite teacher. She was nowhere. She went to the old classroom; she wasn't there either!

"I knew it!" she hollered. "It was all a trick!" I'll never see her again!

Despondent, she walked to the door and started to cry.

Sir Lancelot could feel the little girl shaking and heard her tears. He held her closer.

Then, the little girl heard the singing again, only it wasn't children's voices, it was her teacher's voice. She looked up and there was "Heartsong," which was her name. She was off in the distance on one of the hills and she was waving at the little girl. With that the little girl took off running towards her as fast as she could, which was pretty fast. When she reached her they hugged a long hug and then spent the rest of the day on the hill singing and dancing.

It was then that she woke up and she was singing. She saw Sir Lancelot, Godzilla and Lion sitting there smiling at her.

"Oh, I just had the most wonderful dream."

She then told them all about it, being as quiet as she could so as not to wake the others. They listened, nodding and smiling as she relayed the entire dream story to them.

When she was finished she said, "I feel so free, like something very heavy has been lifted from me and I am a young, happy little girl again. It is like all of these years have never happened. It is wonderful. I can't believe it. And I think I have made a decision that I will tell all of you about in the morning because right now we have to get back to sleep."

"Do you still feel like something is missing?" asked Godzilla.

The little girl thought a moment and then said, "Yes, but it doesn't feel quite as big and as empty as before." With that she was asleep.

After all had finished breakfast the little girl asked for everyone's attention.

"I know this has been a pretty full week with me and Sir Lancelot gone on our journey."

"We missed you," said Sure to Go.

"And I missed you too," answered the little girl.

All eyes were on the little girl because she looked a little serious. She continued, "First, I want to share with you a dream that I had last night that Godzilla and Sir Lancelot already know about." She then shared the dream.

"Wow," said Jacques.

"Yes, wow, my little friend," said the little girl. "So, as a result of that dream and the journey I took this past week I think that the Father is telling me that it is time to leave these woods."

"But where will you go?" asked Pumpkin-Pumpkin.

"Back to the town," she answered.

"But, where will you live?" asked Sabrina.

"I saw a house that would be really nice to live in," she answered.

Nobody said anything. Then Bright Eyes, the little mouse came over and just stood looking up into the little girl's face.

"Oh," she said, "I forgot, and I want all of you to come and live with me, that is if you want to."

Everyone started cheering and the little mouse broke out in the biggest smile anyone had ever seen.

They could talk of little else the rest of the day. And lots of questions, like wondering what they should pack?

"Each of you will have to decide," the little girl said.

Had she told any of her friends yet?

"No," she said.

And of course, when would they leave?

"I thought that Easter Sunday morning would be a good day because it is a day of new life," she answered.

"What about the Easter Bunny?" asked Arp.

"Oh the Easter Bunny will have been here long before we leave," answered Ada B. Green with a bit of a twinkle in her eye.

So, over the next few days everyone was kept pretty busy packing and cleaning things out. Godzilla had reminded them that they really needed to leave the cave in good shape; that they weren't to leave anything behind in case someone else needed to use it one day.

Before they knew it, it was the day before Easter. Everyone, including the little girl were pretty much ready for their journey. They sat around their last fire together and shared memories of the good times, as well as the times that had been a bit of a struggle for all of them. Pretty soon everyone agreed that it was starting to get a little late. Ada B. Green had led her group off much earlier saying that she had a lot to do and so wanted Jacques and Jeanette in bed early.

After everyone had gone to their rooms or sleeping areas Godzilla and the little girl sat up talking for awhile.

"Do you remember the first day we met?" he asked.

"I sure do," she answered. "I didn't know what to think."

Godzilla laughed, "You have come a long ways my young friend and I am very, very proud of you as I know it hasn't been easy for you."

The little girl smiled, "I couldn't have done it without you, in fact, without all of you."

"And the Father," he said.

"And the Father," she answered. She then added, "We had better get to bed so that the Easter Bunny won't still find us up talking."

Godzilla smiled and gave her a hug good night. "Yes," he said, "you have come a very long ways."

Just as with Christmas the younger critters were up early and had snuck into the kitchen where Godzilla was already at work on his special cinnamon, pecan rolls. He had all of them sit in the kitchen and have a glass of juice before he let them go and wake anyone else up.

"Can we do it like at Christmas?" asked Arp.

"Let's try something different for Easter this year," Godzilla responded. "Go and gently tap on everyone's door and ask, 'Did the Easter Bunny bring you anything?'"

Godzilla smiled as he heard all of the little voices echoing throughout the cave. The little girl rolled over and stretched, but wasn't quite ready to get up yet. She just lay there and waited for everyone else. Of course the very last one to get up was Ada B. Green, who still looked very tired.

There were lots of "ooohs and aaaahhhs" as each found the treasures contained in the baskets. For some it was chocolate and for others, especially the bears, it was a jar of honey. The little girl received chocolates but also a beautiful wooden egg that was painted in a very colorful style.

"I remember these from when I was a child," she said, "my Grandmother Rose used to make them."

As they had breakfast Lion read them the Easter Story by John the Writer.

On the first day of the week, Mary of Magdala came to the tomb early in the morning, while it was still dark, and saw the stone removed from the tomb. So she ran and went to Simon Peter and to the other disciple whom Jesus loved, and told them, "They have taken the Lord from the tomb, and we don't know where they put him." So Peter and the other disciple went out and came to the tomb. They both ran, but the other disciple ran faster than Peter and arrived at the tomb first; he bent down and saw the burial cloths there, but did not go in. When Simon Peter arrived after him, he went into the tomb and saw the burial cloths there, and the cloth that had covered his head, not with the burial cloths but rolled up in a separate place. The other disciple also went in, the one who had arrived at the tomb first, and he saw and believed. For they did not yet understand the Scripture that he had to rise from the dead. (Jn 20:1-9)

"What a beautiful story," said P.J.

"And it is one that really happened," answered Lion.

"And we all know how that part of the story finishes," said Lord Percival, "They get to see the Lord again."

"You are correct," said Lion

"OK," began Godzilla, "I think it's time that we get ready for our journey if we are going to be there in time for our main Easter meal."

It didn't take long for everyone to get their backpacks on and take one last look around to make sure they hadn't left anything. They had already packed everything that was too big to carry into a wagon that the Prince had come up with.

Arp had started to ask him where he had found it and then said, "Never mind. I know, you have your sources."

All laughed, including the Prince. But, now everyone also secretly wondered what had happened to things like the three toboggans which were nowhere to be found, or any of the other supplies that he always seemed to simply have. However no one asked as they knew what his answer would be.

The little girl was the last one to leave the cave taking one last walk through and remembering. She stood at the entrance and silently said, "Thank you Father for this gift."

Sir Lancelot said, "Are thee ready my little lady?"

"I am ready my lord," answered the little girl.

Godzilla then smiled and said, "Then it's time to go home Ann."

If anyone had been watching it would have really been a sight to behold as this group of critters of all shapes, sizes and types and a few dolls thrown in, plus a little girl headed for the path out of the woods.

Before they turned the final curve the little girl turned around and looked once again at the cave at the top of the hill and then joined the rest of her friends as they continued on the path towards the town. At the edge of the woods the little girl stopped and looked back one more time and then all of them left the woods together.

Before long they were standing in front of their new home.

"It is beautiful," said P.J.

"And so large," added Raspberry Sundae.

"Yes," said Moose Bear. "I was afraid that there was not going to be enough room for all of us."

Bright Eyes and Sure to Go each took one of Ann's hands and walked through the front door.

It didn't take long for everyone to find their own special spot in their new home. Some were in the kitchen like Miss Louise, D.W.

Duck and Derrière Bear; Sabrina and Charlie. Others found their places on the couch in the living room; Dale E. Woof and many of the winter and Christmas bears found space in the spare bedroom. The protector critters all took places by the many doors in the house; front, garage, and the door to the patio off of the family room. R.T. Cold Nose III, Teresa, as well as many others set up home in Ann's office. Of course The Prince and Arthur were in the library along with their friends. P.J., Godzilla, Sir Lancelot, Sure to Go, Bright Eyes, Lion and a few others kept their places by Ann in her bedroom.

"I think we are going to be very happy here," said Ann and they all hugged her in agreement.

ANN'S STORY
Chapter 14
EASTER

Ann was no sooner asleep than the dream began.

Ann saw herself as she had been so many years ago. It was the happy times with her favorite teacher and it all played out before her like she was watching a movie only it was exactly as it had happened. It was a wonderful dream until she got to the part when it was the last day of school that year. And there it was again, the saddest day of her life ever, or so she felt.

Once again, Ann was the last to leave the classroom; she tried very hard not to cry, especially in front of her favorite teacher, but suddenly she couldn't help it because she just felt so sad and so very much alone.

The teacher asked her why she was crying and Ann said, "Because I know that I will never see you again."

The teacher smiled gently at her and said, "But you will."

The dream moved on through the long summer as she was once again waiting for that first day of school. Finally it arrived and off to school she ran. Only something was different this time. As Ann got closer to the school there was suddenly a crossroad: to the left there was a winding road with the school house at the end, and to the right there was a winding road with the same school house at the end. This was very strange; she had not remembered two school houses before, but she told herself that this was a dream and dreams sometimes do strange things like that. But, which road should she take? It felt as if she had made this decision before, but she couldn't quite remember for sure.

Suddenly, she could hear the school bells ringing in the distance; she would have to hurry or she would be late. Which to choose, which to choose? They both looked identical, so it was very confusing.

Then she remembered some words she had heard somewhere, "Remember, there is a power greater than all of us that will keep you safe and offer you guidance."

"God." Ann said.

Somehow she felt protected and then a voice she had not heard before said, "Look again."

So, Ann looked down the road to the left. There was the school house just as before, but what she could see now is that the road ended there, for right behind the school was a huge mountain. So, she looked to the right and again, it was the same building, but there was a beautiful road that ran beyond it with trees, flowers and beautiful rolling hills. Then off in the distance there was someone waving to her, but she couldn't quite see who it was.

She now remembered that before she had taken the road to the left. Now, it was as if she was being given a second chance, a new start, a new life. She knew what the road to the left had been like before and she didn't want to go that route again especially because she knew for sure that her teacher was no longer at that school. But, she wasn't sure about the road to the right either; what if it was worse?

Then, the voice said, "Follow your heart."

"But, I am not sure what my heart is saying and what if..."

But, the voice cut her off before she had a chance to finish, "Listen," it said.

Then Ann could hear children singing; it was coming from the school on the right road. The songs all sounded familiar and then she remembered; they were all of the songs that her favorite teacher had taught her.

She started to head up the road on the right and then stopped, "Maybe it's a trick. Maybe she's not at this school either and someone is just trying to fool me."

Again the voice said, "Follow your heart and trust. You are being guided."

So, Ann let out a big sigh and continued up the road on the right. She felt more and more nervous and yet more excited the closer she got. She could still hear the singing, which meant there was still hope, but when she got to the school it stopped!

Once again she found herself searching the playground and the halls, looking for her favorite teacher; she was nowhere. She went to the old classroom; she wasn't there either!

"I knew it!" she hollered. "It was all a trick! I'll never see her again!" Despondent, she walked to the door and started to cry.

Then, Ann heard the singing again, only it wasn't children's voices, it was her teacher's voice. She looked up and there was Sister Cecilia. She was off in the distance on one of the hills and she was waving at her. With that Ann took off running towards her as fast as she could, which was pretty fast. When she reached her they hugged a long hug and then spent the rest of the day on the hill singing and dancing.

Ann woke herself up singing. She looked around the room trying to get her bearings. "Wow! That was the same dream that I wrote about in my book. It was pretty wonderful," she said to Sir Lancelot and Godzilla, "and I have the feeling that all of you were there too." She lay there for a moment trying to retain as much of it as she could. "I feel so free, like something very heavy has been lifted from me. What is that feeling?" She got up and danced her way to the kitchen to get her coffee, greeting all of her stuffed animals along the way.

"I know," she said, "I feel like a kid again!"

On one of her waltzes through the living room she spotted her new statue of the risen Christ she had purchased on her trip and she realized, "It's JOY that I am feeling! Thank you Lord."

All through her shower and getting dressed Ann was singing. "What to wear? What to wear?" she said standing in front of her closet. There was a part of her that wanted to wear something really bright, but gratefully, she didn't own anything like that. She finally decided on a long skirt she had with subdued shades of gold, tan, yellow and an off-white top.

She grabbed her large basket with the gifts in it for her friends and headed off to church still singing to herself. It was an incredibly gorgeous day. All of her friends were already there, but Tom of course had saved her a seat.

As he stood up to let her in the pew he whispered, "You look beautiful."

Ann felt a little embarrassed but was able to simply say, "Thank you."

Marie and D.J. were sitting in the pew in front of them and of course Patricia wanted to sit with Auntie Ann.

As Marie handed her over she whispered, "I love that outfit on you."

Marie had Patricia dressed in the most darling dress; it was a light yellow floral print and this year she had a white hat with a yellow daisy, which she kept taking off. Fred and Barb had John Paul in an outfit that looked a bit like a little suit. Every time Ann smiled at him he would give her a huge grin back.

Many of the adults were dressed up too, but not as much as they had dressed their children. The little boys had white shirts, ties and either a jacket or a vest. And the little girls were in pretty dresses and all had hats or bows in their hair. This all seemed to end once they reached middle school age as they then began to follow their parents' and the fashion media's lead. Ann chastised herself a little for thinking, "I bet they wouldn't dress that way to meet the Queen of England or even the Pope and yet here they are in the presence of the King of Kings."

Then the music began for the Entrance or Gathering Hymn and Ann was able to change her focus as it was one of her favorites, "Jesus Christ is Risen Today."

As she sang Tom kept peeking at her and smiling. She pretended not to notice. She knew she was having a wonderful time singing and it felt so good that she really didn't care what anyone else thought, good or bad.

When the choir began singing the "Gloria" Ann felt herself almost being transported to another dimension. And there was that feeling again; like she had when she first awoke this morning, she thought. But she wanted to focus on the words of this praise of God and not on what she was feeling.

As she listened to the Gospel she wondered, what must have been going through the minds of Mary of Magdala, Peter and the "other" disciple that most believed was probably John?

And this was just how Father Jack began his homily. Ann chuckling thought to herself, I know he is a great priest, but reading minds?

"But today," continued Father Jack, "we have been given the gift of the history of over 2,000 years. We KNOW that Jesus is risen. We no longer have to wonder 'what happened here at the tomb?' or 'Where is He?' We know. He rose and overcame cruel torture and death for our sakes and where is He today? He is right here. He is in the person sitting next to you; He is in your spouse, your child, your parent, neighbor or in the person you may have never met. And in a short time He will be present to us in a very special way; right here on this altar when once again we are invited to partake of His beautiful Body and His Most Precious Blood. And at that moment He becomes part of us and we become a part of Him. So with all of the Saints and Angels that are here worshiping with us this Holiest of Days let us sing as we did when we entered the church, 'Jesus Christ is risen today, ALLELUIA!'"

Ann was so moved when she received Holy Communion, that she thought she would just burst right there on the spot. She suddenly remembered a classmate of hers that was so excited at the rehearsal for their First Communion that Sister had told her to try to relax otherwise she might make herself ill. Ann smiled as she remembered what the little girl said in response, "But Sister you don't understand, this is going to be the very first time that I get to receive Jesus." It was almost what Ann was feeling this day.

For the recessional hymn they sang "Alleluia! Alleluia, Let the Holy Anthem Rise" and Ann felt like she was actually floating.

After Mass Father Jack was in the back greeting everyone. Ann gave him the Polish Easter egg and wished him a "Happy Easter."

"And to you Ann," he said, "I can tell by your face that your trip went well."

"It did Father, it did, thanks to your prayers and those of many others," Ann answered, "and I'd like to share it with you sometime."

"Anytime Ann, anytime," he replied.

Everyone met up at the restaurant at their favorite round table that Tom had once again reserved for them. The difference this time was that there was now a high chair for Patricia. Everyone seemed to be able to get through the buffet line quickly as they had numerous stations set up, thus all were able to begin eating at the same time. Randy commented that once he got his own restaurant he was going to remember that idea. Don was asked to lead the blessing before the meal. Everyone made the Sign of the Cross, including Patricia whom D.J. was helping.

Don began, "Thank you Lord for bringing us together once again on this holiest of Holy Days. We thank you for the gift of this food and for the gift of friendship as we pray together:

Bless us O Lord,
and these Thy gifts
which we are about to receive
from Thy bounty
through Christ our Lord.
Amen.

Ann began the conversation by saying, "Don, you look like you belong on that altar."

"I don't know about that quite yet," he answered, "but I have learned so much already."

"How are the classes going?" asked Fred.

"Good," he answered, "as I am considered a 'late' or 'second' vocation I am not having to follow the normal class schedule that works on a rotation as younger seminarians do. The seminary I am at is designed specifically for guys like me so that we can enter when we are ready. We have to take the same classes, but just not in the same order. So, in my classes right now we have a mixture of those who are just starting and those who have been there for a year or two."

"I bet that helps," said J.R.

"Yeah, not only do we have a couple of guys who can 'show us the ropes' so to speak, but it also makes for some really good theological discussions," he answered. "But enough about me. Ann I want to hear about your trip."

Ann could feel herself blushing just a little at being the center of attention but she tried to ignore it. She first thanked all of them for their prayers and support as she knew she couldn't have done it without them and that she had felt their love at every step of the journey.

She didn't go into a lot of detail, but rather more generalities on how it was to see her aunt and uncle and her cousin's family. How it was reading the letters to her parents and her uncle and then the surprise of seeing Sister Cecilia again.

"I remember her," said Marie, "I never had her for a class because by the time I got to that grade she had been transferred, but I remember how kind she was."

Ann agreed and said that she had not changed. "But the most wonderful part was coming home and finding the huge 'WELCOME HOME' sign in my family room that all of you had signed. That meant so much to me. And I brought each of you a special gift for Easter from my trip."

She then handed out her gifts to them.

"Oh Ann, these are beautiful," said Barb.

Ann then gave a little history on the Pisanki eggs, which most of them had not heard.

Maggie then added, "Well something happened to you on that trip because you look simply radiant and much happier, are you?"

Ann said that she was. They then went on to talk of other things and to share the little gifts that each had brought. Randy had made some wonderful Easter cookies and Don gave everyone an Easter Holy card. The rest of the group had decided that it was the year for chocolate in various forms - from bunnies to small boxes of an assortment.

As they all got ready to leave Lynn said, "I love this Easter tradition of ours. This is like my 'Family of Friends' which is so different from my "Family of Relatives.'" Everyone laughed saying they knew just what she meant.

When they got to the cars Tom said to Ann, "I have something else in the car for you." He handed her a deep purple hyacinth plant that was just beginning to bloom. "I know you love these and I thought this one was like you; beginning to bloom." Ann thanked him. "So, are you feeling as good as you look?" he asked.

"I am," she began, "I almost feel like a little kid again; giddy with all of the possibilities of life." Tom smiled. "But..." she continued, "I will admit to you that it still feels like a little something is missing or not exactly right, but I haven't quite figured that out yet."

"But knowing my friend Ann, she will or will die trying," Tom answered laughing.

"I see my therapist this coming week so I am hoping that we can kind of figure it out together."

They gave each other a hug and Ann headed for home taking the long route along the lake simply enjoying the peace of the day. As she pulled into her driveway she noticed something on her front porch but couldn't quite tell what it was as it was wrapped in cellophane. "That Tom," she said to herself, "it's probably a huge Easter Basket." But when she got closer she could see that it was a teddy bear. Once inside she took the cellophane off and inside was the most wonderful bear she had ever seen. She was a kind of vanilla color, with a cute little nose and wonderful big brown eyes. Ann's heart melted as she held the little bear feeling an immediate love for this stuffed critter. "So where did you come from?" she said aloud as she opened the envelope that was addressed to her.

The card read, "Please take care of me like you always wanted to be taken care of when you were little." Immediately tears welled up in Ann's eyes as she held the bear close.

After composing herself she called Tom, "You sure are sneaky," she began.

"What?" he asked.

"I just found a gift on my front porch."

"Sorry Ann, it's not from me. What is it?"

"It's a stuffed bear."

"I know it's silly to ask, but was there a card?"

"Yes, but no name."

"Another mystery to be solved."

When she got off the phone Ann said to the bear, "Well whoever gave you to me, you are a precious gift who needs a name." Ann thought a moment then said, "Of course, your name is Anna." And she gave the bear another hug.

Over the next couple of days she checked with all of her friends but none of them knew anything about the bear. Ann decided to take the words on the card to heart so from that day forward Anna pretty much went everywhere with Ann and she took very good care of her.

Her session with Dr. Pete went well that week as she relayed all that had happened on her trip. Dr. Pete agreed that she had really grown.

When she shared the dream he said, "Now you are in charge of your own destiny and not simply as a reaction to what your parents and uncle did to you. You are now making the choices."

Ann added, "Yes, like you told me a while back, I am now re-raising the little Ann who is still inside."

"Exactly," he said. "Not that you're still not going to make mistakes or revert to old patterns now and again, but at least now the playing field is more even for little Ann." Ann had decided not to tell Dr. Pete about her new teddy bear; at least, not yet.

The women's support group was also glad to see her that week and to hear of her trip. Ann kept her 'trip report' short as she had the sense that one of the women really needed to talk that night and she was correct. The young woman had just met a new guy and on her second date she ended up having sex with him, which was really not something that she wanted to do. Not that she was raped, but more that she was weak. Dr. Pete talked about how very often victims of sexual abuse learn to relate to others only in a sexual manner. It is very difficult for them to unlearn this behavior and it does take awhile. This woman was fairly new to therapy and thus as Dr. Pete said, "You should not judge yourself too harshly nor should we." But, as she was Catholic, he also recommended that if she hadn't done so already, that she should seek the Sacrament of Reconciliation, more commonly known as "confession" as that also serves as a healing grace in these situations.

One woman, who had been with the group for a while then shared that that was how she had also been; even once placing herself in a situation where she ended up being raped, which is also not all that uncommon.

"It takes a while to heal from all of this, but you can do it," she said to the first woman, "I am proof of that."

Then another woman who had also been with the group for some time shared that her problem had stemmed more in the area of sexual self gratification.

"Masturbation," Dr. Pete interjected.

"It has been difficult to overcome," she continued, "because my molest began at such a young age, when I was still a toddler. What I discovered is that was how I learned to cope with everything that was hard, difficult or stressful. It was a challenge to unlearn it, but I did."

Ann was finding all of this absolutely incredible thinking to herself, "And I thought that I had it so bad!"

As if reading her mind Dr. Pete said, "I would like to remind all of you again that the next person's pain is no greater or lesser, it is simply different."

And so the days passed. Ann lived her life, working on research books and tending to Anna. At first it felt a little strange, but Ann kept with it. Anna went everywhere with her, well pretty much. When they were home Ann made sure that she was comfortable, warm enough on cool days and cool enough on warm days. She brushed her fur and kept her clean and when they went for rides together she put the seat belt on her. And of course she was always gentle with her. And somehow, as strange as it sounds, as Ann took care of little Anna, Ann felt better too and that empty feeling that she had inside started to go away.

Finally Ann decided to tell Dr. Pete about little Anna.

He asked, "Do you still have the empty feeling inside, like something is still missing?" Ann answered that she did not. "Do you think that taking care of little Anna had anything to do with it?"

"I'm not sure," answered Ann, "but maybe."

"What have you learned so far by taking care of her?"

Again Ann thought a moment, "I of course learned that gentle is better, but I already knew that. That caring for her is a responsibility, but it can also be fun. And somehow, there is this feeling of loving her unconditionally. I know that really sounds strange because she is only a stuffed animal, but I don't know how else to put it."

"But loving and caring for others seemed to have come easy for you."

Ann sat there for a moment thinking about his last statement. Then with tears in her eyes she said, "I just realized something. You are correct, I have always been pretty good at loving others but there was one person I didn't know how to love and I think little Anna is teaching me that."

"Who was that?"

"Myself. And if I didn't know how to love myself, how could I possibly know how to really love others?"

Both were quiet and then Ann spoke again, but softly, "I think that it goes even deeper than that."

"How so?"

"Despite all that I have learned and all of the growth and healing I don't think I learned the most important lesson of all until this moment..." Again, she was quiet and so was Dr. Pete.

Then Ann smiled at him and said, "I really am lovable."

"Yes you are Ann," said Dr. Pete, "Yes you are."

THE END.

EPILOGUE

Godzilla here again! At this point, usually everyone asks... "What happened to everyone?" "Are all of the stuffed animals still with Ann?" "How and what is everybody doing?"

So, here's the update.

After Ann had completed the major portion of her healing, many of the critters volunteered for new assignments, as they knew their work with her was completed.

Raspberry Sundae, Cotton Candy, and Lion are doing volunteer work with children of all ages at a sexual abuse and rape center. They continue to help children to feel safe and protected.

Pumpkin-Pumpkin, Mr. Bear Claus, Rudy, Rudy Red Nose, Joanne, Little Teresa, the Rabbit, Miss Tali, Miss Amelia and Jean Luc all visited Ann's support group for women who had been molested and were chosen by each of the women to go home with them.

R.T. Cold Nose III, Arp, Fuzzy Wuzzy Woof Woof, Kris, Miss Louise, Bogie and Bacall, J.B. Bear, Artie J., Shawn O'Leigh, Little Donny Williams, Fast Eddy, Sure To Go, and In No Rush, work with other abused children at a university in their counseling center.

The Prince, the Wizard Merlin and Arthur hang out at a couple of different bookstores entertaining all of the children who come in with their parents and they are also really good at helping them to pick out just the right books.

Rudolph Valentino the Heart Nosed Bear, D.W. Duck, Ruthless Bear Hugger, D.J. III, Snowbear, Snowflake, Barely Bear, Sabrina, the Winged Lady of the Snows and Van Gogh the big sheep dog are working with the St. Vincent de Paul Society.

P.J., Lord Percival, Ada B. Green and the twins Jacques and Jeanette, Lucy, Chief Mahka, Front Porch the

Buffalo Bull, Father Charlie, Johann, Beethoven, Nicely, Nicely the Bow-Tie Bear, Carrot Cakes, Nicholas of the North Pole, The Fall Guy, Bear Buns, Derrière Bear, and Bears Watching joined the local police officers to help them with their work.

Dale E. Woof met up with her husband Roy R. and they went back into show business along with R. Rabbit, Topo G., and Peter C. deciding that they were called by the Father to entertain children of all ages. Easy Does It, Jungle Jane and London decided to join them.

Mr. Coyote went to stay with Ann's brother.

Moose Bear, Miss Evelyn, Sir Lancelot and Bright Eyes went to work with a psychologist friend of Dr. Peter's and are also doing good work with children of all ages, helping them to heal from their traumatic backgrounds.

And little Anna was adopted by a very young relative of Ann's as her special playmate after she had to undergo some serious surgery.

As for the family members, friends and neighbors, like Grandmother Rose, Elsie the Keeper of Hearts, Officer Gilbert (a.k.a. Officer Gil Brown), Golden Pockets (Tom), Barrister (D.J.), Storyteller (Marie), Lil Angel (Patricia Jane Michelle), Galahad (Fred), Dancing Girl(Barb), Lil Man (John Paul), Mademoiselle (Maggie), Choo-Choo (Don), Pudie (Lynn), Junior (J.R.), D.W.(Randy), Cousin Lucy, Artist, Songmaker and the Parents of Many Boys,(Ann's aunts and uncles), continue to be supportive, caring and helpful as hopefully relatives and friends are for every child and adult everywhere. Some have passed away or moved on to their own adventures and journeys and others stay always close.

The good teachers of the world, like Heartsong (Sister Cecilia) continue teaching and caring for the children placed in their charge with an eye of extra awareness towards those who might be being abused.

The Dr. Peter Wilhelms also continue with their supportive and healing therapy, understanding just a little more each day the effects of abuse on children whether they are the victims or the perpetrators. They also realize that there is still much that we do not know.

The Father Jacks and Charlies of the world are modeled in the good priests of the Church who comfort, care for and offer the healing touch of Christ through their ministries.

Ann continues to heal and is still writing books. After her stuffed animals went on to new assignments a few new ones showed up to keep her company and to serve as memories of lessons learned. "Mon Petit Chou" is a little grey elephant holding a red heart who reminds her that "Love" always walks at her side. "Sir Edward" is a special bear made for her by a cousin and "Charlotte" is a mink bear made by an aunt; both signs that she is cared for. Then there is a white dog with red paws holding a huge red heart that says "I Love You" named "Signore Amore Cellini" who tells Ann every day that she is loved. Next is Rosie, a little pink bear who always gives Ann roses representing the gift of good friends. "Lil Dahlin" a lavender monkey that says "Don't be so serious; life is also supposed to be fun and silly sometimes." Then there is a little pink and blue mouse named "Veal Chop" who sits on top of her refrigerator reminding her that food is good, but that even too much of a good thing can be bad. And "Little Devil" who really is a little devil admonishing Ann to "be good." Then, a little bear who arrived on the feast day of St. Luke, a physician, artist and writer so was named Luca Bear who is a reminder that Ann is to take good care of herself and to keep writing. And finally, a little doll with pigtails named "Luiza" to let her know that family is always with her.

And me? Well, I have received another special assignment working with a little boy who was abused when he was very little. So you see the work of a Teddy Bear and of all my co-critters is never done; especially if you believe in the loving and healing power of the Father. As Jesus said, "In just the same way, it is not the will of your heavenly Father that one of these little ones be lost."(MT 18:14) Amen.

LITTLE GIRL LOST,
LITTLE GIRL FOUND
RESOURCES

1. TWELVE STEP PROGRAMS

    A. ADULT CHILDREN OF ALCOHOLICS WORLD SERVICE ORGANIZATION INC. http://www.adultchildren.org/

    B. ALANON FOR FAMILY AND FRIENDS OF ALCOHOLICS http://www.al-anon.alateen.org/

    C. ALATEEN FOR TEENAGERS WHO ARE FAMILY OR FRIENDS OF ALCOHOLICS http://www.al-anon.alateen.org/for-alateen

    D. ALCOHOLICS ANONYMOUS http://www.aa.org

    E. COCAINE ANONYMOUS WORLD SERVICES http://www.ca.org/

    F. GAMBLERS ANONYMOUS http://www.gamblersanonymous.org/ga

    G. MARIJUANA ANONYMOUS http://www.marijuana-anonymous.org

    H. NARCOTICS ANONYMOUS WORLD SERVICES http://www.na.org

    I. OVEREATERS ANONYMOUS http://www.oa.org/

NOTE: THERE ARE PROGRAMS THAT FOLLOW THE 12-STEP FORMAT FOR MOST ADDICITVE BEHAVIOR. THIS LIST SERVES AS A SAMPLE.

2. COUNSELING SERVICES

    A. CHILD HELP FOR PREVENTION AND TREATMENT OF CHILD ABUSE http://www.childhelp.org/pages/hotline-home

    B. CATHOLIC THERAPISTS.COM http://www.catholictherapists.com/

    C. AMERICAN ASSOCIATION OF CHRISTIAN COUNSELORS http://www.aacc.net/

3. SUPPORT GROUPS

A. THE COURAGE APOSTOLATE–Catholic support for those with same sex attractions
http://www.couragerc.net/Courage_Apostolate.html

B. ENCOURAGE–Catholic support system for family members and friends of those who have same sex attraction
http://couragerc.net/Encourage.html

4. CATHOLICISM

A. To learn more about the Catholic Faith whether you are:
- Not Catholic
- Not Really Religious
- Are Protestant, Evangelical or Another Faith
- Catholic, But Not Currently Attending Mass
- Want to learn how to return to the Faith
- Want to know how doing so will be helpful in your life
- Are Proud To Be Catholic
- Want to help family and friends to return to the Faith
- Or want to explore the wonders of our Faith

GO TO THE "CATHOLICS COME HOME" WEBSITE FOR INFORMATION
http://www.catholicscomehome.org/

5. OTHER

A. NATIONAL CHILDREN'S ALLIANCE
http://www.nationalchildrensalliance.org

B. SPINOZA BEAR
http://www.spinozabear.com/

C. ST. JOSEPH STATUE
http://www.stjosephstatue.com/

D. Saints.SQPN.com

PRAYER TO ST. GERMAINE COUSIN
Patron of Child Abuse Victims

O Saint Germaine, look down from Heaven
and intercede for the many abused children in our
world.
Help them to sanctify these sufferings.
Strengthen children who suffer the effects of living in
broken families.
Protect those children who have been abandoned by
their parents
and live in the streets.
Beg God's mercy on the parents who abuse their
children.
Intercede for handicapped children and their parents.
Saint Germaine, you who suffered neglect and abuse so
patiently,
pray for us. Amen.

ACKNOWLEDGEMENTS

As always with a work of this type and scope there are numerous people behind the scenes that without their help this never would have been brought to fruition.

Forever first, I thank God the Father who guided and gave me the talents and resources to do this work. To His Son, Jesus, who walks with me every day and to the Holy Spirit who gives me the words to write.

To Msgr. John Schuh for his input, guidance, encouragement, and his support for this project.

To Sister Renita Tadych, OSF, M.C., Lori O'Connor and Wendy Sell who helped tremendously with the editing and proofreading.

To Elizabeth Hall for her review and helpful suggestions on the first draft and her encouragement.

To my former associate Dr. Mary Jayne Carlson for sharing her knowledge and experience.

To Matt Pinto for his insights, suggestions and assistance.

To all of the family members and friends who believed in me, the project, and encouraged me to "write"- Louis Scieszka, Janet Mason, Bruce Altman, Lori O'Connor and Peggy Shallue.

For all of the great teachers and good and wonderful priests who have touched my life but most especially Sister M. Vianney, CSFN, Brother Jeffrey FSC, Father John, Father Jerry, Father Fitz, Father Leo Rock, S.J. and too many others to mention, but you know who you are.

To Mary Elizabeth Sperry and Colin O'Brien of the USCCB for all of their assistance and patience.

To Cheryl Dickow and her staff at Bezalel Books.

And finally, thank you to all men, women and children whose stories are represented in this work. May God continue to heal you.

CPSIA information can be obtained
at www.ICGtesting.com
Printed in the USA
FFOW01n0828230718
47484906-50776FF